CHRISTIAN DOCTRINE

BLOOMSBURY GUIDES FOR THE PERPLEXED

Bloomsbury's Guides for the Perplexed are clear, concise, and accessible introductions to thinkers, writers, and subjects that students and readers can find especially challenging. Concentrating specifically on what it is that makes the subject difficult to grasp, these books explain and explore key themes and ideas, guiding the reader toward a thorough understanding of demanding material. Guides for the Perplexed available from Bloomsbury include the following:

Atonement: A Guide for the Perplexed, Adam Johnson
Balthasar: A Guide for the Perplexed, Rodney Howsare
Barth: A Guide for the Perplexed, Paul Nimmo
Benedict XVI: A Guide for the Perplexed, Tracey Rowland
Bonhoeffer: A Guide for the Perplexed, Joel Lawrence
Calvin: A Guide for the Perplexed, Paul Helm
De Lubac: A Guide for the Perplexed, David Grumett
Luther: A Guide for the Perplexed, David M. Whitford
Pannenberg: A Guide for the Perplexed, Timothy Bradshaw
Pneumatology: A Guide for the Perplexed, Daniel Castelo
Political Theology: A Guide for the Perplexed, Elizabeth Phillips
Postliberal Theology: A Guide for the Perplexed, Ronald T. Michener
Prayer: A Guide for the Perplexed, Ashley Cocksworth
Predestination: A Guide for the Perplexed, Jesse Couenhoven
Schleiermacher: A Guide for the Perplexed, Theodore Vial
Scripture: A Guide for the Perplexed, William Lamb
Tillich: A Guide for the Perplexed, Andrew O' Neill
Wesley: A Guide for the Perplexed, Jason A. Vickers
Žižek: A Guide for the Perplexed, Sean Sheehan

Forthcoming Guides for the Perplexed available from Bloomsbury include the following:

Catholic Social Teaching: A Guide for the Perplexed, Anna Rowlands
Ressourcement Theology: A Guide for the Perplexed, Patricia Kelly
God-Talk: A Guide for the Perplexed, Ryan S. Peterson
Schillebeeckx: A Guide for the Perplexed, Stephan van Erp
Bultmann: A Guide for the Perplexed, David W. Congdon
Postcolonialism and the Bible: A Guide for the Perplexed, Steed Vernyl Davidson and Raj Nadella
The Dead Sea Scrolls: A Guide for the Perplexed, Matthew Collins

CHRISTIAN DOCTRINE

A GUIDE FOR THE PERPLEXED

Geoff Thompson

LONDON • NEW YORK • OXFORD • NEW DELHI • SYDNEY

T&T CLARK
Bloomsbury Publishing Plc
50 Bedford Square, London, WC1B 3DP, UK
1385 Broadway, New York, NY 10018, USA

BLOOMSBURY, T&T CLARK and the T&T Clark logo are trademarks of
Bloomsbury Publishing Plc

First published in Great Britain 2020
Reprinted 2020

Copyright © Geoff Thompson, 2020

Geoff Thompson has asserted his right under the Copyright, Designs and Patents
Act, 1988, to be identified as Author of this work.

For legal purposes the Copyright Acknowledgment on p. ix constitute
an extension of this copyright page.

Cover design: Terry Woodley
Cover image © Jasmina007/Getty

All rights reserved. No part of this publication may be reproduced or transmitted
in any form or by any means, electronic or mechanical, including photocopying,
recording, or any information storage or retrieval system, without prior
permission in writing from the publishers.

Bloomsbury Publishing Plc does not have any control over, or responsibility for,
any third-party websites referred to or in this book. All internet addresses given
in this book were correct at the time of going to press. The author and publisher
regret any inconvenience caused if addresses have changed or sites have
ceased to exist, but can accept no responsibility for any such changes.

A catalogue record for this book is available from the British Library.

A catalog record for this book is available from the Library of Congress.

ISBN: HB: 978-0-5676-7334-3
PB: 978-0-5676-7333-6
ePDF: 978-0-5676-7336-7
eBook: 978-0-5676-7335-0

Series: Bloomsbury Guides for the Perplexed

Typeset by Newgen KnowledgeWorks Pvt. Ltd., Chennai, India
Printed and bound in Great Britain

To find out more about our authors and books visit www.bloomsbury.com
and sign up for our newsletters.

CONTENTS

Preface		vii
Copyright Acknowledgment		ix
List of Abbreviations		x
1	**The Origins, Forms, and Functions of Christian Doctrine**	1
2	**Theologians and Doctrine: Context, Content, and Form**	27
3	**Doctrine in Crisis and Doctrine Renewed**	81
4	**Doctrine, Bible, and Truth**	105
5	**Doctrine and the Christian Social Imaginary**	129
6	**Conclusion**	149
Notes		153
Recommended Reading		181
Index		185

PREFACE

This book is about doctrine, and only as such is it about doctrines. It not an engagement with the various perplexities of specific doctrines (although they are not ignored). Rather, it is about the phenomenon of doctrine as a particular intellectual activity of the church. It is precisely as such that doctrine leaves many people perplexed. An interest in doctrine is often linked to being doctrinaire, something that few people aspire to be. In the minds of many Christians it is the focus of heavy-handed authority and authoritative imposition of beliefs. Many believe it can be avoided, either by relying directly on the Bible or by substituting it with their own "personal" beliefs. Of course, doctrine can be presented in a doctrinaire manner and, in the hands of some, it can be a substitute for engaging the Bible. Both are distortions of doctrine.

There are, of course, other perplexing features of doctrine. These include its contested place in the relationship between the churches of European Christendom and those of the majority world. The former have largely been the source of Christianity's classical doctrines. The latter, now constituting the numerical majority of Christians, often encounter received doctrinal discourse and its underlying concepts as alien and alienating. There is also much perplexity about doctrine's relationship to the Bible and just as much about doctrine's truthfulness. Similarly, in the face of the widespread turn to "practical wisdom," there is often perplexity about doctrine's practical status.

To address these and other issues, this book begins by asking "What is doctrine?" and by proposing a working definition in response. The answer will be then expanded as each chapter addresses some particular aspect of Christian doctrine. Chapter 1 itself will provide an overview of the emergence of Christian doctrine and the various forms it has taken and the functions it has served over the centuries. Chapter 2 will offer a survey of the respective understandings of and engagement with doctrine in ten significant Christian theologians. Chapter 3 will engage the challenge of the Enlightenment criticism of doctrine and observe the resilience of the doctrinal tradition. The latter will involve exploring the way particular

Preface

doctrines have engaged various questions and contexts that are, at some level, the legacy of the Enlightenment. Chapter 4 turns to the question of the relationships between doctrine, the Bible, and truth. It does so by following those discussions specifically as they have unfolded in the debates generated by the emergence of postliberal theology in North America in the 1980s. Chapter 5 begins by offering an expanded definition of doctrine, drawing on the previous four chapters. It then addresses how doctrine, so understood, can be coherently articulated and analyzed. This will be done by placing doctrine within the context of the Christian "social imaginary." A brief conclusion (Chapter 6) will address the truthfulness of doctrine.

In the course of writing this book, I have drawn on the expertise and advice of many colleagues. They have saved me from embarrassing errors, prodded me to write more clearly, suggested nuance when it was lacking, drawn my attention to relevant literature that I had neglected, and, above all, provided generous—and often timely—words of encouragement. For these and other reasons, my thanks go to Alexander Chow, Ian Ferguson, John Flett, Jason Goroncy, Christine Helmer, Mark Lindsay, Ockert Meyer, Gerry O'Collins, SJ, Monica Melancthon, Chris Mostert, David Rankin, Orm Rush, Fotini Toso, and Kevin Vanhoozer. Responsibility for any remaining weaknesses and errors is, of course, entirely mine.

Some of the research and writing was done during a period of study leave generously granted by Pilgrim Theological College. For parts of that leave, I enjoyed the hospitality, both physical and intellectual, of United Theological College in Bangalore and the Mar Thoma Syrian Theological Seminary in Kottayam, India, and the Nanjing Union Theological Seminary, China. I have much more to learn from the insights I encountered in those places. I hope that some features of this book indicate what I have learned so far. I also record my thanks to Anna Turton and Sarah Blake of Bloomsbury for their patience and advice as they guided this book to its publication.

Finally, I thank my wife, Linda, who endured my preoccupation with this project for much longer than was reasonable, but whose love and encouragement helped to bring it to its conclusion.

COPYRIGHT ACKNOWLEDGMENT

Scripture quotations are from the New Revised Standard Version Bible, copyright © 1989 National Council of the Churches of Christ in the United States of America. Used by permission. All rights reserved worldwide.

* * *

Gender-specific terms in English translations of classical texts have been retained. When they occur in modern English texts, attention has been drawn to the limitations of this language.

ABBREVIATIONS

CD	Karl Barth, *Church Dogmatics*, 4 vols., in 13 parts, ed. T. F. Torrance and G. Bromiley (Edinburgh: T&T Clark, 1956–75).
CF	Friedrich Schleiermacher, *Christian Faith*, 2 vols., trans. Terrence N. Tice, Catherine L. Kelsey, and Edwina Lawler (Louisville, KY: WJKP, 2016).
Conf.	Saint Augustine. *Confessions*, trans. R. S. Pine-Coffin (London: Penguin, 1961).
Dialogue	Catherine of Siena, *The Dialogue*, trans. Suzanne Noffke, OP. The Classics of Western Spirituality (London: SPCK, 1980).
Doctr. Chr.	Saint Augustine, *On Christian Teaching*, trans. R. P. H. Green. Oxford World Classics (Oxford: Oxford University Press, 1997).
Ench.	Saint Augustine, *The Enchiridion on Faith, Hope and Charity*, trans. Bruce Harbert, in *On Christian Belief*. *The Works of Saint Augustine: A Translation for the 21st Century*, vol. 1/8, ed. Boniface Ramsey (Hyde Park: New City Press, 2005).
Inst.	John Calvin, *Institutes of the Christian Religion*, trans. Ford Lewis Battles. The Library of Christian Classics (Louisville, KY: WJKP, 1960).
Princ.	Origen, *On First Principles*, 2 vols., ed. and trans. John Behr. Oxford Early Christian Texts (Oxford: Oxford University Press, 2017).
Sentences	Peter Lombard, *The Sentences*, 4 vols., trans. Guilio Silano. Medieval Sources in Translation 42 (Ontario: Pontifical Institute of Medieval Studies, 2007–10).
ST	Thomas Aquinas, *Summa Theologiae*, 60 vols., ed. Thomas Gilby, OP (London: Blackfriars, 1964–81).
TI	Karl Rahner, *Theological Investigations*, 23 vols., trans. Cornelius Ernst et al. (London: Darton, Longman and Todd, 1961–91).

CHAPTER 1
THE ORIGINS, FORMS, AND FUNCTIONS OF CHRISTIAN DOCTRINE

A working definition and its challenges

What is Christian doctrine? Let me propose the following as a working definition: *Christian doctrine is communally recognized and authoritative teaching of the Christian community about Christianity's beliefs and practices.* This definition is at once complicated by the diversity of the Christian community, the processes by which any given teaching is communally recognized, and the nature and extent of its authority. It also begs the question of just how doctrine performs this teaching role. These are all issues that will claim our attention as this book proceeds. For now, they can be put to one side and, for brevity, the working definition will be condensed to: *communally recognized authoritative teaching*. To begin the initial explorations of this topic, consider the following three statements:

Doctrine divides, service unites.[1]

The history of Jesus of Nazareth was and is the crucible of Christian doctrinal possibilities. Whatever the ultimate external reference of Christian doctrine might be, its proximate external referent is this history.[2]

Doctrine is not identical with any existing text—whether it is that of specific theological formulae, or that of a specific theological system; or that of the Church's creed, or even the text of the Bible. Pure doctrine is an event … All the conclusions of dogmatics must be intended, accepted and understood as fluid material for further work.[3]

"Doctrine divides, service unites" had significant currency within the twentieth-century ecumenical movement. Another version of it has enjoyed a certain popular currency in some strands of liberal Protestantism: "doctrine divides, experience unites." Both versions state the obvious: that doctrine has, in fact, been associated with church division, especially among Protestants. Particular doctrines (e.g., the doctrines of justification, Scripture, or baptism) have functioned as fault lines along which various Christian communities have separated themselves from others. The existence of such slogans point to the fact that in many quarters, doctrine is treated with suspicion; it is a problem to be overcome. This both reflects and is reinforced by the fact that "doctrine" is certainly one of the heavier words in the Christian lexicon. Yet doctrine is inevitable. Indeed, particular doctrines, in the form of convictions and beliefs, lie behind the privileging of either service or experience in the slogans just considered. Indeed, neither "service" nor "experience" are either univocal or self-interpreting terms. To invoke them against doctrine is only to open up layers of other doctrines about both service and experience.

If doctrine is divisive, is the working definition of doctrine offered above actually something of a phantom? Is it the case that doctrine is not "communally recognized, authoritative teaching" after all? The answer has to be nuanced. Even as one group separates from others on the basis of, for example, a particular doctrine of baptism, that doctrine simultaneously unites the group separating itself from the others. On the other hand, over time doctrine can again become the point of the reunion of those same Christians as both groups come to some new understanding of baptism that they can affirm together. In other words, doctrine's relationship to community and unity is complex and dynamic. Indeed, this complexity is the reason for using the adjective "communally recognized" rather than (the more usual) "communally agreed" in the definition of doctrine offered in the opening paragraph. Doctrine can perform its community-binding function even if there are differing levels of agreement within a given community about particular doctrines. Within a given community, those who dissent from that community's doctrine do so acknowledging in the very act of dissent that what they are dissenting from is recognized as authoritative. By itself, such dissent does not constitute grounds for exclusion from the community.

By turning to the second of the quotations above, our attention is drawn to the relationship between doctrine and the history of Jesus. The quotation comes from Alister McGrath and its point is hardly contestable. If it wasn't for Jesus there would be no Christian doctrine. Yet, as McGrath implies, the relationship between cause and effect is complex. Jesus himself left no written body of doctrine nor did he teach in a manner that would be recognized as "doctrinal teaching" according to the working definition introduced above. He taught; that goes without saying. Indeed, his teaching was one of the defining features of his ministry. But his teaching, focused as it was on the kingdom of God, was more cryptic and allusive than it was clear and organized. From the beginning, it lent itself to a variety of interpretations. Even more importantly, however, the Gospel records of Jesus' teaching never present it as a self-contained phenomenon. It is framed, albeit in different ways in the various Gospels, by the narrative of Jesus' life, death, and resurrection. This narrative is, in turn, framed by another context of interpretation: first-century messianic expectation and the various complexities of Israel's inherited faith.

Placing Jesus' ministry and identity in the context of Judaism's messianic hope raises another significant issue regarding the relationship between Jesus and doctrine. The charge has been made that the Christian doctrinal tradition gradually let go of that Jewish framework and allowed the fabric of Christian teaching to be increasingly determined by its interaction with Greek philosophy during the second to the fifth centuries. The consequence, so it is said, has been the skewing of Christian doctrine to modes of discourse and substantive topics far removed from the concerns, not only of those who first proclaimed Jesus, but of Jesus himself. Herein lies the foundation of the further claim that Christian doctrine has privileged reason and conceptual systems over the narrative mode of the biblical and foundational Jewish-Christian witness to Jesus. These claims will be addressed at various points in this book.

Finally, in considering the third of the quotations above, words of Karl Barth, we encounter a claim that Christian doctrine is always provisional. Such a claim would at first seem to be in tension with the commonly held idea of the once-for-all character of Christian teaching; indeed, teaching that requires safeguarding (e.g., 2 Tim. 1:13-14; 1 Tim. 6:20). This is often linked, and formally so in the Catholic Church, with the idea of a "sacred deposit of the word of God which is entrusted to the church."[4] The language of "deposit" and "trust" contains resonances of stability and permanence. The notion of doctrine being "fluid material for further work" suggests, on the other hand, instability and an absence of clear or straightforward norms. Behind Barth's remarks is a rather pivotal Christian conviction: to the extent that Christian doctrine seeks to refer to and to articulate claims about the God of Jesus Christ, it speaks of a living God who will always elude complete conceptual, narrative, or doctrinal description. Yet there is another edge, potentially a more problematic one, to Barth's comments. He suggests that even more than simply limited, doctrine is revisable. This raises a question not only about how doctrine might be "authoritative" but also about the relationship of doctrine to truth and the historical context of its interpretation. On this, the following remarks of Christine Helmer are illuminating:

> Truth is not diminished when it is understood in historical interpretation(s). Rather, being attuned to the historical brings truth into the medium of human intersubjectivity, where disagreement and explication, competing perspectives and various proposals—all are part of the process of its formulation ... Doctrine exists—has always existed—in production, negotiated in discussion and debates.[5]

As a historical and intersubjective—or communal—phenomenon, doctrine is inevitably embedded in the realities of power. As Helmer goes on to say, "doctrine is shaped by the formation of concepts; and doctrine is always at risk of error, including or especially the error of mistaking power for truth."[6] To acknowledge the historical nature of doctrine is to acknowledge many of the issues that drive and sustain contemporary discussions about it.

These brief reflections already point to the many aspects of the complexity attached to the topic of doctrine. They will also have reinforced the fact that this book is not, as already intimated in the preface, an overview of various Christian doctrines. While specific Christian doctrines will be studied at appropriate points, the orientation of the book is much more to the very phenomenon of doctrine, its origin, character, and functions. Or to put the issue a little differently, what is the church called to do with doctrine? With what expectations and postures should Christians approach it as they encounter it in sermons, books, and liturgies? How is it to be developed and transmitted? How is it to be judged as true or false? *Should* it be judged as true or false? Is it to be the object of interpretation or is it itself a tool of interpretation? What is its relationship to both Scripture and proclamation? What roles does it play in prayer, praise, repentance, and acts of service and love? Answers to these questions are part of the answer to the question, "What is doctrine?"

Each of the questions just posed is complicated by the vast and seemingly irreducible theological diversity of the twenty-first-century world church. This phenomenon is itself complicated by two of the issues already mentioned in earlier paragraphs: the relationship of Christianity's doctrinal tradition to Greek philosophy, and the power relations in the midst of which doctrinal work is inevitably done. The relationship with Greek philosophy is a particular concern for the churches of the majority world.[7] They have often received the doctrinal tradition as so rigidly fixed in Western patterns of thought that it is an impediment to the non-Western enculturation of the Christian faith. In fact, the charge is even sharper. It is those very patterns of Western thought that are said to aid and abet the church's complicity with colonization. With Western doctrine having the upper hand in the power differential between colonizing and colonized churches, Western doctrinal discourse is seen as a tool for delegitimizing local doctrinal developments. To engage these questions and issues is to engage some of the liveliest debates in contemporary theology.

To continue to get our bearings within these debates, the remainder of this chapter will focus on origins of doctrine, some of the forms doctrine has taken over the history of the church, and the functions it has performed.

The origins of doctrine: The proclamation of Jesus as Messiah

As noted above, Jesus did not bequeath a body of doctrine to his followers. Instead, Christianity and Christian doctrine developed through proclamation about him. The crucified and risen Jesus of Nazareth was proclaimed to be Israel's promised Messiah and came to be known and referred to as Jesus Messiah or, more commonly in Christian discourse, Jesus Christ.[8] The very word, Christianity, bears within itself this messianic orientation. The way of responding to him that came to be known as Christianity depends on this affirmation of his messianic status and the willingness of the early Christians both to defend this conviction and to live with the many puzzles it generated. That there were diverse ways of interpreting this conviction and living it out is known to us through the corpus of Christian literature produced in the decades immediately following Jesus' life, death, and resurrection. Recognizing this diversity is itself important in the context of the present discussion about doctrine, understood as "communally recognized authoritative teaching." The New Testament literature bears witness to various and developing loci of authority. For this reason, it is important to look beyond specific references to "doctrine" in the New Testament. Indeed, in reference to Christian instruction, "doctrine" occurs only six times in the NRSV, that is, Eph. 4:14; 1 Tim. 1:3; 2 Tim. 4:3; Tit. 1:9, 2:1, and 2:10. In each case, the word translates one form or another of the Greek word *didache*, teaching. But the cognates of this word are much more frequent than the occurrence of "doctrine" in the English translation would suggest. Teaching and appeals to authority are a frequent concern of the New Testament writers. Yet the locations and sources of this teaching and authority are diverse.

Christian Doctrine

All the various forms of authority evident in the New Testament are, in some sense, means of mediating the authority of Jesus himself, the Lord of the Christian community. Alongside experiences of his living presence, it was primarily mediated through the memory of his teaching as that was conveyed in both apostolic preaching and the emerging corpus of Christian literature. Apostolic authority was, however, a complicated phenomenon. It could be based on the commission of the risen Jesus to the disciples (e.g., Lk. 24:49, Jn 20:21, Acts 1:8), on being a witness to Jesus from his baptism to his resurrection (as in the case of finding a replacement for Judas), or a direct commission from the ascended Lord, independently even of any engagement with the earthly Jesus (as in the case of Paul according to Acts 9:1-19, 22:4-16, 26:12-18; and in Paul's own words in 1 Cor. 15:8 and Gal. 1:1). Indeed, Paul's own various claims to apostolic authority further complicate the picture of how Jesus' authority was mediated. Paul appealed to his own imitation of Christ's suffering (e.g., 2 Cor. 4:7-12), his reception of preexisting traditions received from other Christians (e.g., 1 Cor. 15:3), and his own innovative interpretations of the Hebrew Scriptures (e.g., Rom. 4:1-25; Romans 9–11). In exercising this authority, Paul could distinguish between what was from "the Lord" and what were his own instructions (1 Cor. 7:10-12) as well as make appeals to "creation" (e.g., Rom. 1:19-20) and "nature" (e.g., 1 Cor. 11:14). Apostolic authority was not a blunt instrument, and its outworking of Christian teaching was a work in progress. This is especially evident in the movement the Christian community made toward its teaching on the matter of Gentile inclusion. Very little, if anything, in Jesus' ministry actually prepared the nascent Christian community for the particular manner in which the question of Gentile membership presented itself.[9] The teaching that Gentiles were to be included in the Christian community without first being initiated into the Jewish community was the cumulative result of the witness of the Spirit, the testimony of authoritative apostles, conciliar debate, and novel interpretations of the Hebrew Scriptures (see Acts 10–15).

The literature of the New Testament also bears witness to the emergence of authoritative, if undeveloped, local offices. There has been much commentary about New Testament references to the offices of bishop, deacon, and elder (e.g., 1 Tim. 3:1-13, 5:17-19; and Tit. 1:5-11). Some have argued that they represent the authoritative foundations for the later threefold ministry of bishop, priest, and deacon. Others have argued that they constitute a departure from Paul's emphasis on the gifts of the Spirit as the basis for ministry. The latter rightly point out that the texts in these so-called pastoral epistles relate the authority of those offices to the personal virtue and social standing of those holding them.[10] It is also argued that the emergence of office is the manifestation of the usual social forces that lead, over time, to the formation of structure and leadership in any developing community.[11] While it is striking that the personal virtues are stressed as heavily as they are in these passages, this should not be understood as straightforward evidence of a separation of office from received belief. These same letters point to a particular concern with doctrine and truth. Indeed, the reference to bishops and deacons in 1 Timothy 3 is immediately followed by a declaration of the church as a "pillar and bulwark of the truth" and by a summary of the "mystery of our religion." And this summary is significant: "He was revealed in flesh, vindicated in spirit, seen by angels, proclaimed among Gentiles, believed in throughout the world, taken up in glory" (1 Tim. 3:16, NRSV). Condensed in this possible creedal or hymnic fragment is an insistence on the theological significance Jesus' earthly life, an allusion to the resurrection's vindication of Jesus, the extension of the church's preaching about him to the Gentiles, and his current exalted state. This, however, is far from the only summary of the faith to be found in the New Testament. Others include Paul's instruction to the Corinthians about the resurrection (1 Corinthians 15), the hymns to Christ in Phil. 2:5-11, Col. 1:15-20, and Eph. 1:3-12, as well as more discursive summaries in Rom. 10:9-10 and Heb. 4:14-15. This brief survey has drawn on what became the canonical literature. For its authors and first readers, whatever authority it had was subordinated to the various authorities it was pointing to. Over time, of course, the very literature that pointed to diverse sources of authority itself came to possess an authority in relation to the authorities it was pointing to. The relationship between the authority of the Bible and that of other recognized authorities in formulating and receiving doctrine is a matter of perennial concern to the study of doctrine.

In sum, during this early period of the church's life, the question of authority and authoritative teaching is complex and diffuse. Yet, at the heart of the emerging body of authoritative teaching were the preaching, example, significance, and identity of Jesus of Nazareth, crucified and risen. Earlier, reference was made to the constancy of convictions about Jesus' messianic identity and status. For all the ways that Jesus' life, teachings, healings, death, and resurrection unsettled assumptions and generated debate about how he related to prevailing messianic expectations, those same expectations provided a theological framework without which the various convictions would have had no currency. For all the variety in messianic expectation in the first century, it presupposed at least three elements: Israel's God is One, Israel's God is creator of the cosmos, and Israel's God is the redeemer of this same creation, a redemption to which Israel's own redemption would be pivotal.[12] Peel away these theological convictions and the proclamation about Jesus as Messiah loses the particular intellectual scaffolding that gave it its meaning and made it relatively coherent, if also puzzling. The challenges of proclaiming this message increased as the church moved into new times and new places. As it did, its communally recognized authoritative teaching began to emerge in somewhat more explicit and organized ways.

Authoritative teaching beyond the canon

Two documents will be studied here. They are quite different in form and were produced almost a century apart near the beginning and end respectively of the second century. Indeed, it is their respective impacts and forms which make them interesting in understanding the diverse pressures and possibilities associated with the construction of communally-recognized authoritative teaching.

The Didache

The *Didache*[13] is a document that appears to have been written from within a largely Jewish-Christian community into which Gentile converts had moved, perhaps in Syria. Estimates of its date of writing range from very late in the first century to no later than the middle of the second century. Although an extant copy was not discovered until 1873, there are at least two positive references to it in other early Christian literature.[14]

The document consists of sixteen chapters. The final chapters reveal something of the context and purpose of the document. That there are references to false and true "prophets" points to the fact that this community was exposed to divergent teaching about the Christian faith and that this document exists to identify what is considered a true interpretation. The content of this "true interpretation" is set out in the first six chapters. It is here that the author, echoing the existing "Two Ways" device of Jewish literature, has set up "two paths," one of life and one of death.[15] The first is announced in the terms of Jesus' own summary of the Law and the Prophets. Once introduced, this way of life is described by references and allusions to Jesus' own teaching as well as (subsequently) to teaching drawn from the

Epistles of the New Testament. Thus, the opening three paragraphs run as follows:

> There are two paths, one of life and one of death, and the difference between the two paths is great.
> This then is the path of life. First, love the God who made you, and second, your neighbor as yourself. And whatever you do not want to happen to you, do not do to another.
> This is the teaching relating to these matters: Bless those who curse you, pray for your enemies, and fast for those who persecute you. For why is it so great to love those who love you? Do the Gentiles not do this as well? But you should love those who hate you—then you will have no enemy.[16]

The second path is that of the Gentiles, presented in descriptions of that way that echo similar summary descriptions of Gentile behavior known from the Epistles. This is the way the document's readers are to eschew. It then sets out instructions for the proper performance of both baptism and the Eucharist, which are followed by teachings about true and false prophets and some material on church order. Its relevance to the present argument is twofold: its appeal to the authority of the apostles (including references to Jesus' teaching), and its genre.

With regard to its reference to the apostles' teaching, the *Didache* is seeking to transmit existing authoritative teaching. Moreover, it does so by weaving into its own text references to Jesus' teaching most likely known from the already-existing Gospels. There are also allusions to material known to later Christians from the Epistles of the New Testament. Its own authority is derivative. With regard to its genre, it consists of a series of (mostly) short statements of instruction. Presented in the form of commandments, it is less discursive and persuasive and more quasi-legal. It is this quasi-legal form that suggests that the community understands its obedience to the teachings of Jesus as obedience to a new Torah. It could thus be argued that that there is a relationship between genre on the one hand and the given understanding of the Christian faith on the other. Moreover, the use of the already existing "Two Ways" form suggests an "ordered programme of initiation" into a particular Christian community.[17] Even if the *Didache* never gained the authority of other contemporaneous literature,[18] its existence indicates the emergence of a more structured and standardized form of teaching entering the Christian community. It also highlights the way both the emphases and genre of the teaching reflect the particular circumstances of the particular community.

Irenaeus's Rule of Faith

Instances of the "Rule of Faith" (*regula fidei*) are found in several of the Ante-Nicene fathers, especially Irenaeus (c130–c202) and Tertullian (c150/60–c225/30). They are summary statements of the normative claims of the faith focused on the oneness of God, the unity of creation and redemption, and, by implication, the unity of the Old and New Testaments. They emerged as responses to claims, mostly associated with Gnosticism and Marcionism, that there were different gods: an inferior god responsible for the imperfect creation, and a superior god offering deliverance from creation to a realm and state of nonmaterial perfection. While both Gnosticism and Marcionism are imprecise terms, their shared resistance to the goodness of creation struck at the heart of the church's claims about, and theological reflection on, the Incarnation. Moreover, the rules were presented as public standards of Christian teaching.[19] As Kathryn Greene-McCreight notes, the Rule is "a basic 'take' on the subject matter and plot of the Christian story, which couples the confession of Jesus the Redeemer with the confession of God the Creator."[20] One extended statement of the Rule, specifically developed in reaction to Gnosticism, is found in Irenaeus's *Demonstration of the Apostolic Preaching*:

> This is the rule of our faith, the foundation of the building, and what gives support to our behaviour.
> *God the Father, uncreated,* who is uncontained, invisible, one God, creator of the universe; this is the first article of our faith. And the second is:
> The *Word of God,* the Son of God, our Lord Jesus Christ, who appeared to the prophets according to their way of prophesying, and according to the dispensation of the Father. Through him all things were created. Furthermore in the fullness of time, in order to gather all things to himself, he became a human being amongst human beings, capable of being seen and touched, to destroy death, bring life, and restore fellowship between God and humanity. And the third article is:
> The *Holy Spirit*, through whom the prophets prophesied, and our forebears learned of God and the righteous were led in the paths of justice, and who, in the fullness of time, was poured out in a new way

on our human nature in order to renew humanity throughout the entire world in the sight of God.[21]

The theological emphases of this Rule are quite clear. The full humanity of Jesus is affirmed. The idea of two gods is resisted and the unity of creation and redemption as works of the one God is upheld. The same Holy Spirit poured out in the redemptive renewal of humanity was already present in the prophecies contained in Israel's Scriptures. The threefoldness of the Rule is not yet fully developed Trinitarian teaching, but this threefold structure already points to the dramatic nature of God's engagement with the world pivoted on Christ. The truth proclaimed is not an abstract principle: there is, as noted above, a Christian story that has a plot.

For the purposes of this study of doctrine as communally recognized teaching, there are several other features of this Rule to note. First, Irenaeus makes a claim for a communal faith: "This is the rule of *our* faith." This is not a private or idiosyncratic belief. Irenaeus seeks (as a bishop) to speak on behalf of a community that has received this faith in the Scriptures and apostolic teaching. Second, it bears witness to the link assumed during the early church between belief and practice. This is not merely an intellectual Rule of Faith; it also "gives support to our behaviour." Nevertheless, it is important to note that the norm being presented in the Rule is theological rather than being explicitly moral. Third, we also see that this is presented as a "foundation." Rather than being a full account of the faith, it constitutes an attempt to define the core beliefs of the faith. There is a "building" that is built on this foundation. Other doctrines and practices have room to develop as occasion demands. But the legitimacy of such developments depends on their relationship to the foundation. Elsewhere, Irenaeus speaks of the coherence and harmony of the faith that the Rule summarizes.[22] The coherence is not simply intellectual; it is the coherence of life, exegesis, and doctrine. Eric Osborn has shown how the Rule points toward such coherence: "Coherence comes from love, the higher knowledge which gives wholeness to life, leads to the knowledge of Christ crucified, holds the system of truth together and points a way through the mysteries of providence."[23]

As an example of "communally recognized, authoritative teaching," Irenaeus's Rule points to the occasion-specific need to indicate what is core and foundational to the faith, in order to provide critical leverage against distortions and alternatives. Yet the emergence of such teaching is also driven positively. Doctrinal teaching points toward the life that corresponds to the teaching. In both the *Didache* and the Rule, we also see how the Christian faith lends itself to being articulated as a coherent and organized vision of God and the world centered on Jesus Christ. Interestingly, while these two documents do not invite direct comparison, it is noteworthy that despite the disappearance of the Jewish Christian communities reflected in the *Didache*, and notwithstanding the Rule's Hellenistic context, the Rule is driven by the fundamental unity of creation and redemption that Christianity inherited from Judaism, and without which the core claim of the Incarnation would collapse. This pivotal conviction survived arguably the most intense pressure Christianity was to experience from its Greek interlocutors. This leads us to the church's Trinitarian debates and the emergence of the Nicene Creed.

The Trinity: Doctrine, creeds, and empire

The doctrine of the Trinity (inevitably linked to the doctrine of the Incarnation) is the most significant and consequential doctrinal achievement of Christianity's formative centuries. The controversies that produced it are mirrored both in extent and vigor by the continuing controversies about its origins, status, and interpretation. To a large extent, it is the paradigm of the possibilities and criticisms associated with doctrine itself. It is also instructive for ancient notions of orthodoxy and heresy that permanently hover over discussions about Christian doctrine.

Through its formal statement in the Nicene-Constantinopolitan Creed of 381, the church went beyond a statement of the threefoldness of the Christian confession already evident in Irenaeus's Rule. It developed a conceptuality that allowed it to confess the relationships between the Father, the Son, and the Holy Spirit, and to affirm that the relationships so defined were integral to the church's understanding of God's redemptive work in Jesus, the Son, Word, *Logos*, of God. During the second and third centuries, various theologians had developed both terminology and analogies to help imagine how "the One" could be coherently spoken of in this threefold way. In the second century, Tertullian had introduced the term "trinity" (*trinitas*) as well as the terminology of three "persons" and of one "substance."[24] He also developed various analogies to imagine, explain, and defend this threefold unity-in-distinction. One was organic: root, tree, and fruit. Another was physical: sun, ray, and apex (or focal point).[25] What the analogies did not decisively clarify, however, was the question of order within, or relationships between, the three. This issue generated much debate in the second and third centuries. Were the Son of God (or the *Logos*) and the Holy Spirit in some sense one with, but also subordinate to, the Father? Or was any such subordinationism a contradiction of the threefold Christian confession already established in the church's worship and assumed in the Rule of Faith? The issue was discussed in terms of preserving the "monarchy" of the Father—the concept that bore the weight of confessing Christianity's monotheism. One summary of the dilemma (albeit focused on the Father–Son/*Logos* relationship) helpfully puts it in these terms: "Speaking of the Logos alongside the Father is unacceptable; either the Logos must be collapsed into the Father, so there is one God unambiguously, or the Logos must be relegated to a subordinate position, so there is one God unambiguously."[26] What the Nicene Creed of 325 did, and reinforced by the Nicene-Constantinopolitan Creed of 381, was authoritatively to formalize a particular conceptuality around these relationships in response to a theological, cultural, ecclesiastical, and political crisis.

With much minimizing of the multiple layers of complexity, the issues at stake can be summarized as follows. In the later third century, a dispute broke out between Alexander (250–328), the bishop of the Egyptian city of Alexandria, and one of his presbyters, Arius (256–336). Alexander's position was that if the Father is eternal, then the Son must also be eternal, otherwise the Father would have become the Father only once he had begotten the Son. The logic is quite straightforward: if God as Father is eternal, then the Son must also be eternal and thus fully divine. To Arius's ears, this was to affirm two gods. His solution, to use the terms of the summary above, was to relegate the Son/*Logos* to a subordinate position, thus removing any ambiguity about there being one God. In the Arian view, the Son was unquestionably exalted, and he was the unique savior, but he did not share in the divine attribute of being unbegotten.[27] Arius summarized his position in these terms in his letter to Eusebius of Nicomedia: "And before [the Son] was begotten or created or defined or established, he was not. For he was not unbegotten. But we are persecuted because we say, 'The Son has a beginning, but God is without beginning.'"[28] It has been argued that Arius "was guilty perhaps not so much of demoting the Son as exalting the Father."[29] Nevertheless, arguments for the Son's subordination to the Father were not, of course, without biblical warrant (e.g., Jn 14:28 and the commonly assumed wisdom Christology derived from Prov. 8:22).[30]

For a complex combination of reasons, this initially localized debate claimed the attention of the wider church and generated widespread division and ferment. Moreover, this occurred just as Christianity had begun to assume greater cultural legitimacy after being decriminalized through the Edict of Milan in 313 and as it was beginning to enjoy the favor of the Emperor Constantine. Anxious about the potential of this dispute to disrupt the Empire, Constantine summoned as many as 250 bishops to Nicaea to resolve the matter. Again, the complexities of Council's proceedings elude easy summary.[31] Its abiding doctrinal significance, however, was its production of the Nicene Creed, the recent English version of which, translated by Wolfram Kinzig, is reproduced here. Note the anathema with which it concludes.

> We believe in one God, the Father, almighty, maker of all things visible and invisible;
> and in one Lord Jesus Christ, the Son of God, begotten from the Father, only-begotten, that is, from the substance (*ousias*) of the Father, God from God, light from light, true God from true God, begotten not made, consubstantial (*homoousios*) with the Father, "through whom all things came into being" [Jn 1:3, 1 Cor. 8:6], both things in heaven and things on earth; who for us humans and for our salvation descended, became incarnate, was made human, suffered, on the third day rose again, ascended to the heavens, will come "to judge the living and the dead" [2 Tim. 4:1, 1 Pet. 4:5];
> and in the Holy Spirit.
>
> The catholic and apostolic Church anathematizes those who say, "There was when he was not," and, "He was not before he was begotten," and that he came to be from nothing, or those who claim that the Son of God is from another hypostasis or substance, (or created,) or alterable, or mutable.[32]

The anathema at the end clearly indicates the repudiation of Arian theology, a repudiation that also included the exile of Arius himself. More subtle—and more consequential—than the anathema, however, is the use of the terms *ousias* and *homoousios* in the body of the Creed. There is debate about which of these terms carried more weight,[33] but *homoousios* became the focal point of asserting the essential unity of the Father and Son that Arius rejected. The term, however, was imprecise. As Stephen Holmes notes, "The claim ... is inchoate: it implies, without actually insisting on, some shared ontology, but gives little content to what that might mean."[34] While the Council symbolizes a certain claim to authority, and while the Creed embodied an authoritative teaching, Nicaea did not end the debate. It was, rather, the beginning of new debates. As John Behr notes, "What Nicaea was to stand for was not a given from the beginning."[35] In the decades that followed, the Arian position attracted new defenders, notably Eunomius (353–393), and even occasional, if unstable, imperial support, notably from Emperor Constantius II (317–361). The Creed produced its critics, especially the so-called *homoians*,[36] as well as its determined champions, notably Athanasius (c296–373). More importantly the Trinitarian faith confessed in the Creed accumulated careful expositors, notably the Cappadocian Fathers: Gregory of Nazianzus (c329–390), Basil of Caesarea (c330–379), and Gregory of Nyssa (c330–394).

Of concern to the Creed's critics was that the term *homoousios* was not scriptural, that it suggested a material understanding of God, and that it implied a form of modalism. Athanasius was pivotal in defending the Nicene *homoousios*, and much of his defense involved directly engaging the resilient Arian position. For Athanasius, the very coherence of the received Trinitarian faith, and its understandings of God and of salvation, were at stake: "If the Son is not the peculiar offspring of the Father's substance but came into existence from nothing, the Triad is composed from nothing, and once there was a not a Triad but a monad."[37] This would be to surrender Christianity's theological uniqueness. Indeed, rather than simply being a contrast between a more and less "exalted" Son, it might be more accurate to say that a qualitatively different meaning of "God" was at issue. Athanasius also engages at length in exegesis of biblical texts to refute the Arian position. His arguments wove together the claims of received apostolic faith, his own exegetical endeavors, and his vocation to defend and explain the gospel. These processes were mutually entwined and mutually defining. They also entailed an understanding of the overall meaning of Scripture. While the Arians could marshal particular exegetical results about such passages as Prov. 8:22, Athanasius rejected such readings because they failed to reflect the underlying meaning running through Scripture. So he writes, "They flee to words of divine Scripture, where in keeping with their lack of perception they do not see the meaning."[38]

As these debates continued, the Council of Constantinople was held in 381. This Council reinforced the use of *homoousios* in the Nicene Creed and clarified the relationships of the Spirit to the Son and the Father, the latter evident in the much-expanded article on the Holy Spirit. The outcome of this Council was the Nicene-Constantinopolitan Creed, now commonly known as the Nicene Creed. While exposition of this Creed and its theology has never ceased, its authority rather quickly achieved a finality that its predecessor did not. This is evident, in part, in that it was soon incorporated into catechesis and liturgy. And this highlights the difference between a Rule of Faith and this Creed. As John Behr notes,

During the course of the fourth century … the Creed of Nicaea became detached from its original context, as rule of faith in a particular controversy and, as a declarative confession, was elevated to a more universal plane. This process continued even more clearly with the Creed of Constantinople, when it became part of the baptismal and liturgical life of the church. In this way, the creed lost its original *ad hoc* character and became a standard and universal point of reference, fixed even its very wording.[39]

Several matters relevant to the study of doctrine emerge from this pivotal episode and its consequences. First, church teaching emerges and is authorized in a form that is declaratory, poetic, and confessional. It invites its use in liturgy, thus placing its teaching at the heart of the church's life. It instructs and regulates those who declare it even as the act of declaration is itself a form of worship.

Second, it emerges from a complex social, political, and spiritual environment. The political dimension of this episode has often been used to attempt to disqualify the teaching that it produced. Such a view is itself politically naive. It assumes that the only valid and trustworthy doctrines are those that emerge in the absence of political entanglements. But there are no such pure cultures or societies untainted by the compromises and alliances symbolized by the word "politics." They are idealized abstractions. This does not mean that either the protagonists or the processes are above scrutiny or that the commonly authorized accounts of this period should be received uncritically. But it does suggest that over and above any political advantage, the Nicene position prevailed at least in part because it proved to be intellectually resilient and spiritually productive in the ongoing life of the church.

Third, in its use of *homoousios*, the Creed was being conceptually inventive. This highlights three different relationships into which church teaching is drawn—to scriptural exegesis, to the received faith, and to culture. The issues at stake in the first two of those issues are summarized by Rowan Williams when he points out that to articulate and teach the faith merely by repeating scriptural terms can be counterproductive. Part of Athanasius's task, Williams writes, was "to persuade Christians that strict adherence to archaic and 'neutral' terms alone is in fact a potential betrayal of the historic faith."[40] This is immensely significant. By the time of this debate there was indeed an "historic faith." Christian Scripture—and its canonization— did not precede this faith. Scripture and the doctrinal articulation of this received faith were mutually formative. As Athanasius's arguments against the Arians demonstrated, the meaning and unity of Scripture was not a function of the exegesis of particular texts but rather of a sense of the plot that held the Christian Scriptures together (and without which there would be no Christian Scriptures at all).

With regard to the relationship between doctrine and culture, the use of *homoousios* and other concerns about the impact of background Greek ideas have fed the charge of Hellenization being made against the production and content of this Creed. Yet the insistence (precisely against Arius) that God had entered time is exactly what distinguished the theology of the Creed from many of the prevailing Greek ideas concerning God's absolute transcendence from creation. In this regard, the Creed's conceptual innovation actually preserves something of the uniqueness of the Christian faith and its claim about God becoming flesh. As Robert Louis Wilken notes in relation to the claims of the Hellenization thesis, "A more apt expression would be the Christianisation of Hellenism … Christian thinking, whilst working within patterns of thought and conceptions rooted in Greco-Roman cultures transformed them so profoundly that in the end something quite new came into being."[41]

The production of the Nicene-Constantinopolitan Creed and its resilience within the Christian community points to the production of communally recognized authoritative teaching as the church's faith is clarified in the midst of controversy. The context of this clarification was simultaneously exegetical, ecclesial, theological, political, and cultural. *This* Creed produced in *these* circumstances, and its *continued* reception by the church, points to the abiding significance for church teaching of the basic Christian confession about God's redemptive and incarnational engagement with the world of which this one God is the Creator. This Creed declares a particular doctrine, and its emergence yields a particular way of producing and using doctrine. A millennium later, a similar combination of exegetical, ecclesial, theological, political, and cultural controversies will produce another chapter in the history of the church that would have immense consequences for the understanding of doctrine: the Reformation.

The Reformation: Doctrine, scripture, tradition, confessions, and councils

While we need to avoid idealizing the "unity" of the Medieval church, the reality is that with the advent of the various reform movements from the fifteenth century onward, European Christianity divided into a variety of movements with one major fault line: on the one side was the Roman church; on the other were diverse protestant traditions that themselves were internally distinguished by some almost equally strong fault lines: Lutheran, Reformed, Anabaptist, and Anglican. In brief summary, the movement that has come to be named "the Reformation" was in fact a series of reformations that began with the protest by the Wittenberg-based Augustinian monk, Martin Luther (1483–1546), against a distorted understanding of salvation that, in his view, prioritized human works rather than divine grace. As his protest deepened, and because it was a protest against this distorted *teaching* about salvation, it also became a protest about ecclesial authority and so a dispute about the respective authority of doctrine and Scripture. Beginning in Germany, the Reformation quickly moved south into Switzerland where Huldrych Zwingli (1484–1531) in Zurich and later John Calvin (1509–1564) in Geneva would develop it in distinctive and influential ways.

A number of particular doctrines were especially associated with the Reformation—notably justification, Scripture, church, and sacraments. Yet, as already noted, Reformation debates about particular doctrines were also debates about doctrine itself, especially about its relationship to Scripture and ecclesial tradition and office. And because it was a debate about these things, it was also a debate about authority. The diverse points of contention are reflected in the various confessions of faith produced by Lutheran and, especially, Reformed churches. Indeed, the genre of confession emerged as a new mode of articulating and mediating doctrine. Arguably, the most famous of the sixteenth-century confessions was the Confession of Augsburg, which was produced by the *Diet* held in the same place in 1530. Called to address a number of diplomatic, political, and theological matters in the wake of the by-then burgeoning Lutheran reformation, the *Diet* published the confession at the meeting's completion. It was the first, and remains the standard, statement of Lutheran doctrines. As the Reformation spread (with varying degrees of reception) into Switzerland, France, Belgium, Holland, Scotland, and England during the sixteenth century, the Reformed communities in those places likewise produced confessions. The connection between place and confession is especially noteworthy and is immediately obvious in any list of the confessions to emerge during this period. Of the twelve gathered in one influential twentieth-century collection, only two do not bear the name of a city or nation.[42] The places or regions named in this list are Berne, Lausanne, Geneva, France, Scotland, and Belgium. These are at once theological and political documents. They are declaratory, expository, and—at least at some level—socially binding. As an example of the latter, the subtitle of the Geneva Confession is illuminating: "Which all the citizens and inhabitants of Geneva and the subjects of the country must promise to keep and hold."[43]

As well as variously affirming the creedal affirmations of God and Christ, these confessions also address the doctrines and practices at issue in the Reformers' disputes with Rome: sin, justification, faith, grace, works, sacraments, marriage, ecclesiastical authority, ministry, and civil authority. Yet a thread running through the teaching on these various topics across the confessions is the basis of the authority for those teachings. There is a repeated claim that whatever is taught about those topics is authorized by Scripture, not least through the use of biblical references as "proofs" of the doctrinal claims. But there are also explicit teachings about Scripture and its authority. Again, to quote the Geneva Confession, Article 1,

> First we affirm that we desire to follow Scripture alone as rule of faith and religion, without mixing it with any other things which might be devised by the opinion of men apart from the Word of God, and without wishing to accept for our spiritual government any other doctrine than what is conveyed to us by the same Word without addition or diminution, according to the command of our Lord.[44]

Alongside the concern to establish Scripture's authority, there are also statements about its correct interpretation. Article 2 of The First Helvetic Confession of Faith puts it this way: "This holy, divine Scripture is to be interpreted in no other way than out of itself and is to be explained by the rule of faith and love."[45] While rejecting any licence for "private interpretation," the Second Helvetic Confession is emphatic in equally rejecting as "true or genuine interpretation of the Scriptures what is called the conception of the Roman Church, that is, what the defenders of the Roman Church plainly maintain should be thrust upon all for acceptance."[46] Countering such views, and the broader assault on its authority and its specific teachings, the Roman church responded, in equally polemical terms, at the Council of Trent. Summoned by Pope Paul III as a "holy, ecumenical and general council" and held in three stages between 1545 and 1563, the Council issued various decrees. Some of these entailed explicit and detailed rejection of Protestant teachings. But not merely defensive, the Council's decrees also led to corrections of some Catholic practices. Though decisive in setting the immediate and later directions of Catholicism, its position on various matters remained contested even among Catholics. For our present purposes, however, the second decree is of greatest interest. Against the Protestant critique of the Roman relationship between Scripture and the church and the claim of the latter to be the determinative interpreter of the former, the Council declared:

> The council ... decrees, in order to control those of unbalanced character, that no one, relying on his personal judgment in matters of faith and customs which are linked to the establishment of Christian doctrine, shall dare to interpret the sacred scriptures either by twisting its text to his individual meaning in opposition to that which has been and is held by holy mother church, whose function is to pass judgement on the true meaning and interpretation of the sacred scriptures; or by giving it meanings contrary to the unanimous consent of the fathers, even if interpretations of this kind were never intended for publication. Whosoever acts contrary to this decision is to be publicly named by religious superiors and punished by the penalties prescribed by law.[47]

The means by which "holy mother church" actually exercised this teaching office was already a matter of controversy prior to the Reformation and would be further questioned and freshly articulated subsequent to this Council (and, indeed, would continue to be so through to the first and second Vatican Councils in the nineteenth and twentieth centuries, respectively). Nevertheless, the fault lines between the church in its teaching office and those who interpreted Scripture "in opposition to that which has been and is held by holy mother Church" were sharply defined. The phrase "held and doth hold" is significant, too, for the way it points to the church's confidence in the constancy of its interpretation of Scripture. This delineation between the Catholic and Reformed theology would be continually sharpened, not least as the Protestant churches became more visibly distinct, both institutionally and theologically.

One of the key instances of that constant sharpening is the Westminster Confession of Faith, regarded by some as the "queen of the Reformed Confessions."[48] It was published in the second century of the Reformation, in England, as that country was sorting out its relationship to the Reformation in the midst of political and cultural crisis. Although short-lived in its English context, it warrants attention for the evidence it provides of the complexities and tensions built into the relationships between the respective authorities

Origins, Forms, and Functions

of church, confessions, and Scripture. Finalized in 1646, the Westminster Confession facilitated an alliance between the Scottish and English parliaments during the English Civil War (1642–51). A Scottish condition of this alliance, and a desire of the English republicans, was the reform along Calvinist lines of the Church of England, including the abolition of the episcopacy. Drafted by an Assembly of Divines meeting at Westminster, on its completion, the Confession became the doctrinal standard of the Church of England, albeit only until the Restoration of the monarchy in 1660. Nevertheless, it retained its authority in Scotland where it remained the "subordinate standard" of the Church of Scotland, subordinate, that is, to Scripture. It continues to hold that status in many Presbyterian churches around the world today.

For present purposes, the focus is its teaching on Scripture, which is, significantly, its first chapter in a total of thirty-three. This opening chapter is broken down into ten paragraphs. The tone is highly polemical. The style is didactic and assertive, more suited to discussion in a theological seminar than for prayer in the liturgy. The content of these early paragraphs pivots around the relationship between the respective authority of Scripture and the church. The main doctrinal emphases of this teaching are as follows. First, the doctrine of Scripture is located in the doctrine of revelation: this written form of revelation is for the "better preserving and propagating of the truth" in relation to the revelation that had occurred in "sundry times" and "diverse manners."[49] By committing this revelation "wholly unto writing," God has rendered any former means of revelation "now ceased";[50] Scripture is described as the "Word of God written."[51] Second, the content of the Bible as the books of the Old and New Testaments is specified and declared to have "been given by the inspiration of God."[52] This fully integrated Scripture functions as the "Rule of Faith."[53] Third, and arguably most importantly, the submission to, and interpretation of, Scripture is directly linked to pneumatology. Indeed, in comparison to the decree of Trent, it is the Spirit that replaces the church as the arbiter both of Scripture's status and its interpretation. This is set out in paragraph 5 and is worth quoting in its entirety:

> We may be moved and induced by the testimony of the Church to a high and reverend esteem of the Holy Scripture (1 Tim. 3:15). And the heavenliness of the matter, the efficacy of the doctrine, the majesty of the style, the consent of all the parts, the scope of the whole (which is to give all glory to God), the full discovery it makes of the only way

of man's salvation, the many other incomparable excellencies, and the entire perfection thereof, are arguments whereby it doth abundantly evidence itself to be the Word of God; yet notwithstanding, our full persuasion and assurance of the infallible truth and divine authority thereof, is from the inward work of the Holy Spirit, bearing witness by and with the Word in our hearts. (1 Jn 2:20, 27; Jn 16:13–14; 1 Cor. 2:10–12; Isa. 59:21)[54]

This link between pneumatology and the acknowledgment of Scripture's authority is echoed in the assessment of the authority of councils and doctrines in paragraph 10: "The supreme judge by which all controversies of religion are to be determined, and all decrees of councils, opinions of ancient writers, doctrines of men, and private spirits, are to be examined, and in whose sentence we are to rest, can be no other but the Holy Spirit speaking in the Scripture."[55] While the rejection of the Roman teaching on this same topic is abundantly clear, a tension significant for any discussion of doctrine, that of its authority and its relationship to Scripture, is sharply focused in these claims. For they do, after all, become the authoritative teachings of any community that adopts this confession. Despite the "yet, notwithstanding" in the above quotation, the confession assumes the right of the church to teach authoritatively, not least doctrines about Scripture and the work of the Spirit. Despite the formal deflection of authority away from the church to Scripture and the Spirit, the confession is perhaps closer than its rhetoric may suggest to transferring the authority it attributes to Scripture and the Spirit to its own teaching. The confessional tradition was not unaware of this tension; it has consistently drawn a distinction, expressed in technical terms, between confessions being *norma normata* (normed norms) and *norma normans* (norming norms). Nevertheless, for the Westminster Confession to declare, as noted above, that Scripture is the "Rule of Faith" is simply to beg the question of precisely how Scripture is read in order for it to perform this "rule" function. And it might be noted in passing that this is a quite different understanding of the "Rule of Faith" from that associated with Irenaeus. For Irenaeus, the "Rule of Faith" was not reducible to Scripture per se but consisted of a way of reading Scripture.

The primacy given to Scripture in the Westminster Confession parallels several of the European confessions of the previous century.[56] Herein lies an issue of momentous import for subsequent developments in Protestant theology. Through the repetition of this confessional move in the Protestant theology of later centuries, Scripture, it has been claimed, became an "isolated piece of epistemological teaching,"[57] obscuring the complexity of the relationship between the doctrine of Scripture and other doctrines. This raises, in turn, the issue of just how different doctrines should be related to each other and with what measure or order and coherence. Of the Westminster Confession it has been rightly said that it "states doctrines with unusual care, clarity, logical precision and caution, showing a theology whose doctrines are richly interrelated and form a coherent whole."[58] The extent to which the body of Christian doctrine should cohere and how to articulate that coherence will become a matter of especially critical discussion in the twentieth century.

Another matter for reflection is the plurality of confessions, something that stands in sharp relief to the singularity of a decree issued by a "general council." It is easy to draw links between the plurality of confessions and the historically documented propensity of the Reformed tradition to fragment and to give rise to the phenomenon of "confessionalism" and the related "denominationalism." It is important to note, however, that the early Reformed churches were not embarrassed by this plurality of confessions. Indeed, acceptance of the plurality has been proposed as one means of limiting the authority of any one confession. There was no desire to develop a universal confession; indeed, the very logic of the confessional genre would have worked against it.[59] As Dirkie Smit observes, the "confessional tradition itself warns against over-estimating any form of human decision-making, standpoints, meetings and documents—including obviously themselves."[60] Again, while there are questions about just how "obvious" this has been in all uses of the confessions, the point is important.

If the plurality of confessions may be used to explain the fragmentation of the Reformed tradition, it might also be used to challenge the capacity of any confession to speak truthfully. This, in turn, raises the question of the provisionality of doctrine per se already discussed at the outset of this chapter. In his defense against any move to employ this provisionality to justify epistemological skepticism, John Webster maintains that the claim that "the creed is conditional or penultimate is worlds apart from the idea that the creed is merely one not very good attempt at pinning down a God we cannot really know."[61] For Webster, confessing the faith while being aware of the provisionality of the confession constitutes an openness to the Spirit: "This is not a matter of promoting instability, having everything open to revision all the time: such an attitude risks denying the reality of the gift of the Spirit to the church."[62]

Indeed, abstracted from the immediate polemics of the Reformation, and of the divisions linked to the plurality of confessions, some

Christian Doctrine

Reformed churches have demonstrated a willingness to acknowledge the provisionality of their own confession and thus be open to the authority of confessions from other times and places precisely because those churches have recognized those other confessions to be gifts of the Spirit to the whole church. We now turn to one such twentieth-century confession whose statement of the gospel's truth has been recognized and acknowledged by churches from other places who have made its teaching their own.

The Belhar Confession: Doctrine, racism, protest, and reconciliation

The example at issue is the Belhar Confession, first developed in the mid-1980s and now one of the "standards of unity" of the Uniting Reformed Church in Southern Africa.[63] Once again, we encounter doctrine—communally recognized authoritative teaching—emerging in the midst of complex political and ecclesiastical conflicts. In the polemical style of the sixteenth- and seventeenth-century confessions, one particular doctrine is affirmed by one church in the face of its de facto denial by other churches. The doctrine is that of reconciliation. The claim was made that the denial of this doctrine was, in fact, a denial of the gospel. Specifically, Belhar was a rejoinder to the denial of the doctrine of reconciliation that came with the theological affirmation of apartheid in South Africa during the twentieth century. In this confession, the rejection of apartheid as a denial of the gospel of reconciliation was considered a matter of *status confessionis*, a matter on which a particular Christian community believes the understanding and proclamation of the faith depends.[64]

Belhar begins with two opening statements of belief: the first in the triune God; the second in the holy, universal Christian church. There follows three pairings of belief and rejection. The first declares belief in Christ's reconciling work and the visible unity of the church that flows from it; the consequent rejection of any "abolustiz[ing] of natural diversity"[65] that breaks the unity of the church constituted by Christ's reconciliation. The second belief is that God has trusted the church with this message of reconciliation and the responsibility to bear witness to it. It is confessed that

> God's life-giving Word and Spirit has conquered the powers of sin and death, and therefore also of irreconciliation and hatred, bitterness and

enmity, that God's life-giving Word and Spirit will enable the church to live in a new obedience which can open new possibilities of life for society and the world.[66]

The second rejection is of any doctrine that, in the name of the gospel, enforces the separation of people on the basis of race or color, and that weakens the experience of reconciliation in Christ. The third belief is built around the convictions that God wishes to bring justice and peace among people and that the church must bear witness to this justice against any form of injustice. This is accompanied by a rejection of both any ideology that legitimates injustice and any doctrine "which is unwilling to resist such an ideology in the name of the gospel."[67] After declaring that it is the church's calling to live out this vision, even at the cost of suffering and punishment, the confession concludes with an acclamation of glory to the Trinity.

Recognizing its significance requires some awareness of the background to its production and its effects both within South Africa and beyond. In 1881, the Dutch Reformed Church (DRC) in South Africa formed the Dutch Reformed Mission Church (DRMC) for people of color. Then, in 1951, the Dutch Reformed Church in Africa (DRCA) was established for "blacks." As the injustices of apartheid were increasingly exposed in the latter half of the twentieth century, the DRMC followed the lead of the World Alliance of Reformed Churches in declaring apartheid a matter of *status confessionis* and, in 1982, issued the Belhar Confession. Four years later, it adopted this confession as one of its four "standards of unity," placing it alongside the Heidelberg Catechism, the Belgic Confession, and the Canons of Dort. In 1994, the same year that democracy was established in South Africa, the DRMC and the DRCA united to form the Uniting Reformed Church in Southern Africa (URCSA). The confession thus performed several functions. It confessed a particular doctrine, it facilitated union between churches, and it took its place alongside other confessions. The latter is especially important. While confessing a matter *status confessionis* at a particular time and place, it stood in a tradition of confessions from other times and places that made their own claim on this later time and different place.[68] And more recently, it has been adopted by other Reformed churches outside South Africa as part of their own collections of authoritative confessions to which they appeal when articulating and teaching the faith.[69]

That Belhar has been adopted outside its own context points to the logic of a confession and the possibilities of the confessional tradition in developing communally recognized authoritative teaching. In the tradition of early Reformed Confessions, Belhar is particular but not parochial. In this regard, it is noteworthy that neither the word "apartheid" nor "South Africa" are referred to in its text. It also demonstrates the positive possibilities of a confession. As noted at the beginning of this chapter, doctrine can divide, but it can also unite. Belhar began as a statement of protest, but it became a means of local church reunion. In regard to content, we can note its opening and closing confession of the Triune God, a significant difference from the Westminster Confession (and some of its predecessors) that began with a confession of Scripture's authority. With this framework, Belhar is salutary for identifying the triune God as the ultimate authority in the church's teaching ministry.

What is doctrine?

At the outset of this chapter, it was proposed that Christian doctrine is communally recognized authoritative teaching of the Christian community about Christianity's beliefs and practices. The rest of the chapter has allowed the definition to be expanded. Doctrine is a product of various intellectual, cultural, political, and spiritual realities. It emerges as the church reads Scripture in the context of those realities. It is also, however, a spark to further enquiry, development, and debate. Recalling Stephen Holmes's comment about the "inchoate" nature of *homoousios*, doctrine employs concepts that both invite and require elaboration and expansion. Doctrine is conceptually innovative, thus often enabling the Christian community to address questions that reliance on biblical idiom alone might limit or even prevent. Doctrine can take the form of summary statements well-suited to liturgical use (e.g., the Nicene Creed). It can also employ a discursive systematic genre suited to structured explanation and teaching (e.g., the Reformation Confessions). Doctrine can be a means of protest against deformations of the faith (e.g., the Belhar Confession) while simultaneously being a source of conversation and mutual learning between churches separated by time and place. Some doctrinal statements have de facto assumed universal authority, whereas others exercise their authority more locally.

In all this, we have observed the church *qua* church generating, debating, and authorizing doctrine. We now turn to explore the way particular theologians have understood, engaged, criticized, defended, and organized the church's doctrinal tradition.

CHAPTER 2
THEOLOGIANS AND DOCTRINE: CONTEXT, CONTENT, AND FORM

In the previous chapter, we engaged the emergence of doctrine as "communally recognized authoritative teaching" and the different genres it generated and/or adopted. The focus was on how the church, collectively, developed, organized, and transmitted its teaching. The focus was on the ecclesial nature of doctrine. In this chapter, we turn to explore how various theologians have received and articulated the church's doctrine. The selected theologians variously expound, adapt, teach, apply, and critique the church's doctrine. They exercise various degrees of freedom with regard to authoritative teaching. They are also diversely located across time and space, as well as inhabiting different alignments of power between the church and the wider world. Some write in the context of ecclesial crisis, others in the midst of cultural upheavals and some in periods of ecclesial and cultural stability. These issues are not treated equally by this selection of theologians, and so the emphases of the respective presentations of them will vary. There is no single template adequate for the diversity encountered here.

Most of those included in this selection have some explicit and articulated understanding of what doctrine is and what they think they are doing when they work with it. It is this that is of interest for the present work. In each case, although some summary picture of their theology will be included, the focus will be on what they understand doctrine to be, how they arrange Christian doctrines in relation to each other, what genre they use, and how the church's circumstances shape their engagement with doctrine. After presenting the overviews of these ten figures, the chapter will turn to a concluding discussion about the relation of content, form, and context in the theological engagement with doctrine. The aim is to deepen the answer to the question of what doctrine is.

Christian Doctrine

Origen

Origen of Alexandria (185/186–253/254) is indisputably one of the most influential and prolific of the Greek-speaking fathers of the church.[1] He was known in his own lifetime for his brilliance as a biblical exegete, the power of his defense of Christian faith, the originality of his thought, and his resilience in the face of persecution (from the effects of which he subsequently died). Yet, for all this, and despite strongly resisting the persistent challenges of Gnosticism, his teachings were condemned at Alexandria in 400. Origen himself was condemned as a heretic by Emperor Justinian I in 543. Justinian also ordered that all Origen's writings be burned. This posthumous rejection was fed by various aspects of his theology: there were certain ambiguities in his Christology, his allegorical interpretation of Scripture was vulnerable to charges of speculation, and his teaching on the preexistence of souls implied a dualism contrary to emerging mainstream Christian thought. Nevertheless, even as he and his teachings were being rejected, he had his forthright and influential defenders, notably Eusebius of Caesarea (263–339).

He warrants inclusion in this chapter, however, for being responsible for what is widely recognized as the first extended and systematic articulation of Christian thought, *On First Principles*. It was, as Ronald Heine has observed, "a new genre for Christian literature."[2] Although providing some of the foundations of the concerns noted above, the framework in which he set out Christian ideas would permanently, if controversially, influence the shape of theology and doctrine in the East. The work is divided into four books, although as John Behr notes, it "is not a thematic division."[3] The concerns of the first three tend to overlap, but the first deals with God and the world, the second with the world itself, and the third with the human creature and the consummation of the world. Book Four is arguably the most thematically concentrated, specifically on the inspiration and interpretation of the Scriptures.

For present purposes, it is actually the preface to the whole work that is of greatest interest. It is here that Origen sets out with considerable clarity the nature of the task that he set himself in writing this work. In many ways, the agenda he outlines articulates what became an influential understanding of doctrine, where it comes from, and what purpose it serves. Origen begins the preface by stating the conviction that all who confess the Christian faith derive the knowledge they need "to live a good blessed life from no other source but the very words and teaching of Christ."[4] These words and teaching are not, however, confined to those Christ uttered during his earthly life.

They are uttered prophetically by Moses and subsequently by Jesus' own apostles. But while there might be common agreement that Christ's teaching is the source of saving knowledge, there is no guaranteed agreement on the content of this teaching. This brings him to his reason for writing *On First Principles*:

> Since ... many of those who profess to believe in Christ differ not only in small and trivial matters, but even on great and important matters—such as concerning God or the Lord Jesus Christ or the Holy Spirit, and not only regarding these but also regarding matters concerning created beings, that is, the dominions and the holy powers—because of this it seems necessary first of all to lay down a definite line and clear rule regarding each of these matters and then thereafter to investigate other matters.[5]

What is this "clear rule"? Essentially it is the "ecclesiastical preaching, handed down from the apostles through the order of succession."[6] Yet there is a distinction between those "certain points that [the apostles] believed to be necessary"[7] and others about which they "stated that things were so, keeping silence about how or whence they are."[8] Origen reinforces this distinction by overlaying it with a further distinction between two different types of believers. On the one hand, there are those who can receive the necessary doctrine "with the utmost clarity to all believers, even to those who seemed somewhat dull in the investigation of divine knowledge."[9] On the other hand, there are "the more diligent ... [and] worthy and capable of receiving wisdom."[10] This distinction is then repeated in Origen's summary of "the particular points, which are clearly handed down by the preaching of the apostles."[11] Those doctrines concern God as Creator, the Son in his humanity and divinity, the Spirit's full and equal dignity with the Father and Son, the substance and life of the rational soul and its free will, the reality of the devil, angels and other spiritual powers, and the origin of the Scriptures in the work of the Holy Spirit. At the conclusion of this Preface, he declares, "Everyone, therefore, who desires to construct a certain structure and body of all these things, in accordance with reasons, must make use of elements and foundations of this sort, according to the precept which says, *Enlighten yourselves with the light of knowledge.*"[12]

Origen is embarking on a constructive work, a "certain structure and body" whose foundation, source, and contours are clear. With these foundations in place, the resultant work sets out both to expound, defend, and develop those foundational claims while also exploring and/or clarifying those matters on which apostolic preaching is ambiguous. While he regards the Trinity as apostolic teaching, he acknowledges that there are points about it "which are yet to be inquired into, to the best of our ability, from holy Scripture, and investigated with the requisite wisdom."[13] That a body of doctrine is constructed is not, therefore, merely the result of the exposition of a given teaching but also the result of investigation into its problems. If the foundation, source, and contours of the work are clear, so too are the criteria for the actual construction. To whoever desires to know this "structured" knowledge, Origen offers the hope that "by clear and cogent arguments the truth about each particular point may be discovered, and he may form, as we have said one body, by means of illustrations and assertions, either those which he came upon in the holy Scriptures or those which he discovered followed from investigation and right reason."[14]

What might be involved in this "investigation" is indicated elsewhere in the preface where he discusses the issue of the incorporeality of God, an issue raised by discussions at the interface of Christian and "Greek and pagan authors,"[15] and which were focused on the meaning of the Greek word *asomaton*. This leads Origen to state the following intention:

> We shall inquire ... whether the actual thing which Greek philosophers call ασωατος (that is, "bodiless") is found in the holy Scripture under another name. For it is also to be investigated how God himself is to be understood, whether as bodily and formed according to some shape, or of a different nature than bodies, a point which is not clearly indicated in our preaching.[16]

Indeed, it is this issue which will consume much of Origen's intellectual energy in the ensuing pages of *On First Principles*. And, the conclusions—or perhaps the ambiguity contained in them—that he reaches on this issue were among the key reasons for the unease with which his theology was received. His critics worried that he did not ultimately sustain a clear distinction between Creator and creature and that he entertained a certain subordinationism between the Son and the Spirit in relation to the Father.[17]

From this brief engagement with Origen's statement of purpose, we can see the many factors at play in his construction of a "connected body of doctrine." It can serve to settle disputes between Christians; it can be a means, at least for some Christians, of developing more sophisticated and more spiritual understandings of the apostolic teaching; it is a constructive enterprise that draws upon Scripture through the use of reason, logic, and understanding. For Origen, this involves the penetration of Scripture for its nonliteral meanings, while always being constrained at some level by received church teaching; and it responds to questions generated at the interface of Christian and non-Christian beliefs and ways of life. Many of these dynamics will be recurring features of the doctrinal tradition as it unfolds over the centuries.

But perhaps the critical issue to be highlighted from this case study is the relation of doctrine to the questions that come from outside the Christian community and how, in answering them, the intellectual and philosophical assumption of the questions are incorporated, or not, into Christian doctrinal discourse. On this, Origen has largely been regarded as a negative example. Perhaps, as David Rankin has suggested, Origen, despite his quest for a scripturally founded theology, was not aware "of the profound influence of Platonist (and other philosophical) thought on his own and thus to what extent he is as self-critical as he might have been."[18] Rowan Williams raises another possibility for the ambiguous reception of Origen's work: that it lacked the doctrinal clarity to which Origen himself aspired and perhaps assumed he had achieved. Or, at least, that it didn't have the doctrinal clarity that later doctrinal theologians expected. Williams contends that despite Origen's ambitions to provide a "comprehensive and coherent reading of the Bible, fit to stand with a conviction about the rational unity or harmony of the universe, [it] fell short in some areas of consistency or systematic thoroughness."[19] Accordingly, Williams writes, "Its loose ends inevitably created problems in a more doctrinally exact and anxious age."[20] Regardless of whether this is the case with Origen and the reception of his theology, this observation raises a question of immense importance for the study of doctrine: How exact must doctrine be? Or, to put it differently, are loose ends a strength or weakness of doctrinal work, and what cultural and intellectual factors within and beyond the church would establish the criteria for such a determination? Such questions are very much to the fore in contemporary discussions of doctrine and will be among the issues explored later in this book.

Augustine

By any measure, Aurelius Augustinus (354–430), better known to posterity as Augustine of Hippo, is, like Origen before him, one of the undisputed intellectual giants of the Christian faith. His work has commanded attention and generated controversy across the centuries. Moreover, living and writing at a pivotal time in the formation of Western culture, his work set trajectories that gave enduring shape to that culture. Indeed, his ideas remain important points of reference and debate well beyond the domains of the church and its theology.

The details of Augustine's life have loomed large even in explicitly theological discussions of his work,[21] partly because the development of his theology followed the various controversies in which he was personally involved and partly because of the impact of the autobiographical genre of his *Confessions*. The first nine "books" of that work are the story of his life told as a story of his own journey through various schools of ancient thought toward the Christian faith.[22] He writes in Book V that even as a catechumen of the Catholic faith, he was weighing up the respective intellectual merits of both Manichaeism and the Academics. From the Academics he had learned to "hover between one doctrine and another" as a consequence of "treating everything as a matter of doubt."[23] This skepticism would give way to sure intellectual convictions that he would come to articulate with immense sophistication and in the posture of prayer. For example, when he addresses the matter of time in the *Confessions*, he writes this: "My mind is burning to solve this intricate puzzle. O Lord my God, good Father, it is a problem at once so familiar and so mysterious. I long to find the answer. Through Jesus Christ, I beseech you, do not keep it hidden away but make it clear to me."[24] Augustine never leaves this posture of prayer in his engagement with church teaching.

Attempts to summarize either his theology or his legacy are perilous.[25] Arguably, however, his most enduring legacies include his understanding of God as "immaterial being," the analogy he drew between the threefold nature of love (the lover, beloved, and love) and the triune nature of God, his view of original sin as inherited (and specifically transmitted by the act of sexual reproduction), his insistence on the priority of grace over free will, the notion of salvation as the reorientation of human desire toward God culminating in the beatific vision, and his *ex opere operato* understanding of the sacraments.

The focus of the present discussion, however, is, first, his understanding of what doctrine is and does, and, second, the general doctrinal shape of his theology. For these, we will briefly focus on his *On Christian Teaching* and *The Enchiridion on Faith, Hope and Love* with an even briefer reference to *On Faith and the Creed*. The first two of these titles do not immediately reflect the actual content of the respective works. In fact, *On Christian Teaching* (written between 395 and 427[26]) has little to say directly on the actual content of Christian teaching and is much more concerned with techniques of interpreting the Bible and instructing others in those interpretations. On the other hand, such techniques are not neutral and are themselves driven by a Christian understanding of the goals of such interpretation. In other words, teaching about the interpretation of the Bible is itself part of Christian teaching. The opening sentence of the work points in this direction: "There are certain rules for interpreting the scriptures which, as I am well aware, can usefully be passed on to those with an appetite for such study to enable them to progress not just by reading the work of others who have illuminated the obscurities of divine literature, but also by finding illumination themselves."[27] The interpretation of Scripture takes place in a community: the rules are "passed on" from teachers to students. Indeed, Augustine is wary of those who would isolate themselves from dependence on other skilled readers and suggests that it is something of an illusion to think that such isolation is possible:

> My argument is with Christians who congratulate themselves on knowledge of the holy scriptures gained without any human guidance ... But they must admit that each one of us learnt our native language by habitually hearing it spoken from the very beginnings of childhood, and acquired others—Greek, Hebrew, or whatever—either by hearing them in the same way or by learning them from a human teacher.[28]

But he is also insistent that those who have such skills must use them for the benefit of the church: "Those responsible for teaching others should pass on, without pride or jealousy, the knowledge they have received."[29] And while a goal of using such rules of interpretation is, as noted above, to illuminate the various obscurities within the Scriptures, the ultimate goal of such illumination is not merely the attainment of exegetical clarity as an end in itself, or even the satisfaction of a certain intellectual curiosity. Rather, the goal of reading the Scriptures is nothing less than the goal of the Christian life itself. This is encapsulated in these famous words: "So anyone who thinks that he has understood the divine scriptures or any part of them, but cannot by his understanding build up [the] double love of God and neighbour, has not yet succeeded in understanding them."[30] So strong is this criterion that Augustine accepts that the evidence of such love can even excuse a poor or erroneous reading of the text: "Anyone who derives from [the Scriptures] an idea which is useful for supporting this love but fails to say what the writer demonstrably meant in the passage has not made a fatal error and is certainly not a liar."[31] Augustine is not suggesting that the hermeneutical error should go unchallenged but that it needs to be kept in perspective. He draws an analogy between such readers and a walker who reaches a given destination by the wrong path. That the destination was reached is to be acknowledged, even if the walker can be shown the more direct route to ensure that making such detours do not become a habit in future walks.

What follows in *On Christian Teaching* is a sophisticated unfolding of the skills required to read Scripture. Augustine engages issues of semiotics, grammar, music, arithmetic, logic, and rhetoric; such is the intellectual depth and cultural observation required to read Scripture well. Yet, as already intimated in the announced goal of all reading, various virtues or dispositions must be attached to these intellectual skills in the process of reading. Augustine identifies seven such virtues or dispositions as stages in the process of skilled reading: fear (of God), holiness, knowledge, fortitude, compassion, hope, and wisdom.[32] Finally, it is important to note that notwithstanding the relative complexity of this framework for reading, Augustine emphasizes that the object of reading is the collection of the books that make up the canonical Scriptures (which he lists[33]) and that familiarity with their content is essential to the development of Christian teaching. He notes, "The first rule in this laborious task is … to know these books; not necessarily to understand them but to read them so as to commit them to memory or least make them not totally unfamiliar."[34] Ultimately, his point is to insist that Christian teaching must begin with the canonical books and the interpretation of them.

The *Enchiridion* (written in 421) provides a much more explicit summary of the content of Christian doctrinal teaching. Written in response to a request from the Roman Laurentius for a "handbook" that would provide answers to various questions,[35] Augustine presents it as something of a summary of his understanding of the faith. Yet, Augustine does not use the handbook idiosyncratically to develop his own ideas. Rather, this handbook is intended as an obedient articulation of the Catholic faith. Moreover, lest Laurentius or any other reader think that their questions will be best answered by particular or isolated pieces of doctrinal information, Augustine suggests that the ultimate answer to all of the questions lies not in knowledge but in faith, hope, and love. The following passage presents Augustine's summary of the questions put to him and his general response:

You write that you wish me to make a book for you to keep ... never to be out of your hands, containing an exposition of what you have asked about, namely, what we should seek above all, what we should chiefly avoid because of the various heresies there are, to what extent reason comes to the support of religion, what lies outside the scope of reason and belongs to faith alone, what should be held first and last, what the whole body of doctrine amounts to, and what is a sure and suitable foundation of Catholic faith.[36]

But how is one oriented to this goal? Such orientation cannot be sustained by the intellect alone. Rather it comes from believing the "evidence of the witnesses by whom those writings that have already gained the name of sacred scripture were compiled."[37] So, if this testimony is to be presented in summary form (what Laurentius had asked for), Augustine suggests that such a summary, indeed two summaries, already exists: the Apostles' Creed and the Lord's Prayer. What follows in the *Enchiridion* therefore includes his own exposition of these two summaries, expositions that are themselves oriented to faith, hope, and love. A particular insight into the theological framework that Augustine derives from these authoritative texts and that give shape to the content of his exposition is given near the end of the *Enchiridion*. The Christian's story is one of beginning in ignorance, moving to a state of sin exposed by the law before being stirred by the Spirit to a life of faith and holiness, which leads, in turn, to the eternal postmortem life of peace. He summarizes: "The first ... is before the law, the second under the law, the third under grace, and the fourth in full and perfect peace."[38] It is, in short, the story of grace, revealed and mediated by Christ, which takes creation to its redemption. According to Augustine, this is the framework of Christian doctrine no less than it is the framework of the Christian life.

For Augustine, therefore, doctrinal work is a matter of the exposition of Scripture oriented to the believers' integration into the fellowship of the church, their life of love of God and neighbor, and their ultimate goal of communion with the triune God. Indeed, what Augustine has set out in the *Enchiridion* was already anticipated in what was perhaps his first attempt to summarize the faith. The occasion, when he was still a presbyter, was the Council of Hippo-Regis in 393. He had been asked to discuss the "Faith and the Creed." It is largely an exposition of the main claims of the Apostles' Creed. At the outset, he explains both the status and function of the Creed and its relationship both to the Scriptures and particular doctrines:

> This is the Catholic faith known as the creed and committed to memory by believers, a vast subject contained in such few words. It is for the benefit of beginners and those still on milk food; reborn in Christ, they have yet to be strengthened by a detailed spiritual study and knowledge of the divine scripture and so are presented with the essentials of faith in a few sentences. However, for those who have advanced further and who, imbued with true humility and genuine charity, aspire to the divine teaching, the Creed would of necessity have to be explained in much greater detail.[39]

This consistent integration of Scripture, the received creedal faith, doctrinal exposition, and the life of charity oriented to union with the triune God presents doctrine as a particular kind of work attending to a variety of tasks. It entails the exposition of teaching authorized and recognized by the church. It serves the purpose of building up the faithful in love. It does this in response to legitimate questions (of Christian and non-Christian alike) as well as to what Augustine deemed to be the heretics' illegitimate answers to those questions.

The links observed between doctrine, practice, and prayer in this brief engagement with Augustine gives his writings a certain contemporary ring. Yet the contemporary attention to such links carries a strongly corrective impulse, precisely because what Augustine held together has often been separated. Augustine reminds us that the separation that has so exercised contemporary theologians is not intrinsic to doctrinal work but is a deformation of it.

Peter Lombard

Peter Lombard, or "the Lombard" (c1100–1161), was born in Italy but is best known for his life and work in Paris. It was there that he taught in the Cathedral School and where he would later become bishop, albeit just a year before his death. Although his immediate influence as theologian was significant, his inclusion in this chapter is warranted by the historical impact of his *Sentences* and by what its genre suggests about the nature, status, and function of Christian doctrine. The *Sentences* not only produced a particular articulation of orthodox belief, but its very style and structure also indicated a way of understanding how doctrine was taught and how orthodoxy was determined. Despite some efforts in the thirteenth century to have the work condemned (at the Fourth Lateran Council in 1215), it became the textbook for theological students and determined the shape of theological education in late medieval Europe. It was replaced in that role by the *Summa Theologiae* of Thomas Aquinas only in the seventeenth century, thus holding an authoritative place in the Roman Catholic Church until even after the Reformation.

During the centuries between Augustine and Lombard, the church's tradition had developed by asking new questions and engaging various issues. Yet, the *tradition* had remained just that, a tradition of belief variously structured around the doctrinal loci generated by the Creed and Scripture. In addition to Augustine, others had emerged as authoritative voices in the development and interpretation of that tradition. In many ways, the *Sentences* was a particular mode of drawing on the variety of voices, being instructed by them, and, where necessary, resolving differences between them. The genre was not, however, invented by the Lombard. The notion of compiling "sentences" of authoritative figures had become a common way of transmitting key teachings of those authorities and of evaluating what differences there were between them. As Philipp Rosemann has pointed out in his survey of the background to the *Sentences*, the Latin *sententia* "signifies an opinion expressed by an authoritative writer," but it also pointed to the "deeper—as opposed to merely grammatical or literal—sense of Scripture."[40] The very title both described the content and the theological significance of such collections: it pointed to "the origin of the authoritative statements of the Fathers in scriptural interpretation."[41] To quote Rosemann:

> In their pronouncements on doctrinal issues, the Fathers do not always speak with one voice. Indeed, even a single Church Father, such as Augustine … does not always seem unambiguous in his positions. Hence the need to collect and compare the Fathers' sentences on given theological topics. In addition, the sentence collections constitute an important move towards the constitution of systematically arranged, comprehensive accounts of theological knowledge.[42]

Of course, as we have already seen, Christian doctrinal writing had long been characterized by a systematic impulse and even by a comprehensiveness. But the sentence genre sharpened both of these impulses by lending itself to the function of instruction at a time when theology was becoming an academic discipline. Theology was being generated less immediately by the pastoral and liturgical ministries of the church, and more by the need to train theologians. In this context, such collections of sentences became textbooks.[43] Yet, they also became the vehicle by which their compilers developed their own stamp on the received material. They "articulated their own views while teaching students to think theologically, and critically, about the legacy of the Christian tradition."[44] Some of this can be seen in Prologue to the *Sentences*.

Lombard announces his task as a work of defense of the received faith. But constructively, he also set out to "reveal the hidden depths of theological investigations."[45] He presents his work as drawn from "the witnesses of truth established from all eternity."[46] Recognizing the authority of the tradition, he announces, "Here you will find the teaching and precedents of our ancestors."[47] There is a certain pragmatism to the genre: "In this brief volume, we have brought together the sentences of the fathers and the testimonies apposite to them, so that one who seeks them shall find it unnecessary to rifle though numerous books, when this brief collection effortlessly offers him what he seeks."[48] Yet he is also clear that in resisting heresies and expounding authorities, his work is not without its own qualified innovations:

> Here by the sincere profession of the Lord's faith, we have denounced the falsehood of a poisonous doctrine. Embracing an approach to showing the truth without incurring the danger of professing impiety, we have pursued a moderate middle course between the two. And if in some places our voice has rung out a little loudly, it has not transgressed the bounds set by our forefathers.[49]

Lombard's own voice can be said to be heard most clearly in his doctrine of God and his insistence, against both the Platonic and apophatic traditions, that God *in se* was the proper object of theology.[50] For present purposes, however, it is important first to note the general structure of the *Sentences* before exploring his treatment of the Eucharist as a brief case study of his engagement with doctrine.

The work is divided into four "Books" with the following headings: Book 1: The Mystery of the Trinity; Book 2: On Creation; Book 3: On the Incarnation of the Word; Book 4: On the Doctrine of Signs. Each book is divided into sets of "distinctions" that are, in turn, divided into chapters. Each distinction establishes a given topic or thesis, sometimes in the form of query, and the chapters present the positions of various authoritative voices, their status and problems, before stating some form of conclusion.

Turning to the case study of the presentation of Eucharist that is located in Distinctions VII–XIII of Book IV, we see how the material begins with comments about the relationship between baptism and Eucharist, followed by discussions, *inter alia*, of its Old Testament "prefiguration," its institution and form, the relationship between sign and reality, participation by the unworthy, the location of Christ's body, and the sacrificial nature of the Eucharist. In this text, we see not only the method in use but also evidence of the medieval notions of sacramental signs and their relationship both to the act of faith and to the reality of the church as the mystical body of Christ:

> ON THE ERROR OF SOME, WHO SAY THAT THE BODY OF CHRIST IS RECEIVED ONLY BY THE GOOD. These words and others like them, where the subject of spiritual eating is discussed, have enveloped in the darkness of error some people who read them with an obtuse heart, some that have dared to say that the body and blood of Christ are received only by the good, and not by those who are wicked. — But without a doubt it is to be held that they are received by the good not only sacramentally, but also spiritually; by the wicked only sacramentally, that is, under the sacrament. These received under the visible species the flesh of Christ derived from the Virgin, and the blood shed for us, but not the mystical flesh which pertains only to the good. This is what is proved by the testimonies appended below.
>
> GREGORY, IN BOOK 4 OF THE *DIALOGUES*. Gregory says: "The true flesh of Christ and his true blood are indeed in sinners and in those who receive them unworthily, but in their essence, not in their saving effectives." —AUGUSTINE, ON THE WORDS OF THE GOSPEL. Also Augustine: "many receive the body of the Lord unworthily, of whom the Apostle says: *Whoever eats [the bread] and drinks the Lord's cup unworthily, he eats and drinks his own judgement.*" AUGUSTINE, ON JOHN: "By this we are taught how much we need to avoid receiving what is good in a wicked way. For, you see, wickedness is done, when that which is good is wickedly received. Just as on the contrary, an evil that was well received became a good to the Apostle, namely when the sting of Satan is patiently born?"…
>
> The same [Augustine]: "One who receives the body of the Lord unworthily does not thereby make that which he received evil because he is wicked, or received nothing because does not receive it for salvation. For it was still the body and blood of the Lord, even in those whom the Apostle said: *Whoever eats unworthily*," etc. —By

these and other authorities, it is plainly shown that the true body and blood Christ is taken even by wicked people, but sacramentally and not spiritually.[51]

As well as demonstrating the general pattern of appealing to an existing and developing doctrinal tradition pursued in the *Sentences*, this brief example also demonstrates something of the tone and assumptions of medieval theology. The point to emphasize here, however, is that the *Sentences*, precisely with this approach, itself became one of the authorities that mediated the tradition and was consulted for its insights as the tradition unfolded and addressed new issues. As Rosemann sets out in his detailed study of the work's reception and use, both expanded and abridged versions were produced within the first few decades of its existence.[52] From the thirteenth century onward, it becomes the object of multiple commentaries and was absorbed into the pedagogical practices of the emerging traditions of university education and the scholastic theology they fostered. It became the text on which later theologians would test and develop their skills as theologians and teachers. Bonaventure, Aquinas, Duns Scotus, William of Ockham, and eventually Martin Luther all produced commentaries on Lombard's text. Moreover, not only did it thus inform and shape the tradition of scholarly theology; through the commentary of Alexander Hales, it also shaped the mendicant Franciscan order of whose theology Alexander was a founding influence.[53]

What does this brief engagement with Lombard tell us about doctrine? It is both the content of teaching and the object of dispute. Its disputes are resolved, not arbitrarily, but through engagement with previous authorities. More overtly than in some of the other examples studied in this chapter, doctrine is not developed, and its disputes are not solved, primarily or decisively by biblical exegesis. There is now a much more developed tradition of doctrine that provides a doctrinal discourse in which the appeals to authoritative figures (which may well include their respective exegetical work) and the deposit of their thought constitute the field of further doctrinal discussion and the resolution of its problems.

Thomas Aquinas

Thomas was born in Aquino, south-east of Rome in 1225. A prodigious student, he was sent to Naples at the age of 14 where he was exposed to the European revival of Aristotle. This philosophical foundation would deeply shape his later theological work and positioned him to address the relationship between the new philosophical learning and Christian doctrine. This in itself has generated a significant and abiding controversy in the reception of his work. Commentators have vigorously discussed whether his work was to be received primarily as that of a philosopher or that of a theologian. Certainly, much recent scholarship has emphasized the primarily theological character of his work.[54] His explicit theological endeavors began following his entry into the Dominican order under whose auspices he continued his education and in which he would ultimately teach, variously in Paris, Cologne, Rome, and Naples. As a young theological teacher he wrote his own commentary on Lombard's *Sentences* and subsequently also various biblical commentaries. His most famous works are *Summa contra Gentiles* and the *Summa Theologiae*. As well as containing his famous discussion of the relation between natural and revealed truths, the former addresses the substantial matters of Christian doctrine in terms of their distinction from those of Judaism and Islam. The *Summa Theologiae*, of greater relevance for the present discussion, is a much longer work and constitutes an extended and detailed engagement with the teachings of the Catholic Church. It was written for theological students to assist them in developing a critical understanding of the faith. It was begun in Rome, continued in Paris, and came to an abrupt end in Naples when, in 1273, after a series of mystical experiences, Thomas resolved to write no further. Indeed, it is said that he declared that he had come to the realization that everything he had written was "straw." He died in 1274. While his teaching had been condemned by the archbishop of Paris, he was recognized as a doctor of the church in 1567.

The *Summa* is divided into three main categories: the *prima pars*, which is concerned with God's existence, the creation of the world, and the human person; the *secunda pars*, which addresses matters of ethics by providing a general moral framework before developing an account of particular virtues and vices; and the *tertia pars*, which considers incarnation, soteriology, the sacraments, and eschatology. This order is noteworthy, not least for the *prima facie* oddness of locating the ethics between God and Christology. More will be said below about this order, but attention will first be given to this pedagogical intent. For this we turn to his Foreword:

> Since the teacher of Catholic truth has not only to build up those who are advanced but also to shape those who are beginning, according to St. Paul, *Even as unto babes in Christ I have fed you with milk and not*

meat, the purpose we have set before us in this work is to convey the things which belong to the Christian religion in a style serviceable for the training of beginners.

We have considered how newcomers to this teaching are greatly hindered by various writings on the subject partly because of the swarm of pointless questions, articles, and arguments, partly because essential information is given according to the requirements of textual commentary or the occasions of academic debate, not to a sound educational method, partly because repetitiousness has bred boredom and muddle in their thinking.

Eager, therefore, to avoid these and other like drawbacks, and trusting in God's help, we shall try to pursue the things held by Christian theology, and to be concise and clear, so far as the matter allows.[55]

The Foreword is something of a clearing exercise. Aquinas is quite clear about the task he faces as a "teacher of Catholic truth" to "beginners." He is determined to avoid the hurdles that others have placed in the way of such students: undue complexity, unnecessary distractions, and the technicalities of conventional discourses. As a self-described "teacher of Catholic truth," Thomas presents this work as an exposition of and inquiry into what has been received as authoritative. The hope for straightforward clarity intimated in the Foreword is, however, rather quickly deflated as the *Summa* begins to unfold in a sequence of questions that are answered through engagement with objections and counterarguments. Nevertheless, the complexity is not to be dismissed as the result of an allegedly academic obtuseness. It simply reflects Thomas's capacity to perceive the multiple lines of enquiry that are opened up by any engagement with "Catholic truth." The element of inquiry is evident straight away in Question 1, "On what sort of teaching Christian theology is and what it covers."[56] Tackling the question from ten perspectives, the reader is introduced to the relationship between reason and revelation, the relationship between Christian teaching and philosophy, the role of authoritative teachers, references to the articles of faith, theological language, and the interpretation of Scripture.

Thomas's comments about the articles of faith indicate how he perceives the relationship between his own work and that of the church's core teaching. But first, what, in fact, are these articles of faith? To answer this, it is necessary to jump ahead to the *secunda pars*. There, in a discussion about the Creed, conciliar and papal authority, and the development of doctrine, he lists fourteen articles of faith—seven clustering around the majesty of the Godhead and the economy of creation and redemption, and seven related to the humanity of Christ. In the former category are the unity of the Godhead, the trinity of Persons, the order of nature, the order of grace, the sanctification of humanity, the order of redemption, and the resurrection of the dead. In the latter category are Christ's incarnation, his virginal birth, his death and burial, his descent into hell, his resurrection, his ascension, and his return in judgment.[57] These articles reflect the main elements of the Creed. Aware that this is what he meant, we can return to our main text of interest, Question 1 of the *prima pars*. There, he writes that holy teaching "work[s] from the articles of faith to infer other things"[58] and that these articles of faith are "the first principles of this science."[59] In other words, holy teaching builds from these articles of faith by inquiry and exposition, and through drawing implications and proposing applications.

But why is this science of holy teaching needed? Answering this question leads into a discussion of the relationship between reason and revelation. Strikingly, the need for holy teaching based on revelation is defended not simply as a matter of theological epistemology but quite explicitly within the framework of soteriology: "It was to prosper the salvation of human beings, and the more widely and less anxiously, that they were provided for by divine revelation about divine things."[60] As he develops this account from this starting point, Scripture is frequently invoked to justify or direct his arguments. While the doctors of the church are also included among "proper authorities," they are subordinated to the witness of Scripture: "For our faith rests on the revelation made to the Prophets and Apostles, who wrote the canonical books, not on a revelation, if such there be, made to any other teacher."[61] Of course, that is not to say that Scripture is not to be interpreted. Entering a conversation with Augustine on this matter, Thomas prioritizes the literal sense of Scripture (over allegory, for example). But this literal sense is not itself "holy teaching," nor is the literal sense necessarily self-evident from the surface of the text. Appealing to something like a rule of faith, Thomas insists that the literal sense of Scripture is what God intends, since "God is the author of Holy Scripture" and has the power of "adapting words to convey meanings."[62]

The soteriological framework of holy teaching is also evident in Thomas's discussion of whether it is a "practical science." His answer is cautiously affirmative but nevertheless unambiguous in relation to the ultimate purpose of any knowledge of divine things:

> Whereas some among the philosophical sciences are theoretical and others are practical, sacred doctrine takes over both functions, in this being like the single knowledge whereby God knows himself and the things he makes.
>
> All the same it is more theoretical than practical, since it is mainly concerned with the divine things which are, rather than with things men do; it deals with human acts only in so far as they prepare men for that achieved knowledge of God on which their eternal bliss reposes.[63]

Awareness of this soteriological orientation can also help to clarify the doctrinal structure of the *Summa*, the *prima facie* oddness of which was noted above. The oddness was perceived to lie in placing ethics between God and Christology. Yet it has been argued that this structure actually reflects Thomas's own understanding of the relationships between God, creation, and redemption. So Nicholas Healy argues,

> The first part [of the *Summa*], for example, moves outwards from God as such through God as Creator to creation as such. The rest of the treatise charts creation's movement back to God, beginning in the second part with an exploration of how it is possible for people to act in accordance with the good (including a full-scale treatment of the virtues suitable for the confessional), and concluding in the third part with an extended discussion of Jesus Christ (who is "our way" to God), followed by an account of the special gifts given through Christ: the Church, the sacraments, and life in heaven. The [*Summa*] as a whole thus describes a process of emanation and return (*exitus et reditus*) that Thomas abstracts from Scripture in order to allow his readers to return to Scripture with greater insight.[64]

These matters take us more deeply into Thomas's thought and to the rest of the *Summa* than is possible to engage here, but allowing for this interpretation, it becomes an illustration of the way a particular theologian's convictions about particular doctrines shape the way that theologian presents doctrine.

The genre of the *Summa*, that of *disputatio*, was an existing method of teaching and enquiry. In Thomas's case, it involves the naming of a theological topic, an acknowledgement of objections to it, followed by a positive statement or statements, leading into rebuttals of the objections. Despite this summary suggesting an overtly adversarial tone, something deeper than that is going on. It reflects a particular way in which holy teaching enquires into and reaches its understanding of the truth. Timothy Radcliffe offers this insight into what is at stake here: "The whole of the *Summa* is founded on considering the arguments of opponents, taking them seriously, modifying then refining one's opinions in the light of their objections, and seeking the larger truth in which we can be one."[65] Radcliffe links this connection between knowledge and a community of knowing to Thomas's Dominican context, but his point has larger significance with implications for how the wider Christian church engages doctrine in its quest to be faithful and true. As Radcliffe further notes, "If knowing is not, then, a private affair of the solitary ego, but is embedded in my belonging to others, then obviously thinking together is part of our communal life. Argument is … but one of the ways in which we build and sustain the community of truth."[66]

We will return to this matter of the relationship between argument, community, knowledge, doctrine, and truth in Chapters 4 and 5.

Catherine of Siena

Catherine of Siena (1347–1380) is frequently described as a mystic and may at first sight seem to be out of place in this study of doctrinal theologians. Of course, the modern understanding of "mystic" may well be inappropriate when applied to Catherine and other medieval figures. More significantly, however, no matter how the so-called mystical element of her teaching might be defined or assessed, her inclusion in this book stems from the fact that within the Roman Catholic Church, she is officially recognized as a *doctor ecclesiae*. In other words, she has the status as an authoritative teacher of the church's faith. She is, in fact, one of only four women to be so designated by the Roman Catholic Church.[67] Her gender explains some of the contemporary interest in her work.[68] But so does the form of her teaching that, as will be noted later, is not unrelated to her gender. Whether the title "mystic" illuminates or distracts from attempts to understand her theology and influence, the fact is that the mode of her teaching is distinctive but no less doctrinal for that. Contemporary understandings of mysticism that present it as a contrast to a doctrinally informed faith do not hold up when the mystics in question are medieval Christian mystics, and certainly not Catherine.

Catherine's short life was marked by devotion from her earliest years, the initial impulses to which were a vision of Christ when she was just 6 years of age and the death of her sister in childbirth when Catherine herself was 15. At the age of 22, she joined the *mantellate*, an order of nuns committed to both active community service and prayer. Catherine became famous for her ministry of letter writing through which she provided guidance, instruction, and counsel. She was involved in church reform and was known for her involvement in papal diplomacy.[69] The main elements of her literary corpus are *The Letters*, *The Dialogue*, and *Prayers*. It is *The Dialogue* that will be the focus of this brief engagement with her work.

The Dialogue is divided into ten sections. Its point of departure is a set of four petitions that Catherine put to God. These are for herself, the form of the church, the whole world, and for God's providence toward an unspecified "certain case that has arisen."[70] As the work unfolds, some of these petitions are differentiated and/or developed. It is, however, as her petitions for the world and the church are further specified that she advances God's answer to these petitions. This directs her to Christ as "the bridge" between God and the world. Walking across that bridge is the way of truth that must be followed if there is to be peace in the church and the world. Indeed, "The Bridge" is the title of the core section of the whole work. The answer to Catherine's petitions is essentially a particular statement of the saving work of the incarnation and its continuation in the work of the Holy Spirit. To the extent that *The Dialogue* addresses the particular concerns Catherine has for the church and world, it does so by an exposition of basic doctrines.

Actually, to describe this as an "exposition" is slightly misleading. So, before attending to details of the core section, it is important to address the genre. When, in the above, reference is made to "question and answer," it is to point out that *The Dialogue* literally presents as a conversation between Catherine and God, although with Catherine speaking either in the first person or obliquely as "a soul." God, however, always speaks in the first person. Yet this is not *merely* a question of genre, as if the one genre might have been exchanged for another. *This* genre actually reflects a particular combination of thought and experience. Catherine's peers and early commentators refer to the ecstatic process by which her writing came about. One of those commentators, Caffarini, reported that he had seen Catherine "rapt beyond senses, except for speech, by which she dictated to various writers in succession sometimes letters and sometimes the book, in different times and in different places, as circumstances allowed."[71] Yet it is also acknowledged that she would edit and modify what had been dictated, thus more explicitly taking responsibility for what would then be published for a wider readership.

In the lead up to the section of *The Dialogue* designated "The Bridge," God has directed Catherine to the divine love as the source of the ultimate response to her petitions. Indeed, the immediately preceding section of *The Dialogue* concludes with Catherine exclaiming, "O immeasurably tender love! Who would not be set afire with such love? What heart would keep from breaking? You, deep well of charity, it seems you are so madly in love with your creatures that you could not live without us! … What could move you to such mercy? Neither duty nor any need you have of us … but only love."[72] The longer engagement with the incarnation that then follows is introduced as a response to this exclamation in order "to stir up even more that soul's love for the salvation of souls."[73]

The bridge "stretches from heaven to earth by reason of my having joined myself with your humanity, which I formed from the earth's clay."[74] Then follows a more specific description of the bridge which has three steps which correspond to the "spiritual stages":

> The first stair is the feet, which symbolize the affections. For just as the feet carry the body, the affections carry the soul, My Son's nailed feet are a stair by which you can climb to his side, where you will see revealed his inmost heart. For when the soul has climbed up on the feet of affection and looked with her mind's eye into my Son's opened heart, she begins to feel the love of her own heart in his consummate and unspeakable love … Then the soul, seeing how tremendously she is loved, is herself filled to overflowing with love. So, having climbed the second stair she reaches the third. This is his mouth, where she finds peace from the terrible war she has had to wage because of her sins.
>
> At the first stair, lifting the feet of her affections from the earth, she stripped herself of sin. At the second she dressed herself in love for virtue. And at the third she tasted peace.[75]

The bridge is the way the "children of truth"[76] pass into fellowship with God. Those who choose instead to cross through the river across which the bridge has been built will drown. The metaphor is placed under some strain once the ascension is taken into account. Catherine builds this into the metaphor as she introduces the work of the Holy Spirit. God is said to acknowledge that following the Son's ascension, "the bridge was raised high above the earth."[77] A bridge still exists, now in the form of the memory of Jesus' teaching brought to mind by the work of the Spirit:

> When he had been raised on high and returned to me, his Father, I sent the teacher, the Holy Spirit. He came with my power and my Son's wisdom and his own mercy. He is one thing with me, the Father and with my Son. He came to make even more firm the road my Truth had left in the world through his teaching. So though my Son's presence was no longer with you, teaching—the way of which he made for you this lovely and glorious bridge—remained.[78]

Catherine then poses the question about how this witness of the Holy Spirit is to be trusted. Her answer, placed on God's lips, points to the church and the works and words of his martyrs, confessors, and doctors. This way to fellowship with God has been

> verified by the apostles and proclaimed in the blood of the martyrs. It has been lighted up by the doctors, attested to by the confessors, and committed to writing by the evangelists. All of these are living witness to the truth in the mystic body of holy Church. They are like lamps set on a lampstand to point out the way of truth, perfectly lighted, that leads to life.[79]

The teaching that makes up the remainder of this section of *The Dialogue* provides more detailed instruction and reflection on how this way to fellowship with God is to be pursued and the consequence for those who choose not to cross the bridge.

Attention has been given here to the content of Catherine's work focused in the metaphor of the bridge. This is to highlight that her way of responding to the presenting issues is to offer an account of some of the fundamentals of the Christian faith. As well as being rich with metaphor, the work is propelled by intensive spiritual dialogue. It is not entirely clear just how the content in this genre address the "certain case" that had arisen. It is on this point, however, that the question of her gender and the work's genre intersect. It has been argued that this heavily metaphorical and mystical discourse is exactly how a medieval woman—denied the formal training of a theologian—would appropriate and mediate the church's teaching. Tina Beattie has highlighted this through dialogue with an essay by Karen Scott. According to Scott, "Catherine sought an ever deeper rooting of Christian doctrine within her soul—memory, intellect and will—through an exchange of words with God. Her mysticism is expressed in speech about divine love, not in visions or silence."[80] Her "speech about divine love" is both shaped by her informal knowledge of doctrine and the genre of her writing, which included speaking God's voice in the first person. Beattie herself has noted how these features of Catherine's work are determined by her gendered social location:

> As a woman, Catherine could not possibly have written in the style of [Aquinas], for she had no access to the conventions and rules of Latin scholasticism. Gendered difference was institutionalized and codified at every level of late medieval life. Women had to speak from within the world to which they were assigned, and to claim such authority as they could through direct authorization by God—which, in Catherine's case, includes "authoring" God's voice within her own texts.[81]

Beattie's observations have much wider significance for the present study. Not only do they press the question of the role of gender in the production and mediation of all doctrine, but they also indirectly pose the question to all doctrinal discourse: Whose voice is being spoken? Appeals to the authority of the church are never benign or transparent. Any discomfort with Catherine's "authoring" of God's own voice should not obscure such "authoring" implicit or unconscious in theologians employing modes of writing and genres where the appeal to divine authority is less direct (but no less real). As we will see in the next chapter, gender has become an inescapable element in the interpretation, reception, and production of Christian doctrine.

John Calvin

John Calvin (1509-1564) was a scholar, pastor, teacher, and civic reformer who, through various editions of his *Institutes of the Christian Religion*, bequeathed a particular doctrinal shape to the theology of Reformed Christianity. Born in France, Calvin was educated in the liberal arts, ancient languages, classical literature, and law. In this respect, he was an heir to, and product of, the flowering of scholarship and the *ad fontes* impulses of the Renaissance. By the time of his legal studies, the

Christian Doctrine

Reformation, initiated by Martin Luther (1483–1546) in Germany, was well underway. It had begun to attract interest and support in France, despite the opposition of most of the country's Catholic rulers. Exactly how and when Calvin was drawn to the new reforming faith is unclear. Nevertheless, by 1535, he was among the French followers of the new faith who sought exile in Basel on account of the persecution of the reforming movement in France. It was in Basel that he wrote and published the first edition of the *Institutes* in 1536.

The warm reception of this work appears to have confirmed Calvin in his vocation to work for and amongst the Reformers. To this end, he intended to travel to Strasbourg. On his way, he was forced to detour via the newly Protestant Geneva where he was more or less commandeered by Guillame Farel (1485–1565) to stay and join in building up the church in that city. As this work began, Farel and Calvin raised the ire of the civil authorities and were forced to leave in 1538. This allowed Calvin to proceed (at last!) to Strasbourg where he pastored a French Reformed congregation for several years until being summoned back to Geneva in 1541. He remained there for the rest of his life.

Controversy was never far away from Calvin. Whether doctrinal (e.g., his doctrine of double predestination) or ethical (e.g., his endorsement of the execution of Michael Servetus) or political (his drawn-out struggle with the city's rulers), these controversies have been well documented and discussed in Calvin scholarship.[82] As with the other case studies in this chapter, however, our interest is in his commitment to, and understanding of, doctrinal work. In fact, Calvin is quite explicit about both these issues, not least in the various prefaces to the respective editions of the *Institutes*. Indeed, the fact that there were various editions of this work, spanning almost a quarter of a century, is itself revealing. As Calvin says in his "Letter to the Reader" of the fifth and final Latin edition of 1559, it had taken him until this edition to be satisfied with the "order now set forth."[83] So, it is worth comparing the order of the first edition with that of the final one. The first edition consists of six chapters of catechetical instruction headed, respectively, Law (with a focus on the Decalogue), Faith (an exposition of the Apostles' Creed), Prayer (an exposition of the Lord's Prayer), The Sacraments, The Five False Sacraments and Christian Freedom, Ecclesiastical Power, and Political Administration. The order of the fifth edition, approximately seven times the length of the first, while not contradicting anything about the first, is less eclectic and more explicitly revealing of a vision of what the Christian faith is. It is divided into four "books," each of which is divided into varying numbers of chapters that themselves divide into numerous sections. The four books are headed as follows:

Book 1: The Knowledge of God the Creator

Book 2: The Knowledge of God the Redeemer in Christ, First Disclosed to the Fathers under the Law, and Then to Us in the Gospel

Book 3: The Way in Which We Receive the Grace of Christ: What Benefits Come to Us from It, and What Effects Follow

Book 4: The External Means or Aids by Which God Invites Us into the Society of Christ and Holds Us Therein

This order could be summarized in various ways, but perhaps the simplest would be to suggest Creation, Christology, Salvation, and Ecclesiology. In each of these books, Calvin displays all manner of significant theological insight. These include his account of the mutual dependence of the knowledge of God and human self-knowledge, his insistence on grace as both justifying and sanctifying, his particular understanding of sacramental mediation that is neither transubstantive nor memorialist, and his developed understanding of the relationship between church, ministry, and civil authorities. As he develops these themes, he does so in dialogue and/or vigorous debate not only with Catholic theology but also with the theologies of his fellow Lutheran and Zwinglian reformers (with whom some of his disagreements are as sharp as those with Rome). Clearly, notwithstanding the neatness of the vision suggested in the headings of the books, it is a profoundly polemical work, rhetorically strategic, and one in which Calvin's heart is as evident to the reader as his intellect. In that respect, the final edition is continuous with the first. In order to grasp that, it is worth noting the English translation of the full Latin title of the first edition.

> *The Institute of the Christian Religion, Containing Almost the Whole Sum of Piety and Whatever It Is Necessary to Know in the Doctrine of Salvation. A Work Very Well Worth Reading by All Persons Zealous for Piety, and Lately Published. A Preface to the Most Christian King of France, in Which this Book is Presented to Him as a Confession of Faith. Author, John Calvin, of Noyon. Basel, MDXXXVI.*[84]

This tells us that Calvin did not simply offer the work as an orderly account of the faith as an end in itself. The *Institutes* begin their life at the hand of a Christian in exile defending his faith to the ruler of the day, and doing so for the sake and comfort of others who were vulnerable to persecution by that same ruler. It is also noteworthy that Calvin retained the preface to the first edition in all subsequent editions when the other intervening prefaces had been omitted, even after King Francis had died. Something of the violent and polemical context into which Calvin writes is set out in the second paragraph of this first preface:

> I perceived that the fury of certain wicked persons has prevailed so far in your realm that there is no place in it for sound doctrine. Consequently, it seemed to me that I should be doing something worthwhile if I both gave instruction to them [the French evangelicals] and made confession before you with the same work. From this you may learn the nature of the doctrine against which those madmen burn with rage who today disturb your realm with fire and sword. And indeed I shall not fear to confess that here is contained almost the sum of that very doctrine which they shout must be punished by prison, exile, proscription, and fire, and be exterminated on land and sea. Indeed, I know with what horrible reports that have filled your ears and mind, to render our cause as hateful as possible to you.[85]

In what ends up being a very lengthy preface, Calvin resists the accusations of novelty, discontinuity with the church Fathers, and socially disruptive behavior that was charged against France's Reformed Christians.

Certainly, by the time of the final edition, the Reformation is a fact and its churches have claimed a more assured, if still contested, place in Europe. But, of course, Calvin's energies are now invested in Geneva and its established Reformed church. His focus now is not so much the immediacy of defending the persecuted but consolidating the ministry of the established church. To this end, his key goal is to teach doctrine in order that Scripture might be read rightly and profitably:

> I believe I have so embraced the sum of religion in all its parts, and have arranged it in such an order that if anyone rightly grasps it, it will not be difficult for him to determine what he ought especially to seek in Scripture, and to what end he ought to relate its contents.[86]

The orientation of the work to Scripture is not separate from its order or from the purpose of deepening his readers' piety. As Randall Zachman has noted, "the order and series of teaching of the *Institutes* is not dictated by logic, or even solely by the order of teaching in Scripture, but rather by Calvin's understanding of the way the awareness and experience of God and ourselves develops and grows."[87] Indeed, according to Zachman, for Calvin, "the pious are taught both by Scripture and by the experience of piety itself."[88] Nevertheless, for present purposes, some brief comment on the status of Scripture vis-à-vis doctrine in Calvin is necessary. It is worth observing that Calvin wrote far more in the genre of biblical commentary than he ever did on doctrine. Indeed, he wrote commentaries on nearly every book of the Bible. Within the *Institutes* themselves, every topic is developed on the basis of biblical warrants. Indeed, it could be said that for Calvin, doctrine simply is the content of Scripture. This tight nexus of doctrine and Scripture is evident throughout *Institutes* I.vi–xi and is especially clearly stated in this comment: "[The] credibility of doctrine is not established until we are persuaded beyond doubt that God is its author. Thus the highest proof of scripture derives in general from the fact that God in person speaks in it."[89] Calvin argues at length that such persuasion is not provided by any ecclesial authority. It is provided by the "inward testimony of the Spirit."[90] The same rejection of ecclesial authority and the contrasting appeal to the Spirit is extended to the reading of Scripture and the teaching of its contents. The "sole office" of the church's teachers "is to teach what is provided and sealed in the Holy Scriptures."[91] Against the "bishops and prelates" of the Roman church who "coin dogmas after their own whim, which … they afterwards require to be subscribed to as articles of faith,"[92] Calvin proposes this rule: "God deprives men of the capacity to put forth new doctrine in order that he alone may be our schoolmaster in spiritual doctrine as he alone is true who can neither lie nor deceive."[93] It must be noted, of course, that any such direct appeals to God's direct teaching or to the Spirit's inward testimony are carefully distinguished by Calvin from the appeals made by the "fanatics" and "certain giddy men" who, "having forsaken Scripture, imagine some way or other of reaching God" and thus "despise the Scripture doctrine as childish and mean."[94] For Calvin, in contrast, Scripture itself is the means of hearing the Spirit's voice: "We ought zealously to apply ourselves both to read and to hearken to Scripture if indeed we want to receive any gain and benefit from the Spirit of God."[95]

Matters of the relationship between Scripture, tradition, and church office have already been encountered in some of the other writers examined in this chapter. But with Calvin they are treated with an exceptionally high degree of polemic. That the unequivocal primacy of Scripture and its direct divine authentication are stressed so strongly reflects Calvin's need to articulate the necessary critical leverage over what he believed was Rome's displacement of biblical authority by ecclesial—indeed, papal—authority. As one commentator has observed in relation to this aspect of Calvin's theology: "If Scripture was not an authority over the church, then it could not be appealed to in cases where the Church had strayed into error."[96] Yet the polemics should not obscure Calvin's constructive point that has already been noted in his various comments about the orientation of his work. If it is the case that Scripture actually contains doctrine that the church's teachers are to draw out, then the work of such teaching, according to Calvin, is to produce wisdom. Indeed, it is the category of wisdom that brackets the entirety of Book 1 of the Institutes (precisely where he locates his extended reflections on Scripture). With the very first sentence he declares, "Nearly all the wisdom we possess, that is to say, true and sound wisdom, consist of two parts: the knowledge of God and of ourselves."[97] After many pages of defending the authority of Scripture and its doctrine he concludes, "For our wisdom ought to be nothing else than to embrace with humble teachableness … whatever is taught in Sacred Scripture."[98]

Even allowing for the polemical context in which they are set, such statements may appear hermeneutically naive to twenty-first-century readers with their assumptions about the inevitable complexities of reading, not to mention the ideological prejudices and self-deception that are at risk in all reading exercises. Ironically, however, in many ways that is exactly Calvin's point. The church errs in its readings of Scripture; indeed, it manipulates its reading of Scripture for its own ends. For him, this was as evident in Rome as it was in the fanatics. Nevertheless, if he placed—at least rhetorically—too much confidence in his own resistance to such errors, Calvin opens the critical space between any doctrinal claim and Scripture, and consequently bequeathed to the Reformed tradition a formal subordination of doctrine to Scripture. But, just as ironically, that same subordination also bequeathed what was a certain biblical foundationalism the effect of which was to isolate Scripture from a wider doctrinal framework that provides Scripture with its meaning and function.[99] How Scripture and doctrine mutually shape each other is a key issue in contemporary discussions of doctrine, often in reaction to this Protestant biblical foundationalism. Yet such foundationalism was not Calvin's. Calvin reaches the sections on Scripture in the *Institutes* only after he has spent the first five chapters of Book 1 discussing the human predicament, God's response to it in Jesus Christ, and the need for Scripture to bring these matters to human awareness. In other words, even if the details are contestable, with Calvin, the doctrine of Scripture is mutually shaped by doctrines of creation, sin, and redemption.

Before leaving Calvin, there is one final observation to make. The question of the intellectual organization of the church's teaching has already been observed in several of the theologians studied so far in this chapter. It has a certain conspicuousness in Calvin precisely because of the manner in which that order developed as he moved from the first to the final edition of the *Institutes*. This order reflected, at least in the final edition, what he described as "the sum of religion in all its parts." The material is not just ordered but also presented as a comprehensive vision of what Christianity is. In later centuries, the link between comprehensiveness and doctrine would become a key criticism of doctrinal work. But Calvin's quest for seeking some unity among "all the parts" of Christianity remains salutary even as suspicion is directed to such a quest.

Friedrich Schleiermacher

Friedrich Schleiermacher (1768–1834) is often described as the father of modern theology and sometimes as the father of liberal Protestantism. That these two descriptions are often interchangeable is itself revealing of his context and significance. For a combination of cultural and historical factors, Protestant theology, especially in its German manifestations, bore the brunt of much of the Enlightenment critique of Christianity.[100] A German theologian in the Reformed tradition, Schleiermacher was instrumental in providing some of the most seminal and influential responses to that critique. Yet the above descriptions of Schleiermacher also obscure, because his impact extended far beyond theology narrowly defined. His influence reached into hermeneutics, philosophy, and even into the conceptual and institutional design of the University of Berlin. He was a famous and popular preacher, something reflected in the estimated twenty thousand people who lined the streets of Berlin for his funeral.

Much of his posture toward the challenge posed by the Enlightenment critique is captured in the title of his first major work: *On Religion: Speeches to its Cultured Despisers*. Schleiermacher was presenting a defense of religion to Europe's newly emboldened critics of it. Much of the boldness stemmed from the "Copernican Revolution" in philosophy effected by Immanuel Kant (1724–1804). The mostly conventional view that knowledge was produced by the impact of reality upon the human knower was turned on its head by Kant. He insisted that the mind itself provides the structure and categories by which reality is known. This might sound a commonplace to contemporary readers. But in the eighteenth century, against the background of long-held and highly developed common assumptions about metaphysics and theological ideas of revelation, this was indeed a revolution. According to Kant, there was no knowledge of things in themselves (what he termed *noumena*); there was knowledge only of things as they were constructed by our minds (what he termed *phenomena*).[101] Unsurprisingly, the extension of this argument to theological claims opened up radically new epistemological discussions for Christianity. For Kant, Christianity could be justified in only essentially ethical rather than metaphysical terms. Yet, Kant's "turn to the subject" and the priority it appears to give to human rationality produced its own critics. These included the Romantics who, while welcoming the elevation of the human subject, also argued that the subject's engagement with reality was mediated by the imagination and emotions as well as by reason. There was depth to human existence that could never be plumbed by reason alone.

Yet the Romantics with whom Schleiermacher himself was engaged did not necessarily include religion in this wider account of human existence. Those who did not were religion's "cultured despisers." Schleiermacher, on the other hand, while sharing the Romantics' rejection of the sufficiency of reason, argued that their broader vision of human existence wasn't broad enough. Rejecting the Kantian binary between ethics and metaphysics, he argued for a concept of religion that would relate to a more integrated account of human existence. To this end, he famously declared in the second of his *Speeches*: "Religion's essence is neither thinking nor doing, but intuition and feeling."[102] The appeal to feeling (*Gefühl*) has often been taken, usually infamously, as evidence of Schleiermacher simply transposing into theology Kant's "turn to the subject" and thereby that he was treating religion as a reality entirely of human provenance. Yet, what was framing this orientation to intuition and feeling was another orientation (which would certainly resonate with the Romantics), an orientation to the infinite. "Religion," he wrote in the same speech, "lives ... in the infinite nature of totality."[103] Religious intuition and feeling is a response to the impact of the infinite on the finitude of human existence. It is receptive before it is active. But he was not advocating an anthropocentric view of religion. Later in this speech, he rejected the view, which he claimed was held by "most people," that "God is obviously nothing more than the genius of humanity."[104] Instead, Schleiermacher insisted, "religion strives for a universe of which humanity,

Theologians and Doctrine

with all that belongs to it, is only an infinitely small part."[105] Obviously, such claims generate their own problems, and there has been no shortage of critical discussion about them.[106] Moreover, for present purposes, it might seem that they are at some remove from the question of doctrine. In fact, they actually provide an important part of the background to Schleiermacher's magnum opus, *Christian Faith*.[107]

The second edition of *Christian Faith* was published in 1830. It is one of the great works of modern theology. It is this, in part, because it represents the first major attempt to construct a doctrinal account of the Christian faith attentive to the challenges of the Enlightenment. But perhaps more tellingly, and certainly in the context of this present book, it is the most influential attempt to articulate a constructive account of doctrine per se against the background of those challenges. The issues Schleiermacher addressed in the *Speeches* remain live issues in *Christian Faith*, even though they are markedly different works. Where the *Speeches* was an apologetic provocation to the cultured despisers, *Christian Faith* is a work directed to the Christian community, and specifically its theological students, inhabiting the Enlightenment milieu. Despite the shift of genre, purpose, and audience, religion and feeling remain in the foreground, and they inform what is ultimately a very precise definition of doctrine. Before attending to this definition of doctrine, and being able to locate its significance, a brief overview of the structure of *Christian Faith* is in order.

There are four major divisions in *Christian Faith*. Their titles, subtitles where applicable, and the number of sections with each of those divisions are as follows:

Introduction: §§ 1–31

The Doctrines of Faith, Part One: §§ 32–61

> *Explication of Religious Self-Consciousness as It Is Always Already Presupposed by, But Also Always Contained in, Every Christian Religious Stirring of the Mind and Heart*

The Doctrines of the Faith, Part Two: §§ 62–169

> *Explications of the Facts of Religious Self-Consciousness as They Are Defined in Terms of Contrasting Features.*

Conclusion: Regarding Divine Threeness §§ 170–2

The further subdivisions of the second and third divisions are strikingly elaborate. Suffice it to say that the second division deals with God and God's relationship to the world, and the third division deals with sin, Christology, redemption, the church, and eschatology. Clearly, Schleiermacher's account of these doctrines warrants close attention by students of doctrine. But of note for this study are the much shorter first and fourth divisions, that is, the Introduction and Conclusion. The former because of the understanding of doctrine set out in it. The latter because of the controversy surrounding this positioning of the doctrine of the Trinity.

The definition of doctrine comes in the fourth section of chapter 1 of the Introduction. In the course of the earlier sections of the chapter, he has developed an argument for the distinctiveness of Christianity. It includes the claim that in Christianity, "everything is referred to the redemption accomplished through Jesus of Nazareth."[108] Doctrine, it turns out, is no exception. His key claims about doctrine are stated in the propositions or theses that introduce §15 and §16. The former reads as follows: "Propositions regarding Christian faith (*Christliche Glaubensätze*) are conceptions of Christian religious states of mind and heart (*Gemützustände*) presented in the form of discourse."[109] The latter: "Dogmatic propositions are statements regarding faith, propositions of the presentational-didactic kind in which the intention is to attain the highest possible degree of distinct resolution."[110] These two propositions clarify the source and nature of Christian discourse and the specific role of doctrinal discourse. The combination of "mind and heart" in the description of these Christian propositions of faith is a reminder that Schleiermacher is pointing to the comprehensive nature of the human reception of Christian redemption. The whole of life is affected so that the experience of redemption generates both cognitive and affective realities. In earlier sections of chapter 1, Schleiermacher had already established the communal nature of redemption. In an important remark in §11.2, he had insisted that Christian redemption is "of a kind with which all Christians confess their faith … in such a way that there is something held in common that all have in mind."[111] So when in §15 he speaks of "Christian religious states of mind and heart," he is not referring to idiosyncratic or individual phenomena as the source of "propositions regarding Christian faith." This point is reinforced when notice is taken of the subtitle of *Christian Faith*, that is, "Interconnectedly Presented in Accordance with Principles of the Evangelical Church." Doctrinal work is an enterprise accountable to a community and its existing received teachings. This needs to be borne in mind in the light of claims that for Schleiermacher, "one's piety can be better than one's religious ideas."[112] This may well reflect aspects of the structure of Schleiermacher's argument, but it evades the nuance that Schleiermacher intends in the relationship between piety and ideas.

So far, the emphasis is on the way doctrine is grounded in the experience of redemption. This extends to the linguistic nature of doctrine. The claim more sharply focused in §15 is that this comprehensive experience of redemption is communicable in words and is appropriated by hearing them. Redemption that is mediated by proclamation itself generates discourse, and not least because the Redeemer himself communicated his "self-consciousness by virtue of discourse."[113] This important point is well summarized by Christine Helmer when she writes, "The reality of Jesus is consistently connected to discourse evoked by his presence … The soteriological dimension of Christian discourse is reproduced in, although not produced by, doctrine because doctrine is grounded conceptually in the language-reality encounter between believer … and Christ."[114] But discourse takes various forms. According to Schleiermacher, Christian discourse displays a threefold differentiation: poetics, rhetoric, and the "presentational-didactic." It is the latter that is the specific domain of doctrine. In the argument set out in §16, the purpose of such didactic doctrinal discourse is to foster an "organised process of knowing,"[115] to "resolve contradictions that rhetorical language had occasioned,"[116] and to provide "logically ordered reflection on the immediate utterances of religious self-consciousness."[117]

Moving on from the connections between redemption on doctrine and its ordering in §15 and §16, Schleiermacher turns to §17, §18, and §19. There, he sheds light on his understanding of the purpose of doctrine. In the discussions of the relevant propositions, he elaborates on the "interconnectedness" announced in the subtitle of *Christian Faith*. Doctrines are not isolated statements; instead, they are "conjoined."[118] The value of a doctrinal statement is a function of its "fruitfulness," which Schleiermacher explains as a function of "how versatile it is in alluding to kindred propositions" and thus contributing to the task of "bringing the structured body of doctrine to an integral whole."[119] This "mass of dogmatic propositions"[120] bears witness not only to Christ's original proclamation but also to the development of the Christian religious self-consciousness that has accompanied Christ's ongoing "replenishing" presence to the Christian community: "When this mass is simply taken together, it comprises the development of that original proclamation, a development increasingly being replenished."[121]

In reflecting on the functions of doctrine, these notions of "development" and "replenishment" warrant further attention. They are related to the idea in Proposition §19, that doctrine "has currency in a given social organization called a Christian church at a given time."[122] Bodies of doctrine are, therefore, *historical* phenomena. The doctrinal projects of earlier centuries cannot be transferred directly to meet the needs of the church in later centuries. Nor are they to be ignored. Attention to the substantive second and third divisions of *Christian Faith* quickly reveals the depth, constancy, and extent of Schleiermacher's engagement with the church's confessions. What he means by "doctrine that has currency" is doctrinal reflection on "what is heard within the church's public proceedings to be a presentation of shared Christian piety."[123] And, as already emphasized in this exposition of Schleiermacher, any reference to Christian piety assumes Christ's living presence to the community, a presence that can lead to "distinctive modifications of Christian consciousness."[124] Once again, however, lest this *historical* nature of Christian piety and the doctrine associated with it be thought to be entirely arbitrary or subjective, one further qualification can be provided, although it is necessary to move to a much later passage of *Christian Faith* to do so. The passage comes from §129, the main point of which is simultaneously to affirm the continuity of doctrine with Scripture while also affirming Scripture's normative role: "The Holy Scriptures of the New Testament are the first member in a whole series of presentations of the Christian faith continued ever since. On the other hand, they comprise the norm for all succeeding presentations."[125] In the body of the discussion, Schleiermacher sketches the nature of this normativity and the room it makes for diversity and novelty:

> We do not understand the Holy Scriptures in such a way that all later presentation would have to be uniformly derived from the canon and be inchoately contained in it already. That is to say, since that time when the Spirit was poured out upon all flesh, no era was also to be without a distinctive originality with respect to Christian thought. Yet on the one hand, nothing is to be regarded as a pure product of the Christian spirit unless it is possible to demonstrate that it is in accord with those original products; and on the other hand, no later product accrues an authority equal to those original writings if the aim is to ensure the Christian character of a given presentation or to point out the non-Christian character of one.[126]

Schleiermacher's Reformed sensibilities are visible. The normativity of Scripture is clear. But as with every other aspect of Schleiermacher's understanding of doctrine, so its relationship to Scripture rightly generates much critical discussion.[127] More generally, any interpreter of Schleiermacher has to engage this normativity of Scripture alongside the openness to genuine "originality" in Christian thought and then bring that dynamic into the equally complex relationship Schleiermacher posits between doctrine, the Christian experience of redemption, and the dialogue with the confessions. Yet, notwithstanding its problems and inherent tensions, his understanding of doctrine per se, shaped as it was by a range of novel intellectual and cultural circumstances, was arguably unprecedented in its sophistication.

There remains one final matter to address, albeit much more briefly, in this engagement with Schleiermacher. It relates to the location of the doctrine of the Trinity in *Christian Faith*. Placed at the very end of the work, Schleiermacher presents it as the "copestone" (*Schlußstein*).[128] The basic claim he makes for the substance of doctrine is essentially orthodox, although he does regard it as "unsettled" since he believes it displays certain "heathen" elements that await their removal.[129] What has generated most discussion, however, is its location. For some, its place (and relatively brief exposition) is taken as confirmation that Schleiermacher's approach to doctrine is based in anthropology rather than theology proper. It could be argued that such criticism sits too lightly both to Schleiermacher's privileging of redemption in the construction of doctrine and to his explicit arguments for why this is the doctrine on which Christianity "stands or falls."[130] The debates about these matters continue.[131] Be that as it may, for present purposes, it contributes to the diversity evident in the ordering of doctrines among the church's doctrinal theologians. Reaction to this location of the Trinity shaped much subsequent doctrinal work, especially in the twentieth century, and not least in the work of the next theologian.

Karl Barth

Swiss Reformed theologian Karl Barth (1886–1968) was one of the most influential theologians of the twentieth century and is often regarded as the most important Reformed theologian since Calvin. After early studies in Bern, he pursued theological study in Germany where, successively at Berlin, Tübingen, and Marburg, he was exposed to the liberal Protestant theological tradition and some of its greatest exponents. On completion of his studies, he returned to Switzerland, was ordained, served briefly as a pastor in Geneva, and then was appointed pastor in the rural town of Safenwil where he served for a decade (1911–21). It was during that period that Barth's dissatisfaction with the prevailing liberal Protestant tradition took root. Not only was he engaged by the usual demands of the pastorate, but he also saw his parishioners suffering the injustices of capitalism at the hands of local industrialists. On a broader horizon, he was observing the upheavals in Europe brought by the ravages of the First World War and the simultaneous collapse of European Christendom. Barth found that the theology he had been taught had no potency in the face of these realities. The ensuing disenchantment with that theology was given powerful literary expression in two commentaries on Paul's letter to the Romans (1919 and 1922). The second, revised, commentary changed the direction of European theology. Barth's diagnosis of the prevailing liberal theology was that it had reduced theology to anthropology, conflated Christianity with European culture, and domesticated God to the needs of that culture. His countermove was to proclaim God as "the Stranger, the Other" who "is finally and everywhere—outside."[132] This God beyond all domestication is God revealed in Jesus Christ. Barth's extended and developed articulation of this protest was worked out as he took up successive academic positions at Göttingen, Münster, Bonn, and finally his native Basel. The move back to Switzerland in 1935 was occasioned by his expulsion from Germany on account of his protests against Nazism. Indeed, while still in Germany, he was instrumental in producing the Barmen Declaration, the confessional document of Germany's Confessing Christians who were resisting the encroachments of Hitler's rule upon the German churches.[133] Barth's major theological legacy, however, is his unfinished four-volume/thirteen-part *Church Dogmatics*, published between 1932 and 1967. Barth was as controversial a figure as was his theology. The reception of his theology has proved to be no less so. It continues to attract significant levels of scholarly attention and commentary. In recent years, there has been much debate about the significance of the long-standing romantic relationship between Barth and his secretary, Charlotte von Kirschbaum. The relationship was an open secret and one that Barth's wife, Nellie, was tragically forced to accept. Until recently, however, it went largely unacknowledged as a factor in the reception of Barth's theology. It no longer is. Debate about how this should impact the assessment of Barth's theology is ongoing and is unlikely to subside.[134]

The development of Barth's theology from the polemics of the *Romans* commentaries through to the commencement of the *Church Dogmatics* is a story in itself, and one that has generated extensive commentary and analysis.[135] A significant part of that story was Barth's reaction against Schleiermacher, whom he saw as the instigator of the liberal Protestantism that he had come to reject. Yet, and this cannot be stressed enough, Barth never ceased to be an admirer of Schleiermacher, albeit a critical one. He acknowledged the legitimacy of Schleiermacher's attempt to respond to modern thought and culture; his disagreement was with the starting point and theological structure of Schleiermacher's response.[136] Schleiermacher (as seen in the previous section) may have believed that even if God is known in the human *Gefühl*, God is the source of that *Gefühl*, not its product. Barth, however, saw this attention to the human subject as the seminal move in the reduction of theology to anthropology, which so troubled him. Of Schleiermacher's theology he famously wrote (fairly or otherwise): "You cannot speak of God simply by speaking of man in a loud voice."[137] Nonetheless, Schleiermacher's presenting issues were, in important ways, his own. While he rejected liberal Protestantism, he did not reject the engagement with modernity. He was, indeed, a *modern* theologian seeking to articulate the gospel afresh within modern culture, albeit in way that was often perceived to be counter to that intent.[138] An awareness of this reaction to Schleiermacher sets the scene for the opening and subsequent development of the *Church Dogmatics*. We will briefly explore the doctrinal structure of the *Dogmatics* before turning to Barth's understanding of doctrine itself. (For clarity, it is worth noting at this point that he uses the term "dogmatics" to refer to the broad disciplined task of interpreting, analyzing, and presenting the church's doctrines. This applies also to use of the word by Karl Rahner, whose work will be the focus of the following section of this chapter.)

In a move that could not be more clearly designed to assert the priority of theology over anthropology, volume 1 of the *Church Dogmatics* presents the Doctrine of the Word of God. In it, the doctrine of revelation and the triune identity of God are presented as mutually defining. What was last in Schleiermacher is first in Barth. The Triune God reveals Godself in Jesus Christ, and human knowledge of God can be nothing other than a participation in what God has revealed. The human subject does not discover God. Rather, humans are addressed by God and are given a share in God's own self-knowledge. By analogy to the Trinity, the Word of God is itself threefold: Jesus Christ is the Word of God revealed, Scripture is the Word of God written, and church proclamation is the Word of God preached.[139] Volume 2, the Doctrine of God, includes matters of theological epistemology and a novel reworking of the attributes of God through the idea of God's perfections. But perhaps most notably, it also includes a Christologically defined doctrine of election designed to correct—and refute—Calvin's doctrine of double predestination.[140] Barth brings his

Christological understanding of election into the closest proximity to God's being, so that faith can confess that from all eternity God is the One who graciously wills to save in Jesus Christ. So presented, the doctrine of election is a reminder that "the good news ... is good news only because it proclaims to us the salvation which is the real will of the real Lord both of our life and of all life."[141] In volume 3, the Doctrine of Creation, creation is presented in a covenantal relationship with redemption. It includes novel (and controversial) treatments of anthropology in which, with regard to the body–soul relationship, Barth himself declared that he "deviated even more widely from dogmatic tradition than in the doctrine of predestination."[142] In volume 4, the Doctrine of Reconciliation, the dramatic character of reconciliation is reflected in the narrative integration of Christology, sin, soteriology, pneumatology, and ecclesiology. A projected volume 5 on eschatology was never written. The unfinished volume 4, however, is the largest of all, and by any measure something of a doctrinal masterpiece. Its internal structure is striking and has generated much comment.[143] Within the Christological dimensions, where the tradition had treated Christ's person and work as distinct doctrinal themes, Barth presents them as mutually defining and integrated dimensions of the one reality, the living Jesus Christ. This is encapsulated toward the end of this volume when he writes,

> We can speak of the being, activity and speech of Jesus Christ only in relation to specific events, only in the form of the narration of a history and histories. If Christology as the depiction of this being, activity and speech is to be anything more than an obscure metaphysics, in all its parts and aspects it can be only the unfolding of a drama.[144]

While the immediate context of this last point is the doctrine of reconciliation, it is not unrelated to the freedom that characterizes Barth's more general approach to doctrinal work. In the above overview of the four volumes, we saw that Barth could develop, correct, and deviate from the tradition. Nor is this unrelated to his resistance to building doctrinal work into a system.[145] Just as Christology narrates a drama, so dogmatics in general can only be "reported" within the contingencies of the church's hearing and confession of the Word of God. Long before Barth developed his doctrine of reconciliation, these concerns were shaping his approach to dogmatics, a discipline that, given its subject matter, cannot but be dynamic. In volume 1, he wrote thus of the Word of God:

The simple reason for this is that whilst its content is indeed the truth, it is the truth and reality of the work and activity of God taking place within it. As such it is not to be condensed or summarised in any view, or idea, or principle. It can only be *reported* concretely, i.e., in relation to what is at any given time the most recent stage of the process or action or sovereign act of which it is the occurrence.[146]

Accordingly, dogmatics "is ready for new insights which no former store of knowledge can really confront on equal terms or finally withstand. Essentially dogmatic method consists in this openness to receive new truth, and only in this."[147] This does not mean that the work of dogmatics lacks intentionality or structure. But that structure requires a metaphorical description to capture its dynamism. It is the metaphor of a wheel with an open center. It illuminates the structure of the four volumes of the *Church Dogmatics* outlined above:

> Concretely applied, all this means that the unfolding and presentation of the content of the Word of God must take place fundamentally in such a way that the Word of God is understood as the centre and foundation of dogmatics and of Church proclamation, like a circle whose periphery forms the starting point for a limited number of lines which in dogmatics are to be drawn to a certain distance in all directions. The fundamental lack of principle in the dogmatic method is clear from the fact that it does not proceed from the centre but from the periphery of the circle or, metaphor apart, from the self-positing and self-authenticating Word of God. From this starting-point, it will draw only a limited number of lines, and even these only to a certain distance; and it will refrain from drawing a second circle round the whole—or, metaphor apart, it will refrain from presenting the whole as a whole.[148]

Doctrinal work occurs, therefore, between the open center and the open-ended lines that extend out from the open center. "Barth's point," says William Stacy Johnson, "is that the theologian has no access to nor can stand within the open centre itself but can only begin from that which falls all around the centre. For Barth this 'inner periphery' is the ongoing discourse of the believing community."[149] Johnson's point is not quite correct. Manifestly, Barth does not ignore the "ongoing discourse of the believing community." But, in this metaphor, if the ungraspable Word of

God is the center, its periphery is actually Scripture and church confession—something more determinate than the church's "ongoing discourse." From this periphery, and working along these "lines," the theologian has specific points of reference in both the "periphery" and the "lines" radiating from the periphery. As we saw from the structure of the *Church Dogmatics*, Barth regards these "lines" as the doctrines of revelation, God, creation, and reconciliation. Notwithstanding the specificity of these points of reference, the task of building upon them cannot be other than provisional:

> Doctrine is not identical with any existing text—whether it is that of specific theological formulae, or that of a specific theological system; or that of the Church's creed, or even the text of the Bible. Pure doctrine is an event ... It cannot in any sense be thought of as a solution already existing somewhere or other, which can simply be taken over. [Of course] where else can it begin ... except with the investigation of the Bible, or the Church's confession ... But it only begins with this investigation. There is far more to it ... than merely the repetition of those texts ... All the conclusions of dogmatics must be intended, accepted and understood as fluid material for further work.[150]

The object of dogmatics is the Word of God that, because it is "God's work and activity, and therefore God's grace," necessarily "escapes our comprehension and control, upon which, reckoning with it in faith, we can only meditate, and for which we can only hope."[151] The doctrinal theologian is not only an active thinker but also one who prays and hopes, and whose praying and hoping is itself an acknowledgement that her work "must have the character of an offering in which everything is placed before the living God."[152]

Yet it is also *placed before* the church. The adjective in the title of *Church Dogmatics* is neither accidental nor cursory. As Barth wrote, "The community in and for which I have written ... is that of the Church and not a community of theological endeavour."[153] Doctrine is that part of the church's theological ministry that is undertaken "not just for free intellectual exchange but also for instruction."[154] This is not "instruction" in any abstract sense. It is instruction in service of "preparation for Church proclamation."[155] Such preparation is not mere exposition awaiting appropriation. It involves "criticism and correction of Church proclamation and not just ... a repetitive exposition of it."[156] For all these reasons, dogmatics "has the character of a challenge, a suggestion and a counsel."[157]

Notwithstanding all this openness and dynamism, doctrinal work so understood is not a "shoreless, rudderless cogitation and chattering."[158] The reason for this, of course, is that the living Word of God at the center of it all is a *revealed* Word. Crucial here is the second of the three forms of the Word, that is, Scripture. As we have seen, Barth says it is only the beginning point, but it *is* the beginning point. There is nowhere else to start since it is the prophetic and apostolic witness to the decisive acts of God in history. Precisely as the beginning point, it is the criterion of doctrinal work in its ministry to the church. The orientation to proclamation means that contemporary Christians do not ask merely about what the prophets and apostles said but "what we must say on the basis of the apostles and prophets."[159] The details of Barth's doctrine of Scripture and his approach to hermeneutics invites close study. But for our purposes, the important point is the role it is given as the second form of the Word of God. And note should also be made of the vast amounts of biblical exegesis included in the *Church Dogmatics*. Its style is novel and its scale is perhaps unsurpassed in Christianity's corpus of doctrinal writings.[160]

To conclude this summary, let me return to Barth's metaphor of the circle, center, periphery, and its radiating lines. For Barth, doctrinal work begins its work at the periphery listening, via Scripture, to the living Word of God. It proceeds with its work by confidently but humbly walking along the established lines of revelation, Trinity, God, creation, and reconciliation, being always ready to check the stability and even to correct the direction of these lines by what it has learned at the periphery. And all of this for the church's ministry of proclamation. The point is partly caught by Joseph Mangina when he writes that for Barth, "doctrine … means not the generating of theories, but concrete teaching intended to shape people's hearts and minds so that they may hear the Word of God."[161] But it needs to be added, not only shaping people's hearts and mind but also keeping them on their spiritual and intellectual toes.

Karl Rahner

Karl Rahner (1904–1984) was a German Jesuit and one of the most influential Roman Catholic theologians of the twentieth century. Born in Freiburg, he began his Jesuit formation in 1922. During this period, he became immersed in the texts of the Fathers, the medieval scholastics, Aquinas, and the modern philosophers, notably Martin Heidegger (1889–1976). He was also drawn to the insights of Ignatius Loyola, insights that deeply shaped his own faith and spirituality. He held teaching positions at Innsbruck, Vienna, Munich, and Münster. He served as a *peritus* at Vatican II and is known to be have been a significant influence on the documents *Lumen gentium* and *Dei verbum*. His vast literary output was not confined to technical works of theology; it extended to sermons, reflections, and spiritual guidance. Tempting though it is to treat his one-volume *Foundations of Christian Faith: An Introduction to the Idea of Christianity*[162] as a summary of his thought (not least because it was written relatively late in his life), that volume is what its title says: an outline of the *foundations* of Christian faith. In the terms of its subtitle, it sets out what he terms "the idea" of Christianity on the foundation of which the faith can be believed and lived. Some of his historical and expository work was distilled in reference works that he either edited or coauthored.[163] Above all, however, it was the publication of his twenty-three-volume *Theological Investigations* (sixteen volumes in the original German) that constitutes his most important legacy to theology. The *Investigations*, unfolded as collections of his various essays, were collated and published (between 1961 and 1984 in German and between 1961 and 1991 in English).[164] The genre and scale of this output bears witness to the fact that the vast majority of Rahner's theological writings were occasional, exploratory, and worked out in relation to specific and diverse issues and questions.

Living during a period of immense cultural change and ecclesial ferment, Rahner worked on multiple fronts. Nevertheless, two broad impulses were dominant: one negative, the other positive. The negative impulse was his rejection of the neo-scholasticism of nineteenth- and early twentieth-century Catholic theology. This was a "textbook approach to theology" consisting largely of the exposition of authoritative Catholic doctrinal teaching. It was not the teaching he was rejecting. It was the mode of engagement with it that worried him. In this, Rahner was part of the movement known as *nouvelle théologie*. The positive impulse involved bringing Catholic teaching into conversation with the culture and philosophy of modernity. In pursuing this positive impulse, he employed a transcendental understanding of human existence and an existential understanding of grace. This involved insisting that "grace is not thought of as a thing."[165] Rather, it is "God himself, the communication in which he gives himself to man as the divinizing favour in which he himself is."[166] Moreover, the grace of God is not conceived as "an isolated intervention on God's part at particular points in an otherwise profane world."[167] Rather, grace is a "constantly present existential of the [human] creature and of the world in general."[168] On this basis, "man is who he is always confronted with the holy mystery."[169] It was this idea of the "supernatural existential" and its debt to themes of twentieth-century existentialism that was perhaps the most distinctive substantive feature of his theology and remains one of its most discussed.[170] It has been the focus of ongoing discussions about Rahner's use of philosophy and whether he privileged it over theology.[171] This same network of ideas also fed into another of his much-discussed idea, that of anonymous Christianity.[172]

The first of these impulses is the one that most directly impacts upon his understanding of doctrine and will be the focus in what follows. It can be seen in what he explicitly says about doctrine, or, to use his terms, dogma and dogmatics (by which he means the technical theological engagement with the dogmas held and taught by the church). Some of the most pertinent material is actually included in the first volume of the *Theological Investigations*. Indeed, in the first essay, "The Prospects for Dogmatic Theology,"[173] Rahner registers his dissatisfaction with the state of dogmatics. He complains that the "textbooks" display an inexcusable "uniformity and stagnation."[174] They content themselves with stating positions clarified in the past without any attention to the questions to which those positions were answers. Those questions are "allowed to escape … in favour of a convenient clarity and comprehensiveness."[175] This approach cannot "elicit the hidden energies of the old theology"[176] and thus while seeking to preserve the past actually obscures it. The issue is not just a matter of having a better historical awareness; what is actually needed is a "theology of history,"[177] not least because what the church teaches is a "report on the history of salvation."[178] For these reasons, Rahner also addresses himself to the "development of dogma," in an essay by the same name.[179] This is a very significant theme for Catholic theology but not just because of a modern historical consciousness. Rahner states the obvious when he says—with the doctrine of the bodily assumption of Mary as his example—that many of the doctrines that have become part of the church teaching were not always part of that teaching. They have "'come to be' within the course of Christian history."[180] In one sense, "development" appears to understate what Rahner is proposing. *Prima facie* there seems to be genuine novelty, potentially a problem for a tradition that understands that it was entrusted with the truth in its fullness from the beginning. Rahner counters this by presenting dogma as itself "the process in which its own mystery is progressively unveiled."[181] He resists proposing any formula that indicates how and when such progression may unfold, for that would deny the genuine *mystery* of the truth first given. The church is to be receptive and discerning rather than active and intentional in this phenomenon: "It is in the very act of developing, and not in any prior reflexion, that the reality of the Church's consciousness in faith comes progressively into a full possession of itself."[182] Rahner is also quite insistent that any such "progress" is not in any sense the acquisition of "a sort of plus quantity of knowledge (as though the Church were somehow to become 'cleverer')."[183] It is rather that Christ gradually leads the church "sometimes by new ways, through a changing reality to his own single Truth."[184]

Inevitably, this entails a certain posture toward any existing proposition of faith—or doctrine—because while it is true, it may yet come to point to other as yet undisclosed dimensions of Christ's "single Truth." This does *not* mean, however, that existing statements are only, as it were, *partially* true. All doctrinal teaching is *adequate* to the truth without being exhaustive:

> The statements which we make about [spiritual and divine realities], relying on the Word of God which itself became "flesh" in human words, can never express them once and for all in an entirely adequate form. They are not for this reason false. They are an "adequatio intellectus et rei" in so far as they state absolutely nothing which is false. ... Anyone who proposed to regard these propositions of faith, because they are wholly true, as in themselves *adequate* to the matter in question, i.e., as exhaustive statement, would be falsely elevating human truth to God's simple and exhaustive knowledge of himself and of all that takes its origin from him.[185]

In all of this, of course, Christian faith must be alert to the distinction between "genuine developments" and "wrong turning[s]."[186] Such alertness and the judgments that come with it do not lie with the preferences of individuals but is cultivated and exercised with the church "recognized as the court of last appeal."[187] In the magisterium, the "Church possesses an organ of perception by which she can tell whether something which ... emerges from theological activity, is in fact objectively something more than the result of human speculation; whether it is still God's Word, though now expressed propositionally in a new form, in a new articulation and explication."[188] In this last remark, Rahner simply assumes the ongoing existence of theological activity in the church. It exists alongside the magisterium while deferring to it. This is where the doctrinal theologian works, not merely as an expositor but as one who engages the church's teaching through the work of "rational, conceptual deduction and historical investigation."[189] Over time, that work may lead the church to consider some "new proposition,"[190] but it is the church, through the magisterium, that makes this decision. Of course, quite apart from Rahner's particular exposition of these matters, the relationship between theologians and the magisterium are controversial matters within the Catholic Church, and those controversies are beyond the scope of the present book.[191]

In passing, it might be noted that Rahner is no less aware of the historical contingency of church teaching than were the modern *Reformed* theologians studied in the immediately preceding sections of this chapter. But, as have we just seen, Rahner always understood this historical dimension of doctrinal work within the context of both the idea of an original authoritative deposit of faith and of the Catholic Church's magisterium. In other words, Rahner is in a *similar* cultural world to that of Schleiermacher and Barth, but in a vastly different ecclesial world. There are overlaps in the various approaches, but Rahner's approach to ecclesial authority renders a very different understanding of the contingency of doctrinal statements and the scope of the doctrinal theologian's work. At the same time, this comparison should not be taken as license to ignore Rahner's own creativity as a theologian, and as a doctrinal theologian at that. This is born out in his own proposal for new brief creedal statements, itself an unusual move for a Catholic theologian.

Notwithstanding the occasional nature of so much of his writings, he accepted, indeed assumed, the necessity of constructing a vision of the whole reality of Christian faith. This is *partly* what he is doing in *Foundations of Christian Faith*, which does give some idea of the doctrinal structure of that overall vision. It begins (controversially) with a theological anthropology in which God and the human in relation are mutually the point of departure. This is followed by attention to the history of salvation and revelation, after which follow, in order, Christology, ecclesiology, Christian life (which includes the sacraments), and eschatology.[192] In an epilogue to this work, however, he makes an attempt to "bring the whole of Christianity into view"[193] by means of proposing three brief creedal statements. Of course, providing such a "view" is what the Apostles' Creed does, and although that Creed remains a "permanent and binding norm of faith,"[194] it has lost its capacity to communicate to the "contemporary intellectual and spiritual situation"[195] characterized as it was (in mid-twentieth-century Europe) not only by an increasingly confident atheism but also by the diversity of "cultures and social milieus"[196] in which the gospel is preached. The latter, he observed, was all the more obvious now that "theological European imperialism no longer possessed its obviousness and power."[197] The cultural diversity points, in turn, to a need for a diversity of any such creedal statements, each of them intelligible to their particular users and hearers. While none of them will have the binding normative role of the Apostles' Creed, they must "give expression to our faith in the historical Jesus as our Lord and as the absolute saviour."[198] The brief creeds Rahner offers for consideration are respectively "A Brief Theological Creed," "A Brief Anthropological Creed," and "A Brief Future-Oriented Creed."[199] Alert to his own critique of Western theological imperialism, he offers them only to the "European situation."[200] Despite this limit, it is nevertheless difficult to see that they meet the criterion of communicability given their conceptual and linguistic density. But that is not the point for these present considerations. Their very existence demonstrates Rahner's particular combination of respect for the binding statements of the past, the orientation of occasional theological work to a sense of the whole, a sensitivity to the demands of context, and a recognition of the limits of such work in the face of the wisdom of the whole church. In one sense, all the theologians considered in this chapter would share some or another similar combination of such commitments. They have a particular edge in Rahner's case because of the intersection of his respect for the authority of the Catholic magisterium and his alertness to the claims of modernity.

Sarah Coakley

Sarah Coakley (1951–) is a British academic theologian and Anglican priest who has taught in both the USA and the United Kingdom. After several years as Mallinckrodt Professor of Divinity at Harvard, she served as Norris-Hulse Professor of Divinity at Cambridge University from 2007 to 2017. The broad body of her work covers a range of themes and at first glance might more likely attract the designation of philosophical theology rather than doctrinal theology. This, together with a wide range of interdisciplinary interests, would seem to remove her from the field of theologians surveyed in this chapter. While much of her work has been more identifiably related to the analytical traditions of philosophical theology, this, together with her much-contested relationship to feminist theology,[201] adds a certain edge to the way she pursues the constructive engagement with doctrine that has been part of her recent work. In 2013, she published the first volume of a projected four-volume systematics that will bear the overall title, *On Desiring God*.[202] Reflecting contemporary Western concerns, this title points to an intention to explore the connections between Christian faith and the phenomena of sex, sexuality, and gender. As yet, only volume 1 has been published, but it is precisely her intention to produce such a work, and her reasons for doing so, which leads to her inclusion in this chapter. She is engaged in a quite explicit attempt to produce an ordered, comprehensive, if particular, vision of the whole. But there are notable polemical edges to this attempt that make it of special interest and that open up dimensions to the question of the ordering and functions of doctrine that have been explored throughout this chapter.

Volume 1, *God, Sexuality and the Self: An Essay on the Trinity*, explores the relationship between sexual desire and desire for God, within the framework of a Trinitarian understanding of prayer. Her outline of the projected three remaining volumes indicates how different areas of doctrine are ordered within this particular vision after this this opening Trinitarian move:

> The second volume (*Knowing Darkly*) will adumbrate ... theological anthropology of the "spiritual senses," and at the same time turn to the vexed modern category of "race." The third volume (*Punish and Heal*) will address the public realm of the polis with its secular institutions of prison and hospital, and so re-examine the doctrines of sin and atonement. Christology (*Flesh and Blood*) will advisedly be left till last, not as a demotion but as a climax: the mystery of the incarnation will be approached via a theology of the eucharist.[203]

This overview suggests not only a novel arrangement of doctrines (especially in view of its placement of Christology) but also an equally unusual *explicit* orientation of such a work to social and ethical realities. In fact, this orientation to the social and ethical is related to her definition of "orthodoxy" and illustrates something of her posture to the authority of past theological formulations and doctrinal teachings. Rather than a benchmark received from the past, orthodoxy is "a project."[204] It is no "mere creedal correctness, no imposed ecclesiastical regulation."[205] Rather, within the "horizon of true orthodoxy, theology, 'spirituality,' and ethics are fully united."[206] This novel order and the orientation are deliberate and are related to each other. They reflect her declared "freedom to *recast* the central categories of thought and to sit light to the burden of traditional loci"[207] and even "add new loci as needed."[208] This novelty is justified if it is "the best way to recapture the contemporary imagination for Christ."[209] So, attention to the ordering of doctrinal topics is partly for the sake of coherence between the parts but also because it is part of the "attempt to provide coherent, and alluring, vision of the Christian faith."[210] This quest for some sense of the whole is reflected in the name she gives to her method, that is, *théologie totale*. Nevertheless, even the fact of seeking to offer such a doctrinally integrated presentation of Christianity leads her directly into conflict with various kinds of suspicions toward such comprehensive visions and the perception that order is often "a front for abuse."[211] There are three strands of such suspicion: the fear that such comprehensiveness turns God into an idol; concerns about a hegemony of the discourse that suppresses the voices and insights of the powerless; and, most potently, that of feminist theory that sees such theology as "phallocentric," being determined by the "'male mode of thinking which seeks to clarify, control and master,'"[212] thus relegating matters to do with the feminine, and especially the female body, to the subconscious.[213] They hold in common the concern that the quest for a vision of the whole necessarily involves a "complete understanding of God, a regnant position in society, or a domination of the gendered 'other.'"[214]

Coakley offers considered responses to the validity of these criticisms and a theological interpretation of what they are rightly criticizing: they expose the place of desire in theological work, but it is a case of theology pursuing unredeemed desire. Her own quest for a vision of the whole involves the redemption of that desire. Within the confines of her project, the strategy for orienting doctrinal work to the redemption of desire takes two principal forms. One is to counter the view that the quest for totality is hegemonic, precisely by suggesting that it is exactly such a quest that prompts attention to the excluded and neglected. The other is to integrate theological work with prayer, whereby theology involves an ongoing "unmastery" of theological knowledge. The first is seen in her explanation of *totale* in the name she gives to her approach. It points to the attempt within her theology

> to do justice to every level and type, of religious apprehension and its appropriate mode of expression. Thus it is devoted precisely to the excavation and evaluation of what has previously been neglected: to theological fieldwork; … to religious cultural productions of the arts and the imagination; to neglected or side-lined texts; and to the examination of the differences made to theology by such factors as gender, class, or race … In short, *théologie totale* makes the bold claim that the more systematic one's intentions, the more necessary the exploration of such dark and neglected corners; and that precisely as a theology *in via*, *théologie totale* continually risks destabilisation and redirection.[215]

In other words, the more oriented the theologian is to the whole, the more disciplined she must be in attending to the breadth of experience and circumstances. The effect of doing so, Coakley argues, is not the hegemonic consolidating of knowledge but its "destabilisation." This, however, is aligned with a different mode of knowledge; it entails a knowledge that is inseparable from prayer and contemplation. This is her other strategy for properly directing desire. By contemplation, she means something quite specific; it is associated with the Trinitarian understanding of prayer that, in turn, is based on her reading of Rom. 8:14-26. Her Trinitarian interpretation of this text carries a lot of weight not only in her understanding of the role of prayer in theological work but also in her attempt to read patristic Trinitarian theology, alert to what she claims is the neglect of the role pneumatology played in the conventional presentations of its development. These matters are at the heart of the published first volume and have generated significant discussion, but they are not the present focus.[216]

The practice of contemplation, she writes, "is the condition of new 'knowing in unknowing'. It must involve the stuff of learned bodily enactment, sweated out painfully over months and years, in duress, in discomfort, in bewilderment, as well as in joy and dawning recognition."[217] For all the openness this approach involves, this reference to "dawning recognition" must not be bypassed. It points to the fact that this particular kind of apophatic theology is not simply "mere verbal play, deferral of meaning."[218] It yields actual knowledge, albeit provisionally. This also contrasts it with a "dogmatic 'liberal' denial that God in Godself can be known *at all*; it is not mysterious in *this* sense."[219] Moreover, in the role she thus gives to contemplation, something more than a simple appeal to "experience" over "knowledge" is going on here. Elsewhere, she has addressed this issue by clarifying that she is not just privileging one of the four commonly cited sources of theology (i.e., Scripture, tradition, reason, and experience):

> I am not here appealing to "experience" in a naively empiricist way, as if some particular "experience" could offset deficiencies in what is otherwise provided by Scripture or tradition or "reason." Rather, the regular undertaking of an intentional form of what I term "dispossession" underwrites and progressively transforms all that one goes on receiving from those other sources: it sets them in a progressively new light.[220]

The "dispossession" mentioned here combines with the other themes of "unmastery" and "unknowing" to produce a very particular understanding of theological knowledge and how it cultivates a vision to move toward a vision of the Christian faith without that vision ever being exhaustive. The spiritual and intellectual comprehensiveness of this proposal is well summarized by Michael Allen in an appreciatively critical response to it: "Contemplation cannot be myopic ... but must be drawn upward and out to consider not only God and certain divine things of prestige. No, such would be to set the gaze upon the easily ossified."[221] On the other hand, it is not without its critics, not least from feminist theologians who remain troubled by the role given to suffering, reinforced as it is by the place suffering is given in prayer. One such critic makes the further point that no explanation is given on how this approach to theology *actually* "undoes patriarchal idolatry."[222]

Notwithstanding such criticisms, for our purposes, it can be noted that her detailed attention to the relationship between prayer and the production of theological knowledge, precisely in the context of developing a doctrinally aware and doctrinally structured vision of the Christian faith is striking. Clearly, critical discussion of this intended "coherent, alluring vision of the Christian faith" must await the completion of her multivolume work. Yet, even at this stage, her voice is an important inclusion in the conversation generated by the theologians surveyed in this chapter.

Context, Content, and Form: Some Observations

Following on from Chapter 1's broad historical overview of the origins, form, and functions of the Christian doctrine, this chapter surveyed selected individual theologians' engagement with the church's doctrine. Following the three categories of the chapter's subtitle, some general observations will be drawn from the survey before summarizing its contribution to the question, "What is doctrine?"

The respective *contexts* of these theologians were multilayered. As all contexts are, they were constituted by matrices of language, cultural practices, social structures, and the highly variable ways in which Christianity (in its various forms) was itself culturally located. For instance, Origen's presentation of doctrine was developed for a relatively nascent Christianity with little cultural prestige and which was facing persecution. Aquinas's *Summa* presented doctrine in a context where Christianity (and its institutional forms) were mutually defining. Likewise, Calvin spoke into an established Christian culture, but one where doctrine played a particular role in the fragmentation of that culture. Schleiermacher, Barth, and Rahner developed their confessionally defined accounts of doctrine in a context where a once-dominant Christianity and its established doctrinal discourses were being rejected, dismissed, or simply ignored by the culture and toward which many of the churches' own members were uncertain and questioning. Additionally, Barth's work was shaped by the direct confrontation of the church with violent totalitarianism. Coakley's work explicitly responds to the revolution within the contemporary West's understanding of gender and the claims that it makes on knowledge and justice. The theologians varied in their explicit consciousness of those contextual dynamics, but the work of none of them could ever be reduced to or simply explained by those contextual factors. An obvious element in the immediate context of each of these theologians was the Christian community itself. Nevertheless, variety could be observed in each theologian's respective posture toward the church and its doctrine: Lombard and Aquinas were expositors and teachers; Catherine was a loyal, pastorally driven guide; Schleiermacher was an apologetically driven revisionist; Rahner was as loyal and constructive critic; Calvin and Barth were prophets to church and society, and Calvin was an institutional innovator; Coakley is an intellectual innovator, but one who draws deeply from the tradition as well as from the church's present experience. These different contexts were also reflected in a variety of purposes that doctrine served: providing clarity of conviction to a minority community; offering regular instruction to an established and culturally legitimated Christian community; explaining, defending, and/or generating differences between Christians; and articulating the faith anew for a church that had lost is cultural legitimacy.

Although the substantive *content* of each theologian's theology was not the focus of this survey, the matter of the ordering of doctrinal topics is closely related to it. The various arrangements of doctrinal topics do provide some sense of what each theologian believed was the substantive content of the Christian faith, or some sense of what Christianity is about. Even though there was variety in the order, there was some constancy in what the order implied about the faith overall. One way or another, every theologian considered in this chapter has understood Christianity to be about the creation and redemption of the world by the God first identified as Israel's covenantal God and then by the life, death, and resurrection of the one proclaimed as Israel's Messiah, Jesus Christ. Nevertheless, even within *this* selection there are those who have been considered (either temporarily or permanently) as heretics or whose orthodoxy has been regularly questioned on account of some element in their presentation of this set of conventional Christian claims. Be that as it may, some of the more notable and controversial examples of ordering can be noted: Scripture last in Origen, theological anthropology first and Trinity last in Schleiermacher, and Trinity first and Christology last in Coakley. It is arguable, however, that any controversy about the ordering of doctrinal topics should not be about what is first or last but about what overall picture is presented by all the doctrines in their interconnection. In this regard, Sarah Coakley's concern to generate a "coherent and alluring vision of the Christian faith" is noteworthy. It is also connected to the third theme of this final section of the chapter.

The question of *form* is perhaps most obviously addressed through the question of genre. Again diversity is apparent, although the dominant genre has been that of a carefully designed multivolume treatise produced over long periods of time. Indeed, the duration of production invites a qualification of the somewhat flat notion of "treatise." Most of the theologians studied here who employed this genre included conversations with various interlocutors and even with their own earlier works. The latter is certainly true of Calvin's *Institutes* and Barth's *Church Dogmatics*. Perhaps "conversation" may not quite describe the encounter with the traditional authorities in Lombard's *Sentences* or Aquinas's *Summa*, but their works are definitely not monologues. Alongside this dominant genre, there was also Augustine's (relatively) short advisory *Enchiridion*, Catherine's visionary and hortatory writings, and Rahner's ad hoc academic essays. Further reflection on these issues would invite consideration of the relationship between genre and the vision communicated. Form and content influence each other. While this raises many issues, one that should briefly be mentioned concerns the matter of just how "systematic" Christian doctrine should be. We have already encountered this implicitly in the attention given throughout the chapter (including in the immediately preceding paragraph) to the question of the ordering of doctrines. We have also encountered Barth's explicit rejection of theological "systems." For Barth, the issue was the nexus between systems and the attempt to produce comprehensive and exhaustive accounts of doctrine. He was alert to the potential of the theologian to fail to acknowledge the freedom of God and the living nature of God's Word. We also noted that Coakley's defense of her *théologie totale* had to confront similar objections. As discussed above, the question is not so much whether there is a normative ordering of doctrines but rather what is the vision they represent in their interconnectedness. That can be granted, but the question remains: What place does the systematic ordering of doctrines have in any particular doctrinal vision of the Christian faith, and what justifications are offered for that ordering? In his *Hermeneutics of Doctrine*, Anthony Thiselton points to two positive uses of system in doctrine (after firmly rejecting the idea of a "final" system). One is system as *coherence*, which he presents not so much as a function of logical or conceptual consistency but as a motif that point to a unity that embraces dialogue and diversity.[223] The other is system as a self-regulating means by which a community maintains "stability, identity and boundaries,"[224] which provide a framework for "ongoing history, experience and hermeneutical life-worlds."[225] Thiselton's embrace of system in doctrine largely draws on modern discussions of philosophy and hermeneutics without extensive attention to actual doctrinal projects. In another recent work addressing such issues, Gale Heide drew attention to the way the nature of the justifications for any given ordering of the doctrine shifted at the Enlightenment.[226] Pre-Enlightenment theology, he argues, treated system as a tool to enable doctrine to meet its pastoral and pedagogical roles. The Enlightenment, however, led some theologians to link the systematic nature of theology to a philosophical and universal foundation for Christian truth.[227] For Heide, the former is legitimate; the latter is problematic. It is the former that we have observed in, for instance, Augustine, Aquinas, and Calvin, whose respective presentations of doctrine were specifically oriented to drawing readers into encounter with God. The details of Heide's study warrant closer attention than can be given here, but his general insight is worth bearing in mind in the study of any doctrinal theologian. His observations prompt the question: If a theological work shows a systematic impulse, what is the reason for it? Is it a means of intellectual justification or a pedagogical tool employed to enhance the life of the Christian and the Christian community? Either way, in addition to this effect of the Enlightenment on doctrinal work, a further decisive one was the critique of the very legitimacy of the doctrinal enterprise. A brief description of the Enlightenment, its critique of doctrine, and some of the possibilities of doctrinal work beyond the Enlightenment will be the concern of the next chapter. But first, some further elements will be added to the answer to the question, "What is doctrine?"

What is doctrine?

We had already observed in Chapter 1 that doctrine is the focus of conceptual and intellectual activity. The material covered in this chapter points to the sheer scale of that activity. Christian doctrine is an intellectual enterprise that generates further investigation, clarification, criticism, commentary, and construction. We have seen that one of the key results of this activity is the generation of intellectual visions of what Christianity is: the parts of Christian faith are integrated into a whole. Produced by particular theologians, such visions address the intellectual challenges of their contexts. But it is not intellectual activity for its own sake. Certainly, all the theologians studied in this chapter present their constructive doctrinal work as a means of variously teaching, strengthening, and provoking Christian people and the church as a whole. Such doctrinal work has been diversely assessed by the church, whether institutionally (some have been formally deemed heretics; some of the theologians have been acknowledged as "doctors of the church") or through its reception, usually contested, in the more diffuse realms of individual faith and discipleship. Doctrine teaches the faith; it does so by recalling old teachings and articulating new insights, by unsettling and consolidating piety, and by offering a big-picture vision of Christianity.

CHAPTER 3
DOCTRINE IN CRISIS AND DOCTRINE RENEWED

In the previous chapter, we explored the work of some of the church's significant doctrinal theologians. Attention to the themes of context, content, and form revealed a mixture of continuities and discontinuities. It also revealed a range of critical questions about each of those themes and how they inform an understanding of doctrine. Common to all those studied, however, was an assumption that doctrinal work was a coherent and credible intellectual undertaking. We turn now to explore both the challenges and possibilities of Christian doctrine when that assumption is not taken for granted. The point of departure for this exploration is the European Enlightenment. This movement and its challenges were briefly introduced in the previous chapter, specifically in the section on Schleiermacher. By noting it only in passing, however, the extent to which the Enlightenment was a watershed for the Western doctrinal tradition was potentially obscured. As various intellectual criticisms were leveled against Christianity, key doctrinal claims were inevitably the target of those criticisms. Just as importantly, however, the Enlightenment generated a general posture of suspicion toward the *authority* of tradition as well as specific criticisms of the *origins* of Christian doctrine. All of this located Christian doctrine in a newly emerging intellectual world, one where matters of epistemology, history, and new methods of textual exegesis dominated.

Although they will be discussed briefly, these intellectual challenges will not be the focus of this chapter. Instead, the focus will be on the way the Enlightenment diversified the cultural and intellectual circumstances in which Christian doctrine was produced and received. The Enlightenment reshaped not only the intellectual world but also the cultural world and Christianity's place in it. Moreover, the Enlightenment's criticisms of authoritative institutions, first directed against the church and monarch, could easily be transferred to other institutions and other contexts. As Dorinda Outram observes in her *The Enlightenment*, "Once 'critique' began, it was difficult to stop."[1] Notably, as the Enlightenment's rhetoric and strategies moved into non-European contexts, those same criticisms were, over time, turned back on the Enlightenment and Europe. In these circumstances, which overlapped with the growth of Christianity in non-European contexts, Christian theology began to move into a range of conversations reflecting a level of cultural, social, and intellectual diversity to which the construction and reception of Christian doctrine had not been exposed since the patristic era. In what follows, we will observe how, as the cultural consequences of the Enlightenment took hold during the twentieth- and twenty-first centuries, *specific* doctrinal loci became the particular focus of enquiry, exploration, and development in specific intellectual and cultural conversations.

With all this in mind, this chapter will begin with a brief overview of the Enlightenment's critique of doctrine. This will be followed by five examples of where doctrine has engaged a particular audience or issue that, in one way or another and at least in part, is a legacy of the Enlightenment. These will be as follows: a discussion of the humanity of Jesus in the light of the post-Enlightenment critical study of Jesus; attention to the Trinity in the conversation between doctrine and the gender-aware Western church; an exploration of cosmic Christology in the conversation between doctrine and the church of the majority world; an overview of one discussion about salvation, also in the majority world; and attention to anthropology in the Western church's conversation with scientific claims about sexuality and gender. The main point will be to demonstrate the sheer vitality of doctrinal work following what was presented as a crisis of its very possibility. In turn, this will allow a further expansion of the answer to the question, "What is doctrine?"

The Enlightenment and doctrine

As noted in the brief discussion of the shortcomings of the term "*the* Reformation" in Chapter 1, to speak of "*the* Enlightenment" is also somewhat misleading. The issue is crystallized in the title of Gertrude Himmelfarb's 2008 book, *The Roads to Modernity: The British, French and American Enlightenments*. After noting their respective features, Himmelfarb indicates what was common to these three movements. "To be sure," she notes, "all of them shared some common traits: a respect for reason and liberty, science and industry, justice and welfare. But these ideas took significantly different forms and were pursued in different ways in each country."[2] Himmelfarb does not include the German Enlightenment in her work, but the same themes apply. Certainly, it was the German Enlightenment that produced the most potent of the criticisms of doctrine, specifically in the form of the Hellenization thesis. But before coming to the specifics of that thesis, it is important to address just why the Enlightenment had the consequences it did for the study of doctrine and its history. One relatively straightforward answer to this question can be gleaned from the much-quoted definition with which Immanuel Kant begins his famous essay, "What is Enlightenment?" It reads as follows:

> Enlightenment is man's release from his self-incurred tutelage. Tutelage is man's inability to make use of his understanding without direction from another. Self-incurred is this tutelage when its cause lies not in lack of reason but in lack of resolution and courage to use it without direction from another. *Sapere aude!* [Dare to know.] "Have courage to use your own reason!"—that is the motto of enlightenment.[3]

Bearing in mind even the working definition of doctrine introduced in this book ("communally recognized authoritative teaching"), the very appeal to authority intrinsic to doctrine is anathema to proponents of the Enlightenment so understood. Moreover, when, as we have seen in Chapters 1 and 2, doctrine is characterized by acknowledging the wisdom of the past, and when the Enlightenment is presented as release from the darkness of the past, the clash between doctrine and Enlightenment is intensified. But Kant's essay raises the stakes even further. Later in the essay, he declares that he has deliberately placed the "main form of Enlightenment … chiefly in matters of religion."[4] This is because, in his view, "religious incompetence is not only the most harmful but also the most degrading of all."[5] In other words, the religious person's deference to an external authority was an affront to the understandings of human dignity and autonomy prized by the Enlightenment.

It is against the background of such ideas that the Hellenization thesis and its impact is best understood.[6] In brief summary, the Hellenization thesis maintained that Christian theology invested in, but never divested itself of, its potent engagement with Greek philosophy during the second to the fourth centuries. This argument held the force it did because of other ideas associated with the Enlightenment, namely its historical consciousness and the way reason was used to critique truth claims generated at particular times in history, which were then enforced with the authority of tradition. In the famous remarks of G. E. Lessing (1729–81), "If no historical truth can be demonstrated, then nothing can be demonstrated by means of historical truths. That is: accidental truths of history can never become the proof of necessary truths of reason."[7] Adolf von Harnack (1851–1930), and others before him, sharpened this critique by developing the school of *Dogmengeschichte,* the history of dogma. By showing that dogma and doctrines had histories, the occasion-specific circumstances of their origin could be demonstrated, and any claims to their absoluteness could thus be challenged. Moreover, the Hellenization thesis was about more than the priority of reason over tradition and more than a simple claim to historical consciousness. It included the further claim that the substance of the doctrines so produced during Christianity's engagement with Greek philosophy were actual distortions of the gospel proclaimed in the New Testament. This passage from the Prolegomena to Harnack's *Outlines of the History of Dogma* indicates these various themes:

> The claim of the Church that the dogmas are simply the exposition of Christian revelation, because deduced from the Holy Scriptures, is not confirmed by historical investigation. On the contrary, it becomes clear that dogmatic Christianity (the dogmas) in its conception and its construction was *the work of the Hellenic spirit upon the Gospel soil*.[8]

He continues with the charge that not only can the history of dogma prove the illusory nature of basing the status of dogma on its origin but also that "historical investigation destroy[s] the other illusion of the Church, viz.: that the dogma, always having been the same therein, have simply been explained, and that ecclesiastical theology has never had any other aim than to explain the unchanging dogma and to refute … heretical teaching."[9] In a statement that echoes the emancipatory intent and rhetoric of the Enlightenment, he suggests that the history of dogma, precisely as it "sets forth the process of the origin and development of the dogma, offers the very best means and methods of freeing the Church from dogmatic Christianity, and hastening the inevitable process of emancipation."[10] Yet, on a more hopeful note, the history of dogma, precisely through its historical work, is also able to highlight the "*unity* and continuity of the Christian faith in the progress of its history, in so far as it proves that certain fundamental ideas of the gospel have never been lost and have defied all attacks."[11] What exactly Harnack himself argued was that the "fundamental ideals of the

Gospel" need not distract us here. Suffice it to say, positively, they involved a particular focus on Jesus of Nazareth, and negatively, they excluded any metaphysical elements.[12] For our purposes, two points from this cluster of remarks from Harnack warrant comment. The first is his claim that the function of dogma is to provide constancy of teaching and thereby to refute heresy. This reveals a radical intellectualizing of doctrine that ignores the many other things it does even as it performs its normative teaching role. As seen in the previous two chapters, doctrine fosters, among other things, prayer, forms a vision, and cultivates discipleship. To intellectualize doctrine is to truncate it. The second point is to highlight how *Dogmengeschite*, as presented here, is completely embedded in the Enlightenment's rhetoric of emancipation. Even if suspicion of doctrine preexisted the Hellenization thesis, this particular notion of it being an authority from which the church needed to be liberated carried much of its force (and its resilience in many quarters of the contemporary church) from its Enlightenment provenance. Nevertheless, even if the Hellenization thesis itself has been subject to effective historical and ideological criticism, perhaps the more telling critique of it is the way many of the church's received doctrines have actually been major resources in Christianity's post-Enlightenment reconstructive work, including that of its own emancipation from the Enlightenment's prejudices and ideologies. To these and other examples of this fruitfulness of particular doctrines we now turn.

Doctrine and the study of Jesus: Jesus' human nature

The contours of relationship between the study of doctrine and the study of Jesus have been permanently shaped by the impact of the Hellenization thesis.[13] The relationship between these two fields of study remains highly contested and is frequently characterized by mutual suspicion. Nevertheless, the most enduring and undeniable challenge of the Hellenization thesis to the doctrinal tradition is that of the need to acknowledge the Jewishness of Jesus in any theological account of his significance. To accept the critique of the Hellenization thesis that classical Christology paid insufficient attention to Jesus' Jewishness is not *a priori* to deny what classical Christology affirms. It is, however, to raise the legitimate question of whether Christological discourse can be broadened, enhanced, and/or modified by attention to this matter.

One theologian who has engaged such questions is the German Reformed theologian Jürgen Moltmann (1926–). Retrieving and appropriating the

Jewish roots of the Christian faith has been a persistent theme of his writings, not least in his two early and groundbreaking works, *The Theology of Hope* (1964, ET 1967)[14] and *The Crucified God* (1974, ET 1974).[15] In the context of the present book, the focus will be on his incorporation into Christology of Jesus' identification with Jewish messianic hopes via his proclamation of the kingdom of God. This is part of his later work, *The Way of Jesus Christ: Christology in Messianic Dimensions*.[16] Attention to the Christological significance of Jesus' proclamation of the kingdom of God is an interesting move in its own right, and hardly unique to Moltmann. Yet in the context of an investigation of doctrine, Moltmann's engagement with these issues is an interesting development. He proposes an addition to the church's creeds. This is an unusual step for a doctrinal theologian. It is certainly more radical than even Rahner's proposed context-specific creeds that were noted in the previous chapter. Moltmann is proposing an addition to the universal creed. It is also notable that Moltmann offers this proposal precisely as an addition, not a revision as such. After all, the creedal tradition (in both the Nicene and Chalcedonian Creeds) affirm Jesus' full humanity. He sets out to "arrive at a fuller, richer portrait of the person of Jesus Christ."[17]

The path by which Moltmann comes to this proposal is relatively straightforward. Rather than appealing to any putative "historical Jesus," Moltmann works with the accounts of Jesus given in the synoptic Gospels where Jesus is placed squarely in the context of messianic hope and his own messianic identity. Retaining but qualifying the term "person" from classical Christology, Moltmann argues that doctrinal enquiry should ask about the nature of Jesus' "messianic person."[18] He defines this not in terms of the classical categories of nature or essence but in various dynamic categories that point to Jesus' simultaneous existence in three sets of relationships. The first is his relationship to the eschatological messianic kingdom of God, the second is to the one he called Abba, and the third is his relationship to his human brothers and sisters. Essentially, he argues that Jesus' personhood "acquires its form in living relationships and reciprocities, and becomes an open identity in the course of Jesus' history."[19] It is not "determined and fixed from eternity"[20] as it is, according to Moltmann, in the metaphysical categories of patristic discussions. Rather than invoke the various messianic titles attributed to Jesus in the Gospels to define Jesus' identity, Moltmann argues that it is Jesus' history, especially his experience of suffering, that "provide[s] the key to titles."[21] It is this line of thought that leads Moltmann to propose that the church's creeds should say more about the humanity of Jesus, and that what is said should point to how it was formed and developed in the course of his messianic vocation. Moltmann points to the failure of the Nicene and Apostles' Creeds to say "either nothing at all, or really no more than a comma"[22] between their references to Jesus' birth and death. So he offers a suggestion for an addition to the second clause of the Creeds. It should, he says, be "something along the following lines":

> Baptized by the John the Baptist,
>
> Filled with the Holy Spirit:
>
> to preach the kingdom of God to the poor,
>
> to heal the sick,
>
> to receive those who have been cast out,
>
> to revive Israel for the salvation of nations, and to have mercy on all people.[23]

Critical discussions will ensue regarding the validity of Moltmann's critique of the Greek tradition and its impact on Christian theology. There will also be legitimate debates about the veracity of the general shape of his messianic Christology.[24] It might also be suggested that even in their classical form, the Creeds achieve their theological purpose through their affirmation of the Son's incarnation and that the specific attention to the details of his earthly life do not add to that. Having allowed for all those possibilities, however, Moltmann's proposal is important in its suggestiveness, regardless of whether the church universal might ever accept such an addition to the Creeds. It is suggestive in the first instance because it brings to the summary of the faith the actual contours of Jesus' life. While creeds—and confessions—might be used and defended as summaries of the faith (as we observed in Chapter 1), their content, exactly as summaries, must be interrogated by and, at least in some measure, reflect the breadth of the biblical witness. It is suggestive in the second instance because it explicitly connects Israel and the church in manner that means that in any use of an expanded creed, the church would be reminded of Jesus' and its own Jewish roots, the denial or forgetfulness of which is writ large in the tragic history of Christianity's attitudes toward, and relationships with, the Jewish people. Absorbing the details of Jesus' life and its Jewish context into the doctrine of Jesus' humanity allows this doctrine to take its place in a highly contested part of Christianity's history and present existence. It is important in the third instance, and especially to be noted in the present work, for highlighting how engagement with the doctrinal tradition can be simultaneously critical and constructive. It was highlighted in Chapter 1 that no creed or confession can be exhaustive, even in relation to the questions to which it was initially a response. Moltmann's example suggests ways in which a particular doctrine, in this instance, the humanity of Jesus, can be deepened and expanded, rather than necessarily rejected, by addressing new questions to it. While the creeds might de facto be beyond formal revision, attention to the particular doctrines that they contain can illuminate their overall claims and point to their intellectual and spiritual capaciousness.

Doctrine and women: Trinity

One of the most enduring legacies of the Enlightenment's emancipatory forces are the various strands of feminism that have become an established part of cultural, intellectual, and political landscapes, especially in the West but also in other parts of the world. Feminist theology has similarly become an influential element of the global theological community. Strikingly, even though feminism was an extension of the emancipatory trajectories of the Enlightenment, it has also been at the forefront of criticisms of the Enlightenment's rationalism.[25] In some respects, the presence of these two forces within feminist theology converge in some feminist approaches to the doctrine of the Trinity. Although, before turning to a particular example of feminist engagement with this doctrine, it needs to be noted that feminism is a fluid and contested concept and that "feminist theology" is a very loose term for the wide variety of intellectual disciplines by which women engage Christian theology.[26] For some, the term "feminism" is simply too narrow, and Womanist and Mujerista theologies are needed to broaden the agenda.

Having said that, the growing influence of some Western strands of feminist theology coincided with the renaissance of interest in the doctrine of the Trinity more broadly during the twentieth century. Both Karl Barth and Karl Rahner brought the doctrine to the attention of their respective traditions. At stake for both of them was the very identity of the one God revealed in Jesus Christ and worshipped by Christians. In Barth's case, it was partly in reaction to Schleiermacher's alleged relegation of the doctrine and what he perceived were the doctrinal consequences of that move.[27] In Rahner's case, his concern was the de facto irrelevance of this doctrine to the life of Christian people.[28] Their influence, combined with the growing attention by Western theologians to the Orthodox traditions, led to a proliferation of reflection on this neglected doctrine. The parallel between these developments and the emergence of feminist theology is not merely chronological. The doctrine of the Trinity, with all its Greek philosophical conceptuality, was inevitably one of the chief targets of Enlightenment criticism of Christianity. On the other hand, the renewed attention to it also manifested a new confidence in the appeal to modes of analogical and relational knowledge broader than the rationalism of the Enlightenment. At the same time, the doctrine of the Trinity, with its naming of the three persons as Father, Son, and Spirit, embodied with particular potency the problem of gendered language and the patriarchy it represented and legitimated. Accordingly, it became an object of particular suspicion in many strands of feminist theology. But it also attracted new positive interest by others.

One of the notable examples of a critically constructive feminist approach to the doctrine of the Trinity is that of American Catholic theologian Elizabeth A. Johnson. Her work reflects many of the dominant concerns of feminist theology: the critique of patriarchal language, the rejection of objectivist theories of knowledge, and the appeal to women's experience as a decisive theological resource. These various themes converge in her engagement with the doctrine of the Trinity in her book *She Who Is*.[29] Johnson describes her feminist perspective as oriented toward "reflection on religious mystery from a stance which makes an *a priori* option for the human flourishing of women."[30] Clearly, this has the goal of correcting the neglect of, and even blindness to, such concerns in the history of theology. Yet her posture toward the tradition is not one of rejection. She draws on the church's core doctrines (incarnation, Trinity, creation, etc.) for "fragments of wisdom, fruitful possibilities" to resource her feminist concerns.[31] A more general feature of the classical tradition that she especially highlights is its attention to the incomprehensibility of God. She makes the point drawing on Augustine's dictum on this matter: "*Si comprehendis, non est Deus*: if you have understood, then what you have understood is not God."[32] She perceives connections between these concerns and the "overrationalized condition"[33] of Trinitarian discourse, especially its tendency toward literalness and abstraction. This also allowed the doctrine of the Trinity to succumb to the abstract theism that became the easy target of Enlightenment criticism. To all these problems, there was also the "deeply masculinized" nature of the doctrine that, in turn, pointed to "an essential divine maleness."[34] It is in the context of such considerations that she speaks of feminist theology "intersecting with these other concerns at every point."[35] Through such "intersecting," her engagement with the doctrine of the Trinity displays a mixture of critical appropriation of the tradition and her own innovations.

Johnson begins with the affirmation of the basic concerns of Trinitarian theology as it first emerged. She insists that the doctrine of the Trinity confesses that the Christian experiences of Christ and the Spirit are experiences of God. Against claims to the contrary, the doctrine affirms that in Christ and the Spirit, God is involved in and related to the world *as God*. The doctrine is "shorthand for the dynamic, inexpressible Sophia-God of compassionate, liberating love who is involved in history."[36] Accordingly, she adds an anti-modalist note by affirming that God *pro nobis* is consistent with God *in se*. On the other hand, she resists what she believes is the patristic and later preoccupation with relations of origin within the Trinity. Such discussions, she argues, sit too lightly to the diversity of patterns of relationships between Father, Son, and Holy Spirit portrayed in the New Testament.[37] Ignoring this diversity, these discussions unnecessarily legitimated the persistent concern with hierarchy in Trinitarian doctrine. To Johnson's mind, this has obscured the deeper insight of Trinitarian reflection: the mutuality of the divine persons. This, in fact, is her main emphasis and it is where her concern with language and metaphor is highlighted.

While arguing that all three persons of the Trinity transcend gender, she nevertheless uses female categories and metaphors aligned with feminist concerns as a necessary corrective. Her aim is not merely to substitute certain male terms with female terms. It is, instead, to develop a language around this doctrine that resonates with feminist concerns and that does greater justice to the diversity of biblical language for and about God. To this end, she employs the category of Wisdom/Sophia and confesses the Trinity's three in these terms: "God is God as Spirit-Sophia, the mobile, pure, people-loving Spirit … releasing power that enables fresh starts … God is again God as Jesus Christ, Sophia's child and prophet … God is God again as unimaginable abyss of livingness, Holy Wisdom unknown and unknowable. She is the matrix of all that exists, mother and fashioner of all things."[38] To these designations Johnson adds the metaphor of friendship to describe the relationships between the three, echoing the ancient doctrine of perichoresis: "Holy Wisdom, the horizon encircling all horizons, is a profound mystery of relatedness, whose essential livingness consists in the mutuality of friendship. The love of friendship is the very essence of God. Hidden Abyss, Word and Spirit mutually indwell in a companionable communion of unimaginable strength."[39]

Thus, she proposes a language by which the doctrine of the Trinity may be "confessed as critical prophecy in the midst of patriarchal rule."[40] Positively, it also resonates with "so many studies of women's ways of being in the world,"[41] thus providing a means by which women in particular can be called "to grow into the abundance of their human powers" as full participants in the *imago Dei*.[42] By no means, however, does she argue a simple "cause and effect" relation between this doctrine and the attainment of women's full freedom and the undermining of patriarchy. Doctrine does not do its work that easily. In a very sobering remark, she comments on the power that such an account of this doctrine might produce. It "flashes like a beacon through a dark night, rather than shining like a daytime sun." This is a reminder of the complexity of how doctrine does in fact shape behavior, a theme to which we will return in Chapter 5.

The question of the Trinitarian names is a controversial issue in contemporary theology. The argument is made by some theologians that Father, Son, and Spirit are biblically authenticated proper names for the persons of the Trinity and not mere substitutable metaphors.[43] Johnson herself draws on biblical warrants for her own use of female imagery pointing to the "interesting fluidity of usage" evident in the New Testament.[44] Moreover, Johnson's particular project has drawn the heavy criticism that it arbitrarily makes women's experience normative for the articulation and development of the doctrine of the Trinity.[45] Be that as it may, the question of her revised language raises another issue of importance for doctrine. It parallels the use of the non-biblical terminology of "persons" and "substance" in the patristic debates. Recall the comment of Rowan Williams cited in Chapter 1 about how an insistence on the repetition of biblical terms can actually be counterproductive. The language can become ossified and its use might fail to address any new issues that arise in new contexts. Similarly, by introducing new terms, concepts, and metaphors, a doctrine is not necessarily abandoned; rather, it is renewed and its basic concerns can be mediated anew. As with the use of non-biblical concepts to articulate biblical teaching, so new concepts and metaphors can articulate and renew received doctrines.

Doctrine and church of the Majority World 1: Cosmic Christology

Even as the Enlightenment was sealing the end of European Christendom as a stable and fixed cultural phenomenon, Christianity was growing in Asia, Africa, Latin America, and the Pacific. Although parts of the former two regions were already home to ancient Christian communities, the impact of the modern missionary movement had resulted in new and expanding forms of Christian communities throughout the non-Western world, or to use the term used and explained in Chapter 1, "the majority world." This development is itself riddled with theological and ethical ambiguity, not least because of the now evident overlaps between the missionary movement and European colonialism. Nevertheless, as those churches grew and as Western Christendom declined in its impact and numbers, the churches of Asia, Africa, Latin America, and the Pacific exercised their independence of their Western counterparts and began to develop theological agendas alert to their respective contexts.

The example to be drawn on here is Cosmic Christology (or the doctrine of the Cosmic Christ). This doctrine has not been without some interest among post-Enlightenment Western theologians who have appropriated it, in part, as a means of resisting the undue narrowing of Christological discourse by the authority given to the modern academic discipline of "history."[46] It has also attracted the interest of various Asian theologians for some overlapping but distinct reasons. The work of two Chinese theologians is to be considered here: K. H. Ting (1915–2012) and Wang Weifan (1927–2015).[47] The example of the Chinese theologians is especially instructive for several reasons. They too see cosmic Christology being a correction to the reductionist Christologies developed in response to the European Enlightenment (and which had become a problematic presence in modern Chinese Protestantism). In a manner that echoes the strategies of the second-century Apologists, they appeal to the universality of Christ to legitimate Christianity in modern China against the view that it is a Western religion alien to China. In the hands of one of them in particular, the development of cosmic Christology provides an illuminating example of the subtleties of contextualizing received doctrinal discourse into a new context. Such matters are heightened in view of the seemingly infinite complexities of Christianity's relationship to modern China, and especially following the Communist Revolution in 1949. Ting and Wang (and their peers) were so enmeshed in the very survival of the church, including experiencing its suppression during the Cultural Revolution, that their engagement with doctrine was always ad hoc and necessarily oriented to the ever-changing and permanently delicate circumstances of the Chinese Christians. Indeed, Ting—the high-profile leader of the Chinese church during this tumultuous period—once compared the nature of his and his colleagues' work to that of the apostles: "We have no time to sit down to do systematic theology. But we write letters, much like the early apostles."[48]

Ting is explicit in stating that the doctrine of the cosmic Christ generated interest in China precisely because the circumstances of Chinese Christianity have "driv[en] Christians to go back to the New Testament and meet there familiar words glistening with splendour and meaning as if for the first time."[49] Drawing especially on the relevant Colossians and Ephesians texts, and the respective prologues from the Gospel of John and Hebrews,[50] he asserts Christ's place and status in creation: "He is the pre-existent Logos, the crown or fulfilment of all creation, the revealer in all fullness of its nature and meaning. His incarnation is not an intrusion into an alien world, but a divine yes to creation and God's means for human redemption and renewal."[51] This line of thought is substantiated with references, albeit in passing, to both the *logos spermatikos* idea of Justin Martyr and Aquinas's view that grace completes nature.[52] Substantively, the universality of Christ in both creation and redemption leads in two related directions. The first is a soteriologically hopeful posture toward the world beyond the church. Drawing on Romans 5, he argues that if Christ is Lord of the cosmos, then he "is stronger than Adam, his gift stronger than disobedience, and grace stronger than sin."[53] Or, in one especially poignant statement: "Too often, we make sin universal while limiting grace only to the few who profess a belief in Christ. It really amounts to saying that the Incarnation of the Son of God has made less of an impact on humanity than the fall of Adam."[54] The second, echoing Justin's *logos* ideas in particular, points to historical movements and thoughts being regarded as "aids in illuminating" God's creative and redemptive work.[55] Thus, Ting suggests, they can be critically welcomed by Christians.

The first of these points allows him to critique pessimistic Augustinian/Calvinist anthropology, which he contends is characteristic of much modern Chinese Protestantism. The second allows him to encourage Chinese Christians to work together with their non-Christian neighbors whatever their politics. This does not qualify Christological particularity. Any affirmation of the "universal creative and redemptive activity of God for all humankind" rests and is grounded in the "the particular redemptive activity of God in the history of Israel and in the person and work of Jesus Christ. This is implied when we say Christ is cosmic."[56] Ting's approach resists any easy categorization, although what he rejects also illuminates his own position. He is especially critical of modern reductionist accounts of Jesus as merely a great ethical teacher, a "Christology" that is transparently at odds with any claim to the cosmic *lordship* of Christ. He points out that such Enlightenment-inspired Christologies confused many Chinese Christians when they sought to understand the relationship between Christianity and Communism.[57]

It is important to note that, as outlined so far, Ting develops these ideas largely in terms familiar to Western discourse. He does, however, also draw on certain ideas from traditional Chinese teachings to illuminate his cosmic Christology. He suggests a parallel between the cosmic nature of Christ's rule and Lao Tze's description of the supreme Tao:

> The supreme Tao, How it floods in every direction!
> This way and that, there is no place where it does not go.
> All things look to it for life, and it refused none of them:
> Yet when its work is accomplished, it possesses nothing.
> Clothing and nourishing all things, it does not lord it over them
> Since it asks for nothing from them,
> It may be classed among things of low estate;
> But since all things obey it without coercion, it may be named supreme.
> It does not arrogate greatness to itself, and so fulfils its greatness.[58]

Although such parallels might suggest some kind of *preparatio evangelica* status for Chinese traditions and religions, he speaks less systematically of the ways such insights are, as we saw above, "aids to illumination" of the Christian faith. The ad hoc nature of his writings make it difficult to offer a definite judgment on how systematically coordinated with Christianity Ting believes Chinese traditions are.

Similar themes are found in Wang's work. Like Ting, there is an explicit orientation to the development of a specifically Chinese Christian theology. Appealing to Jn 1:14, he writes, "When the revelation of God and the gospel of Christ enters a particular culture it must 'put on the flesh' of this culture."[59] For our purposes, however, there are two features of his work that warrant attention. One is his development of the ancient Chinese idea of *shengsheng shen*. The other is his sensitivity to the authority of received doctrine. Apart from one explicit reference in an untranslated article, Wang does not explicitly engage the language or discourse of Cosmic Christology.[60] But he does develop a Christological reading of the unity of creation and redemption that orients his ideas to the universal lordship of Christ. It is in relation to this that he develops the concept of *shengsheng*. Drawn from the *Book of Changes* of the Zhou Dynasty (1045–256 BCE), Wang uses it to speak of God as the "ever generating God" (*shengsheng shen*). The term could also be translated as "unceasing generation" or even "life-birthing life."[61] Wang highlights the presence of this term in Chinese Christian writings from the Tang dynasty (618–907) and in the writings of the *Yelikewen*, a Christian group present in China during the Yuan dynasty (1271–1368).[62] This in itself is important. It highlights how he draws on an already existing (if mostly obscured) Chinese Christian theological tradition that had already appropriated aspects of traditional Chinese beliefs. Drawing on this concept allowed the earlier Chinese Christians to contextualize their discourse about God. Wang notes,

> Ancient Christians in China called their God "Ever-generating God." This was a God who created, sustained and enriched life, a God who ceaselessly generated and regenerated life. They saw Jesus as the "Holy One," whose saving grace fulfilled the life created by God and brought it to completion. From this they gained a view of human life which responded straightforwardly to heaven, a life which continued to strengthen them by borrowing strength from heaven, a life which took the safeguarding of life (guarding the life which God had created) as the highest good and the greatest virtue.[63]

Christ is the universal Lord who, being one with God, is the source of life in both creation and redemption. He summarizes as follows: "Therefore, God is an ever-generating God who creates and sustains life and Christ is an invitation to life through the destruction of death, making life more complete and full."[64]

Presented as briefly as they are here, these ideas will prompt many questions. Nevertheless, aside from the content of the idea itself, Wang is very clear about what he understands is at issue in drawing on ancient Chinese concepts. He seeks to pursue "theological thinking which can be refined into a theology with Chinese characteristics [and thus allow] Chinese theology [to] guide the Chinese Church and Chinese believers through the process of modernization in China."[65] What is just as interesting, however, is what he says next: "and make a fitting gift to the Church worldwide."[66] The same point is made when he articulates the hope that such a theology "will be more easily appreciated and accepted by the sons and daughters of the yellow Emperor—and welcomed and treasured by the Church ecumenical."[67] Clearly, this is not an attempt to develop a parochial Chinese theology. Indeed, echoing Ting's resistance to reductionist Christologies, Wang was wary of some Chinese influences on Chinese Christian thought, notably the pressure of Confucianism to "lower the status of Christianity to that of an ordinary ethical system, ignoring its transcendent aspects."[68] Rather, he was attempting to develop a Chinese theology that could take its place in the whole church. This raises an important issue with regard to the relationship between this proposal and received doctrine. Wang is not an unqualified innovator. He is explicitly drawing on an earlier teaching of the Chinese church that he also understands to be a Chinese interpretation of the biblical teaching of the lordship of Christ. Moreover, the reference to the Chinese concept is not used for any foundationalist purpose. His point about the earlier appropriation of this term is not that the God of Jesus Christ was prefigured in the concept of *shengsheng*.[69] It is much more the case that this concept is used to illuminate an existing Christian belief. In the *Book of Changes*, *shengsheng* was embedded in processes of divinization based on numerograms. In a departure from earlier techniques of divinization, the *Book of Changes* was not seeking wisdom from the ancestral spirits. Instead, it "attempted to explore the hidden patterns of change in order to predict the future."[70] It involves the exploration of *yin* and *yang* as the elemental forces causing change. Patently, Wang is not suggesting that either he himself or the earlier writers are wanting to appropriate divinization techniques of the Zhou dynasty into contemporary Chinese Christianity. Rather, the concept is given Christian meaning while also being used to illuminate an existing Christian concept.

What does this case study tell us about Christian doctrine? It is striking that for all the emphasis upon orienting Chinese theology to Chinese concepts, and whatever level of doctrinal development or innovation is undertaken, both Ting and Wang see themselves as receiving and transmitting an already existing Christian doctrine. While their developments of this doctrine do not take catechetical or formulaic form, their discourse is clearly that of persuasion. They are using this doctrine to teach the Chinese church. But in also transmitting it, they develop it. And in developing it, they bring it into relationship with other doctrines in order to correct what they perceive to be doctrinal imbalances in Chinese Christianity. There is a Christological reordering of the doctrines of creation and redemption. Moreover, while they are critical of some aspects of the theology of the modern Protestant missionary movement, they resist this not (at least in this instance) by anti-Western rhetoric but by a deeper penetration into the teachings of the church.

Doctrine in Crisis and Doctrine Renewed

They are also alert to what they perceive to be distortions of this doctrine that had developed under the pressure of the European Enlightenment, notably in their shared resistance to a reductionist Christology focused on Jesus as merely a teacher. Most tellingly, however, is the fact that, at least in Wang's case, the doctrine has been received from an ancient Chinese Christian source. Here, doctrine, as a teaching of the earlier Chinese Christian community, is being retrieved for the sake of both current concerns and the catholicity of doctrinal teaching. Doctrine is being developed, but not in a way that is either cavalier or parochial. Here, a particular doctrine becomes the focus of a conversation across time and place; it is a conversation with elements of polemic, correction, and mutual encouragement.

Doctrine and church of the Majority World 2: Salvation

The nexus between the churches of the majority world and colonization was already noted in the previous section. Undoing that nexus has been and remains a challenge not only for those churches but also the churches of colonizers. In the middle of the twentieth century, however, the challenge of doing so coincided with the various movements for independence and the tasks of nation building. Just as the churches of Africa, Latin America, Asia, and the Pacific were finding their own voice vis-à-vis the churches of European Christendom, they were also finding their voice amid the political and cultural realities of their immediate national contexts. This was certainly the case in India. Although there had been a continuous and visible Christian presence in India since at least the third century,[71] the consequence of the modern missionary movement was a greater denominational diversity and geographical spread of the Christian presence. Indian Christian leaders had emerged and were playing a significant role in civic leadership and in orienting the Indian Christian community to this new context. One such leader was Madathilparampil Mammen Thomas (1916–1996), more commonly referred to as M. M. Thomas. As well as being a prolific writer and activist, he served as Moderator of the Central Committee of the World Council of Churches (1968–75) and was briefly Governor of the Indian state of Nagaland (1991–3).

Of Thomas, it has been said that "his theology is at core Christology."[72] It is, moreover, a Christology directly and explicitly oriented to and interrogated by the challenges of human existence and suffering, specifically as they were experienced in twentieth-century India.[73] For Thomas, therefore, there is no legitimate discussion of Christology abstracted from anthropology and soteriology. These concerns come together in an influential lecture he gave in 1970, "Salvation and Humanization."[74] The lecture has been described as Thomas's "most mature thinking on the subject."[75] Twenty-first-century readers of this lecture may well find its concerns very familiar, largely due to its parallels with concerns of liberation and contextual theologies. Where those theologies tend to make extensive use of various critical theories, one of the striking features of this lecture is the way the argument is based on quite direct appeals to the doctrines of Christology, anthropology, sin, and soteriology.

As the title suggests, the presenting issue is a theology of mission "for India." Part of the background is the then recent discussions within the World Council of Churches, which had raised the question of the "relation between the gospel of salvation and the struggles of men [sic] everywhere for their humanity, constituting as this does the contemporary context of the world in which the Gospel has to be communicated."[76] These struggles are located not only at an individual level but also in the "dehumanizing spiritual forces of corporate life"[77] in caste, class, family, and nation (the first two of which presented especially forcefully in India). While these "evil forces are never totally done away with from history,"[78] the Christian gospel grounded in the resurrection of Christ calls for confronting them within history. The theological structure of the argument is set out in this passage:

> The mission of salvation and the task of humanization are integrally related to each other, even if they cannot be considered identical. The ultimate destiny of man [sic] in the Resurrection beyond sin, guilt and death must have its realization, however partial it may be, in terms of his [sic] historical destiny—even as no humanism which does not take into serious account the reality of sin as self-righteousness, guilt and fear of death in the light of the Cross of Christ, can grapple responsibility with the forces of dehumanization emerging in ever-new forms and achieve even tolerable conditions for human living in history.[79]

It is important to note how the more generic idea of humanization is described in specifically Christian terms of salvation and Christology. In sum, "This means our mission is to make clear that salvation is the spiritual inwardness of true humanization, and that humanization is inherent in the message of salvation in Christ."[80] Whether through "dialogue, presence or proclamation," the purpose of mission is "to make Christ known as the source and foundation of true humanization" and that it should be characterized "by constant awareness of the mystery of the death and resurrection of Christ."[81]

Thomas extends these arguments to the particularities of the Indian situation. This includes drawing on the specific Christologies of earlier Indian theologians. "The most characteristic feature of the Indian understanding of Jesus Christ," he writes, "is as the Divine Man, or the New Adam, the bearer of the New Humanity, New Creation. And they all see in the bodily resurrection and ascension of Christ the assumption in the Godhead of Christ's historical humanity."[82] This is the fundamental ground of the link between salvation and humanization: "Salvation itself could be defined as humanization in a total and eschatological sense. And all our struggles on earth for the fragmentary realization of man's [sic] humanity point to this eschatological humanization as their judgement and fulfilment."[83] Alongside the Christological insights of Indian theologians, he also places the experience of India's "outcastes, the poor and the orphans [who] saw Christian faith as the source of a new humanizing influence and the foundation of a human community … It was the promise of humanization inherent in the gospel of salvation that led to the influx of the oppressed into the Church."[84]

As noted earlier, the basic contours of Thomas's understanding of salvation—its grounding in an interpretation of the resurrection and its realized eschatology—are familiar. While this particular lecture continues to be discussed by Indian theologians, contemporary Indian theology addresses a wider range of presenting issues than those that claimed Thomas's attention.[85] Nevertheless, the link he draws between salvation and humanization warrants attention here as an example of the confident use of a basic Christian doctrine—salvation—and its underlying doctrinal structure to both describe and respond to the particular challenges of a specific context. Implicitly, Thomas sees doctrine as intellectually and spiritually fertile in directing the church to an understanding of its situation as well as in its response to that situation.

Doctrine and new knowledge: Anthropology

With its privileging of reason over revelation, indeed even its dismissal of revelation, the Enlightenment provided the cultural legitimation of intellectual disciplines and sources of knowledge that were independent of revelation. This included the already emerging natural sciences. The relationship between modern science and Christian theology is complex, but the common assumption that it is *necessarily* conflictual in nature is true neither of the origins of modern science nor of the majority of Christian theology's contemporary posture toward science.[86] One Christian doctrine that has been brought into conversation with scientific knowledge is anthropology, specifically the doctrine of the human person bearing the *imago Dei*. The doctrine has certainly been vigorously interrogated in the light of new cultural assumptions and scientific understandings of both gender and sexuality. At the same time, the gendered nature of human being as the image of God as declared in Gen. 1:26-27 had already become an influential tool of criticism against the widely assumed and theologically legitimated normativity of the male. Yet the same binary that proved liberating in one context has become problematic in more recent discussions of sexual- and gender diversity, a diversity that has been reinforced by scientific analyses of those phenomena. Theology has, of course, always been in conversation, consciously or otherwise, with "natural" knowledge of sex and gender.[87] In the engagement with *modern* science, however, the knowledge generated is often presented and/or used precisely to deconstruct theologically generated understandings of sex and gender. Christian theology is thus often involved in a demanding discernment of how such knowledge might actually provide resources, or even norms, for doctrinal claims. The example to be presented here is that of the exploration of the doctrine of the *imago Dei* in the light of the reality and claims of intersex people and the scientific interpretations of that reality. The work in question is Megan DeFranza's *Sex Difference in Christian Theology: Male, Female and Intersex in the Image of God*.[88]

The reality of intersex is not new. Essentially, it refers to the phenomenon in which a person's anatomy and physiology do not match normative definitions of either male or female. Many cultures have produced conventions and practices by which intersex people have been acknowledged, classified, and/or marginalized. In recent centuries, one such convention was to medicalize the condition, treating it as an illness or a deformity to be healed. This has been a factor that has further marginalized intersex people, as well as leading to some destructive medical interventions. It is this particular response to intersex that DeFranza challenges. She does so on scientific, exegetical, and doctrinal grounds. As DeFranza notes, "intersex" is an umbrella term that covers a "wide range of variations"[89] in both sexual development and sexual anatomy. The scientific community, with access to genetic analysis and knowledge of chromosomal structures, is able to explain these variations in terms of natural genetic variety. DeFranza argues that such knowledge, combined with the witness of intersex people resisting the medicalization of their reality, calls for a fresh questioning of the male–female binary associated with the doctrine of the *imago Dei*.[90] The question driving her enquiry is this: "What are the implications of intersex for theological anthropologies built upon a binary model of human sex differentiation?"[91] Finding an answer to this is intended to resource the church in its "ministry to/with/by the intersex."[92]

One part of her strategy is to attend to the biblical witness to eunuchs (which itself is also an umbrella term). Against the background of widespread ancient prejudices against eunuchs, she points to their full inclusion in Isaiah's vision of the messianic age in Isa. 53:3-7. She also, more importantly, draws on Jesus' teaching in Mt. 19:12. There, Jesus refers to three classes of eunuchs: those who are born as such, those made so by others, and those who have become eunuchs for the sake of the kingdom of heaven. DeFranza acknowledges that the later reception of this teaching had the possibly unintended consequence of transforming the eunuch "from the immoral other into a new model of Christian perfection,"[93] a perfection manifest in the putative virtue of sexual renunciation. Yet, DeFranza seeks to reclaim this teaching from its consequences. She argues that in its immediate context of teaching about the kingdom of heaven, "Jesus was not afraid of eunuchs. He was not disgusted by them. He did not ridicule them as did Jews, Romans and Greeks."[94] Drawing on other scholarly work, she also highlights that in this declaration by Jesus about eunuchs, there is no hint, as there was in his encounters with blind and diseased people, that they needed restoration. The main point she draws from Jesus' teaching is that in "calling his disciples to learn from eunuchs, Jesus was calling them to learn from those whose gender identity was not secure, to learn that gender identity is not the central value in the kingdom of heaven."[95] Drawing on this teaching is important in resisting the view, based on a certain reading of Gen. 1:26-27, that the body has an essential nuptial meaning, directing men and women to marriage. Jesus' teaching points to the fact that "there are those whose bodies do not carry a nuptial meaning—they naturally do not marry" and there are those who place the values of the kingdom above this nuptial possibility.[96]

Another, closely related, part of her strategy involves "recovering the canonical place of Adam and Eve"[97] and rejecting the tradition that claims the unity of their gender distinction to be constitutive of the *imago Dei*. Such arguments are often reinforced by invoking the Trinitarian language of unity-in-difference to present the unity of gender difference as the image of the triune, social God. To note the "canonical place" of Adam and Eve is to recognize that their role in the canon is *not* to provide "the paradigmatic forms of difference."[98] Rather, they are the "fountainheads of even greater differences."[99] Genesis does not, she points out, provide a full list of all the diversity contained in God's good creation. "It is the beginning of the story, painting in broad brush strokes, with so much more to come."[100] Recognizing this can also be a check on the "overemphasizing of sex and gender difference and its essential or constituted relation to personhood."[101] It can also avoid the "conflation of sexuality and relationality" that often flows from this reading of Genesis. Nevertheless, it is this broader diversity and the richer notions of difference of which Adam and Eve are "fountainheads" that should be brought into conversation with the Trinitarian unity-in-difference. These lines of thought are summarized as follows:

> Relocating love from the binary model of spousal sexuality into the wider community of extended family, neighbourhood, and *ecclesia* retains the social *imago* whilst delivering it from sexual distortions … Such a vision makes space for the unmarried, for the nonsexually active, for eunuchs, and for intersexed persons to be recognized as fully made in the image of God.[102]

Further consequences of canonically "locating" Adam and Eve include the recognition of the New Testament emphasis on Christ as the image of God (Col. 1:15) and the parallel teaching that those in Christ are "no longer male and female" (Gal. 3:27). Not only does this reframe the status of the human beings as the *imago Dei*, it also adds to the relativization of the place of the gender binary in that image. All of these arguments combine in a challenge to "construct better anthropologies,"[103] ones that make room for the many forms of difference, of which intersex is one.

This summary barely skims the surface of a rich and complex argument. By no means is it the only possible theological response to new knowledge about gender and sexuality.[104] Yet it does provide an example of doctrinal reflection that responds to new knowledge and moreover shows doctrinal reflection taking place in relation to a highly controversial matter in the life of the church. It also teaches us something else about doctrine. This particular case shows how the reconsideration of one doctrine has been pursued both by exegetical concerns and by allowing one doctrine to be interpreted and shaped by others. DeFranza's argument allows anthropology, Trinity, and Christology to converge in such a way that a particular aspect of anthropology could be restated. As we have seen in the previous chapter and in the earlier sections of this chapter, particular doctrines may have their own integrity even as they are part of larger wholes, but they are not discrete or isolated. It might be said that just as Scripture interprets Scripture, so there is room for doctrine to interpret doctrine when a particular doctrine is subject to new knowledge. New knowledge is not self-justifying, and the more that multiple doctrines are brought into relation to its challenge, the less the chance that any one doctrine will be swamped or over-determined by that challenge.

What is doctrine?

After two chapters looking at the larger doctrinal projects of the church and individual theologians, the focus in this chapter has been on particular doctrines. Moreover, this focus has been against the background of the Enlightenment's challenge to Christian doctrine. This challenge was twofold. On the one hand, it was a challenge to the origins and content of Christian doctrine. On the other hand, the cultural impact of the Enlightenment included the fracturing of the institutional, political, and intellectual cultures that had sustained the work of Christian doctrine and provided many of its shared assumptions. Ironically, however, when the Enlightenment was confidently calling doctrinal discourse into question, it was simultaneously creating the space for doctrine to enter new conversations. Those conversations suggest that doctrine has defied the doubts cast upon it, even as particular doctrines have been renewed, reformed, or developed in the process. From the small sample of such conversations explored in this chapter, and by attending to particular doctrines, the answer to the question of what doctrine is can be further developed.

Arguably the most important point is that there is no doctrine without doctrines. There is no vision of the whole without its constituent parts. Indeed, one of the lessons to be gleaned from this chapter is just how much intellectual heavy-lifting particular doctrines do in theological engagement with a range of issues and in varying contexts. This includes their capacity to interpret and illuminate particular contexts (as in the case of M. M. Thomas). This can be obscured when the focus is on, for example, broad theological movements or programs in which attention is paid to the possibilities of theology per se in a particular context. There is an intellectual parallel here to the social dynamics that accompany Christianity's encounters with new contexts or changed social conditions. Of such encounters, Kathryn Tanner has observed: "Christian engagement with other ways of life rarely involves a face-off between distinct wholes."[105] Similarly, Christian theological visions and alternative intellectual visions do not necessarily encounter each other as "distinct wholes." They intersect and engage through incremental steps, for which, from the Christian perspective, particular doctrinal loci are often the place of focused and intense conversation, intellectual work, and pastoral concern. Feminist theology, for instance, has some very expansive agendas, but its capacity to meet them will depend in part on the fine-grained work that particular feminist theologians do in relation to particular doctrines, such as the Trinity. Any constructive and engaged Christian response to the monumental shifts in Western cultural sensibilities around sex and gender will likewise require much attention to the details of anthropology. In such contexts, doctrines emerge from the doctrinal whole and have much important work to do. Nevertheless, while particular doctrines might *emerge* from the vision of the whole, they should not be *abstracted* or *disconnected* from the whole. Referring to the Apostles' Creed, Nicholas Lash suggests that its threefold structure points to a "pattern of self-correction" whereby anything said in one article cannot "appropriately be said except in relation to the other two."[106] His point can be applied more generally to Christian doctrine with regard to the relationships between the part and the whole.

A second point to take from this chapter, especially from the engagement with Ting and Wang, is how particular doctrines can be the focus of conversation across time and place in a diverse and divided church. It might be said that this simply states the obvious. Nevertheless, Wang's hope that Chinese reflection on the cosmic Christ might actually be a gift to the world church struck a note that is quite different from the polemics that often accompany discussion of diverse theological methods generated by diverse contexts. There is potential for different doctrinal loci to be points of conversation between different parts of the church. Nevertheless that assumes some common acceptance of shared doctrinal loci and their validity. That, of course, is not an assumption that can be made easily in the contemporary church.

The larger picture of how doctrine and doctrines actually function in a globally diverse and divided church is one of the matters to be addressed in more detail in Chapter 5. Before that, however, the question of the relationship between doctrine, the Bible and truth will be explored in Chapter 4.

CHAPTER 4
DOCTRINE, BIBLE, AND TRUTH

The case studies of the previous chapter demonstrated how particular theologians could explore, interrogate, reform, exploit, or expand particular doctrinal loci in order to respond to new challenges. They provided further material for answering the question of what doctrine is. To continue pursuing this question, we turn now to a particular contemporary debate. For present purposes, the engagement with this debate serves a double function. Beginning in the 1980s, it is a debate that has been especially preoccupied with what doctrine is. Yet as the debate has unfolded over the subsequent decades, it has opened up underlying questions about the relationship between doctrine, the Bible, and truth. Indeed, engagement with this debate strongly suggests that there can be no answer to the question of what doctrine is without articulating the relationships between doctrine, the Bible, and truth. This chapter will, therefore, provide the opportunity to introduce and engage one important and lively debate about doctrine while simultaneously attending to the wider and inevitable questions about its relations to the Bible and truth. These questions were already broached in Chapter 1 in the discussion of Reformation Confessions. They were part of the discussions of many of the theologians discussed in Chapter 2, especially Calvin, Barth, and Schleiermacher. They now take on new form in this contemporary debate.

The seminal moment giving rise to the debate at hand was the publication in 1984 of *The Nature of Doctrine: Religion and Theology in a Postliberal Age* by the American Lutheran, Yale-based theologian, George Lindbeck (1923–2018). That and two more recent proposals will be the focus of this chapter. The latter are those of Kevin Vanhoozer (1957–) and Christine Helmer (1965–). Vanhoozer engages directly with Lindbeck whereas Helmer's work is an engagement with what she perceives to be the narrowing of doctrine in the post-Lindbeck era. Because the issues at stake in the proposals are at the heart of the contemporary discussions about doctrine, a quite close reading of each of the texts will be presented. It happens that all three of these theologians link their basic understanding of doctrine to a particular and, in each case, quite potent, metaphor. The descriptions of doctrine in terms of their respective metaphors will be the point of departure for the engagement with each of their proposals. For Lindbeck, doctrines are "rules"; Vanhoozer presents doctrines as "prompts"; for Helmer, doctrine is a "catalyst."

Doctrine as rules: George Lindbeck

The use of the adjective "postliberal" in the title of his book locates Lindbeck in a wider cultural context and, more specifically, a particular theological school of thought associated with the Yale Divinity School during the 1970s and 1980s. Gaining some purchase on the meaning of this adjective will be important for what follows. This brief definition is helpful.

> Postliberal theology has always been more a loose connection of narrative theological interests than it is some monolithic agenda. It represents an overarching concern for the renewal of Christian confession over theological methodology. Rather than reliance on a notion of correlative common experience, postliberal theology moves towards the local or particular faith description of the community of the church.[1]

Additionally, in employing the descriptor postliberal, those associated with it indicated their alliance with other disciplines (especially in the humanities) that were also questioning the dominance of the culture and intellectual convictions of modern liberalism, not least the quest for universally held intellectual foundations. In other words, being "postliberal" was not simply an intra-theological matter.[2]

Nevertheless, Lindbeck's primary concern in writing *The Nature of Doctrine* was actually an ecumenical one. Long involved in ecumenical discussions, he was concerned with the role of doctrine in ecclesial division and unity.[3] As noted in the opening pages of this book, the fact that churches divide is often an immediate result of doctrinal disagreement. Conversely, the quest for (re-)unity has often placed a high premium on the resolution of those doctrinal disagreements. This was certainly the case in the twentieth-century ecumenical movement. Lindbeck pointed out, however, that the role that doctrine had come to play in both division and unity presupposed a particular understanding of doctrine, one that actually impeded ecclesial reunification. The notion of doctrines as rules was developed as a way to rethink the function of doctrine so that it would not be such an impediment. Nevertheless, it took on a life of its own quite apart from its ecumenical provenance. For present purposes, however, the focus will be on Lindbeck's understanding of doctrines as rules and how this is related to doctrine's role in making truth claims and its relationship to the Bible.

Doctrine as rules: A new typology

The easiest way of entering Lindbeck's understanding of doctrine is to note his threefold typology. His "rule" understanding of doctrine is contrasted with the understandings of doctrines as "propositions" and "expressions." He has relatively little to say about the propositional type. The real force of his own proposal emerges in the contrast between it and the notion of doctrines as expressions. In what follows, brief descriptions of the three types will lead into Lindbeck's background understanding of "religion" to which his own proposal is strongly tied.

In the propositionalist type, doctrines are what the name says: propositions. As informative statements, doctrines are regarded as direct truth claims about objective realities. In this type, a doctrine once true is always true, and once false always false. Doctrine is the locus of truth.

In the expressivist or, more fully named, the experiential-expressivist type, doctrines are culturally and psychologically conditioned expressions of inner feelings and experiences of the divine. In this model, doctrine is a potentially dispensable religious artifact and is only incidentally related to the truth that actually lies in a precognitive, prelinguistic realm of the human experience of God. It is to be noted that Lindbeck cites Friedrich Schleiermacher as the representative of this type[4] (this is significant for discussions later in this chapter).

As "rules," doctrines are to religion as grammar is to the language of a given culture. In fact, Lindbeck also names this as a "cultural-linguistic" understanding of doctrine. So understood, doctrines regulate the religion's various modes of speaking of God. In short, "doctrines [function] as communally authoritative rules of discourse, attitude, and action."[5] As such they are almost the inverse of how doctrines are understood in the experiential-expressivist model. Rather than expressing prior experiences, in this model, doctrines produce the experiences. Accordingly, and in direct contrast to the propositional type, doctrines do not carry the burden of being the primary locus of truth; that is borne by the religion as a whole. This places a religion as a whole and its doctrines in a particular order: "First come the objectivities of the religion, its language, doctrines, liturgies, and modes of action, and it is through these that passions are shaped into various kinds of what we call religious experience."[6] This focus on religion as a whole is very significant. At issue for Lindbeck here is not simply different understandings of doctrine. Also at issue are different relations of religion and doctrine to the claims of modernity. So, for instance, Lindbeck argues that the experiential-expressivist model of doctrine is a product of distinctly modern views of religion and therefore prevails in cultures and religions shaped by modernity. Accordingly, "the structures of modernity press individuals to meet God first in the depths of their souls and then, perhaps, if they find something personally congenial, to become part of a tradition or join a church."[7] In contrast, an understanding of religion unconditioned by modernity has a much more expansive and comprehensive understanding of itself as a public or a culture. Accordingly, its communal nature is constitutive rather than derivative. Thus, in a passage that crystallizes many dimensions of his proposal, he argues that as a cultural-linguistic phenomenon, a religion

> is not primarily an array of beliefs about the true and the good (though it may involve these), or a symbolism expressive of basic attitudes, feelings or sentiments (though these will be generated). Rather, it is similar to an idiom that makes possible the description of realities, the formulation of beliefs, and the experiencing of inner attitudes, feelings and sentiments. Like a culture or language, it is a communal phenomenon that shapes the subjectivities of individuals rather than being primarily a manifestation of those subjectivities. It comprises a vocabulary of discursive and nondiscursive symbols together with a distinctive logic or grammar in terms of which this vocabulary can be meaningfully deployed. Lastly, just as language … is correlated with a form of life, and just as a culture has both cognitive and behavioural dimensions, so it is also in the case of a religious tradition. Its doctrines, cosmic stories or myths and ethical directives are integrally related to the rituals it practices, the sentiments or experiences it evokes, the actions it recommends, and the institutional forms it develops.[8]

Some of the influences on Lindbeck noted earlier will be evident in this quotation. Perhaps the only critical issue to note at this stage, and bearing in mind some of the claims for doctrine already quoted above, regards the extent to which doctrines do in fact generate experiences in the way Lindbeck suggests. As we will see below from one of Lindbeck's own examples, mere enculturation into doctrines does not ensure their embodiment or performance in a manner integrated with all the religion's other "discursive and non-discursive symbols." It is striking, as Simeon Zahl has noted, that Lindbeck does not give any further account in *The Nature of Doctrine* of how exactly "this shaping and constructing of experience and emotion takes place in concrete instances and settings."[9] That is not to say that they don't, or that arguments can't be made to demonstrate that they can and do.[10] It is, however, important to note this claim and its significance for when we enter a more comprehensive discussion of the function of doctrine. Nevertheless, allowing for at least some constructive and formative role for doctrine, and noting these general claims which Lindbeck makes for doctrine, we turn now to the question of its truth.

Doctrine as rules and the question of truth

In rejecting both the propositionalist and expressivist views of truth, Lindbeck invests instead in what is known as a "performative" or "pragmatic" notion of truth. So, for example, it is not that a religion makes true statements about reality and is therefore true; rather, it is that a religion lives the truth and only as such is it true. He speaks about a religion as a "gigantic proposition":

> As actually lived, a religion may be pictured as a single gigantic proposition. It is a true proposition to the extent that its objectivities are interiorized and exercised by groups and individuals in such a way as to conform them in some measure in the various dimensions of their existence to the ultimate reality and goodness that lies at the heart of things.[11]

In a much-quoted example, he suggests that the claim "Jesus is Lord" is a true statement when it is confessed as the framework for an act of charity, but it is a false statement when it is uttered by a Crusader as he cleaves the skull of an "infidel."[12] When used for that purpose, *Christus est Dominus* "contradicts the Christian understanding of Lordship as embodying … suffering and servanthood."[13] This example reveals Lindbeck's commitment to "intrasystematic truth" that he distinguishes from truth claims associated with ontological correspondence and the kind of realist truth claims linked to it. Again, he provides an example that has also been much quoted in the subsequent discussion. The example is drawn from Shakespeare's *Hamlet*.

Lindbeck suggests that "the statement 'Denmark is the land where in Hamlet lived' is intrasystematically true within the context of Shakespeare's play, but this implies nothing regarding ontological truth or falsity unless the play is taken as history."[14] On the basis of this line of argument he states, "intrasystematic truth is a necessary but not sufficient condition for ontological truth."[15]

If, then, ontological correspondence exists at the level of Christianity as actually lived, what then is the role of doctrinal statements? Drawing on the analogical nature of theological language, Lindbeck does allow for what he terms a "modest cognitivism" to be included in the cultural-linguistic model.[16] Returning to the *Christus est Dominus* example, he writes, "For Christian theological purposes, that sentence becomes a first-order proposition capable … of making ontological truth claims only as it used in the activity of adoration, proclamation obedience, promise-hearing, and promise-keeping which shape individuals and communities into conformity to the mind of Christ."[17]

Lindbeck extends this argument from such confessions as "Christ is Lord" to the more technical, second-order statements of doctrine. Thus, he argues, doctrines *regulate* the use of first-order confessions in the matrix of practices that constitute authentic Christian witness. For instance, in relation to the classic Trinitarian doctrine of the Nicene-Constantinopolitan Creed, Lindbeck proposes that this doctrine entails (at least) three regulative principles:

> First, there is the monotheistic principle: there is only one God, the God of Abraham, Isaac, Jacob, and Jesus. Second, there is the principle of historical specificity: the stories of Jesus refer to a genuine human being who was born, lived, and died in a particular time and place. Third, there is the principle of … Christological maximalism: every possible importance is to be ascribed to Jesus that is not inconsistent with the first rules.[18]

An inevitable question to this rule-based, cognitively modest, intrasystematic approach is whether it can either account for or allow for change. Anticipating such concerns, Lindbeck writes that theology can be "intratextual, not simply by explicating religion from within but in the stronger sense of describing everything as inside, as interpreted by the religion."[19] The tools for doing so are the "relatively fixed canons of writing that they treat as exemplary or normative."[20] These "canons of writing" are not only normative or exemplary but are also generative: "For those that are steeped in them, no world is more real than the ones they create. A scriptural world is thus able to absorb the universe. Its supplies the interpretative framework with which believers seek to live their lives and understand reality."[21] These ideas are distilled in a much-quoted comment: "Intratextual theology redescribes reality within the scriptural framework rather than translating Scripture into extrascriptural categories. It is the text, so to speak, which absorbs the world, rather than the world the text."[22] In sum, therefore, the critical issues are sharply focused around two questions. First, in terms of doctrine's truth status, does the confession of Jesus Christ as Lord invite something more than a "modest cognitivism"? Second, in terms of the text absorbing the world, how "relatively" fixed are the "relatively fixed canons of writing"? This latter question directly raises the question of the relationship between doctrine and the Bible in *The Nature of Doctrine*.

Doctrine as rules and the Bible

As we saw above, Lindbeck writes of "Scripture absorbing the world" and of how for those "who are steeped in them," no world is "more real" than the worlds created by the canonical writings. Reality is "redescribed within the scriptural framework." These are certainly very strong statements about the role of Scripture in the process of the meaning-making within the cultural-linguistic system. But here lies a key problem. For instance, recall the already quoted definition of religion where Lindbeck refers to the "doctrines, cosmic stories or myths and ethical directives [which] are integrally related to the rituals it practices."[23] Not only is the Bible itself not mentioned, but (and assuming it is implied with reference to cosmic stories, myths, etc.) there is nothing there to clarify just how and where the Bible sits among those doctrines and cosmic stories. As observed in the immediately preceding section, he notes that the "relatively fixed canons of writing have a 'normative' or 'exemplary' role." Of course, the use of the Bible will always be located within a wider canon of authoritative literature (e.g., liturgies, confessions, and creeds), but just how it is so located warrants careful specification.

On the other hand, there is much in what Lindbeck says about how the Bible functions in "intratextual theology" which, while undeveloped, is suggestive. His comments combine his commitment to a typologically unified canonical narrative, an insistence that the canon is to be read (in literary terms) as a "realistic narrative" with the centrality or climactic status of Jesus in that narrative.[24] When the canon is so read, "it is Jesus' identity as thus rendered, not his historicity, existential significance, or metaphysical status, which is the literal and theologically controlling meaning of the tale."[25] The canon is oriented to producing a certain outcome for the reader who reads in this way: the Bible leads the believer "to be conformed to the Jesus Christ depicted in the narrative."[26]

Lindbeck does not deny that such a position begs certain hermeneutical questions.[27] Perhaps, however, an even more critical question to put here is whether his depiction of the literary unity of the canon is too blunt. As already noted, he applies the category of "realistic narrative" to the whole of the canon. He elaborates this point with the following questions and his own answers: "What is the literary genre of the Bible as a whole in its canonical unity? What holds together the diverse materials it contains: poetic, prophetic, legal, liturgical, sapiential, mythical, legendary, and historical? These are all embraced, it would seem in an overarching story that has the specific literary features of realistic narrative."[28] This "overarching story" is that of "a being who created the cosmos … for his own good pleasure … appointed Homo sapiens stewards of one minuscule part of this cosmos, permitted appalling evils, chose Israel and the church as witnessing peoples, and sent Jesus as Messiah and Immanuel, God with us."[29] So construed around this—what is essentially a Rule of Faith—the canon renders an identity description of God climactically revealed in the Gospels' account of Jesus of Nazareth. Yes, all of this is genuinely suggestive. Nevertheless, certain questions are going begging here too. Is there not also a *theological* diversity in the canon that, even if it centered around the Gospels' witness to Jesus, actually shapes how the center itself is to be read and how that witness illuminates the rest of the canon? And how does a theologically diverse canon, even centered as it is on the witness to Jesus Christ, shape both the formation and function of doctrine?[30]

There is a further question that needs to be asked of this approach to the Bible: How does the Bible relate to revelation? Indeed, one commentator referred to Lindbeck's "studied evasion of the central question of revelation—in other words, whether the Christian idiom, articulated in Scripture and hence in the Christian tradition, originates from accumulated human insight, or from the self-disclosure of God in the Christ event."[31] This is an issue that is confronted much more directly in the proposal of Kevin Vanhoozer to consider doctrine as "prompt." To that we now turn.

Doctrine as prompt: Kevin Vanhoozer

The idea of doctrine as "prompt" is part of Vanhoozer's larger appropriation of theatrical metaphors developed in his 2005 book, *The Drama of*

Doctrine: A Canonical-Linguistic Approach to Christian Theology.[32] The use of theatrical metaphors emerging out of the controlling one of "drama" in the title of the book is not merely a matter of rhetorical convenience. It is related to Vanhoozer's understanding of the gospel itself.

> At the heart of Christianity lies a series of divine words and divine acts that culminate in Jesus Christ: the definitive divine Word/Act. The gospel—God's self-giving in his Son through the Spirit—is intrinsically *dramatic*, a matter of signs and speeches, actions and sufferings … What faith seeks to understand is inherently *dramatic*.[33]

Moreover, the manner in which drama combines "signs and speeches" is intrinsic to its application to the gospel in which there is "a cosmic stage and covenantal plot; there is conflict; there is climax; there is resolution."[34] Vanhoozer's use of the dramatic metaphor is not limited to God's direct works of creation and covenant. It extends to the role of the Bible itself and then also to theology. Indeed, theological work is itself a means of participating in the drama: "Scripture is a human-divine communicative act; theology oriented to the Scripture principle is a means of participating in the theo-dramatic action."[35] The allusions here to twentieth-century speech act theory, and its idea that words do things, are not accidental and the weight they carry in Vanhoozer's proposal should not be underestimated, even if they need not detain us here.[36]

While Vanhoozer has been accused of overworking the theatrical metaphors,[37] even this foregoing summary of the nature of the appeal to dramatic indicates it richness. Indeed, Part Four of *The Drama of Doctrine*, precisely because of its extensive development of the theatrical metaphors within the church's life, offers a strikingly suggestive description of the relationships between doctrine, the ministry of the church, and the vocations of its ministers. Be that as it may, it is time to turn to the specific claim about doctrine as prompt.

Doctrine as prompt and its many resonances

The notion of doctrine as prompt may well be used only once in *The Drama of Doctrine*, but perhaps more than any other single term, it captures the intent and many of the resonances of Vanhoozer's proposal. It is shorthand for a fuller claim that "[d]octrine is direction for the fitting participation of individuals and communities in the drama of redemption."[38] This dramatic notion of doctrine is developed as a direct counter to Lindbeck's three types of doctrine. According to Vanhoozer, each of Lindbeck's types tends to privilege only one of the informational, volitional or expressive. The prompting function of doctrine, in contrast, integrates all three: "Doctrine is not merely a proposition or an expression, or a grammatical rule, but a *prompt*: a spiritual direction for one's fitting performance of the script, and hence a means for continuing the pattern of communicative action that lies at the heart of the gospel as theo-drama."[39]

The very notion of prompt carries very different, and arguably more engaging, resonances than Lindbeck's rule metaphor. The regulative resonances of "rule" can easily imply a certain formalism if not legalism. On the other hand, "prompt" can imply related notions of patience, encouragement, and even comfort. After all, a nervous actor can take great comfort from the knowledge that someone will be offstage ready to remind her when her memory fails. But Vanzhoozer does not intend merely this compensatory or corrective function of prompt. It has a definite constructive intent oriented to the faithful context-specific performances of the "script." And because it has this role in the church's commissioned theo-dramatic witness to the gospel, doctrine, too, has a designated role in this drama. In sum: "Doctrine is one of the means the Spirit uses to direct the church to abide in the biblical word and to follow the script into new situations."[40] The "biblical word" looms large in *The Drama of Doctrine*. It will be explored first before addressing the question of truth.

Doctrine as prompt and the Bible

Vanhoozer articulates the role of Scripture in the drama of doctrine through what he terms a "revised Scripture principle" that "views the Bible not simply as a deposit of revealed truths but as the result of God's multifaceted communicative action … Scripture serves as authority for theology, then, because it is caught up in the triune economy of communicative action … *The ultimate authority for Christian theology is the triune God speak-acting in the Scriptures*."[41] Such claims inevitably lead to further claims about inspiration and canon, both of which are also presented in theo-dramatic terms.

Scripture is produced in the "very messy historical processes" through which the Spirit is involved in "prompting, appropriating, and coordinating human discourse to present God's Word."[42] And it is the same Spirit who acts to bring about an "understanding of Scripture among present-day readers."[43] Inspiration involves the Spirit also working as a *prompt*. It is a matter of the

"Spirit's prompting the human authors to say just what the divine playwright intended. Prompting—urging, assisting, recalling to mind, supplying the right words—is the operative notion."[44] This does not deny that texts have "natural histories,"[45] but the emphasis falls on the way that the Spirit takes these texts up into the theo-drama "in such a way that the biblical texts may also be considered to be the result of the Spirit's sanctifying action."[46] And as the individual texts are produced, so too is their canonization: "The Spirit sanctifies the church's judgment, enabling it to perceive and acknowledge scripture as God's word written."[47] So construed, the canon is more than authoritative; it is normative: "While Christ is faith's form, the canon, as the normative specification of the gospel, is faith's *norm*."[48] The spirit's inspiring—or prompting—action unites the authors of the texts and the church's acknowledgment of those texts. Such prompting, however, is also oriented to the church's performance in the present.

> While doctrine is direction for our fitting participation in the drama, the canon, as the authorized account of the theo-drama's form and content, is doctrine's supreme norm. It follows that the canon is … a criterion for truthful speech and righteous action, for embodying the wisdom of Jesus Christ and for continuing the theo-drama in new situations.[49]

The role of doctrine in "new situations" is most concrete in Vanhoozer's discussion of confessions which are presented as examples of "regional theatre."[50] Confessions and the churches that generate and confess them are "performance traditions … that combine elements of stabilization with elements of innovation."[51] That there is a multiplicity of confessions is a strength of the church's unity in diversity: it enables the church "to form the most adequate conception of the whole."[52] Indeed, that unity in diversity "is the condition of theology's being able to address different kinds of situations" and also "the enabling condition of creative theological understanding."[53] Nevertheless, confessions are "means of doctrinal stability."[54] The combination of "stabilization" and "innovation" does not, of course, escape the norm of the canon.

In a manner that echoes the remark of Lindbeck (noted in the first section of this chapter), Vanhoozer speaks of the canon as "society of biblical literature"[55] in which diverse literary forms play their various roles: narrating, praising, foretelling, anticipating, and so on. Above all, however, Jesus Christ is the center of this literature. He is, in a quite striking image, the one around whom the Bible is "wrapped [at] its centre"; he is the "hermeneutical key to the biblical canon as a whole."[56] Such a claim at once brings the discussion to matters of interpretation and its boundaries. Vanhoozer stresses that his own use of dramatic and performance metaphors does not lead to the indeterminacy of interpretation that they do in the hands of some self-consciously postmodern interpreters.[57] The fact of interpretative boundaries raises the issue of heresy, "the worst possible improvisation, an example of clever ad-libbing that pays only scant attention to what the other players are saying and doing."[58] It "develops not simply by employing new concepts but from making *judgements* that go against the canonical grain."[59] In this context, doctrine (with Vanzhoozer now introducing another striking, but nontheatrical, metaphor) "is the antibody that counteracts the heretical antigens that threaten the health of the body of Christ."[60]

Following the Fathers, Vanhoozer sees in the "Rule of Faith" a key doctrinal tool that prompts the church to a faithful reading of the canon and thus to a faithful performance of the gospel. He acknowledges that there is no uniform formulation of the Rule and that it cannot be thought of as a "hermeneutical panacea."[61] The Rule is itself ruled by the canon because, ultimately, Scripture interprets Scripture. Nevertheless, it has a role to play. He summarizes it thus:

> The Rule states that the creator God and the covenant Lord of Israel is also the Father of Jesus Christ; the one who brought Israel out of Egypt is also the one who raised Jesus from the dead. The Rule thus holds the two testaments together, theologically and hermeneutically, what we may call the Christian "metadrama": the story of the cosmos and the story of the covenant as these come together in the story of Christ.[62]

Even this brief summary of Vanhoozer's extensive writing on doctrine as prompt and the normative role of the Bible in it being that prompt has barely touched the surface of what is an extensively and intricately developed proposal. Essentially, doctrine serves its role as prompt to the church's performance of the gospel by subordinating itself to the canon that is, in turn, received in its sapiential function of directing behavior rather than merely advancing beliefs. The distinctiveness of the Scriptures and their origin in the "prompting" work of the Spirit has no parallel in Lindbeck. Nevertheless, there are some critical issues to note.

For all the resonances of "prompt," and despite the various references to the interaction between "stabilization" and "innovation," the final impression is of doctrine being oriented to stabilization rather than to innovation. This is not to imply that innovation is a self-evident virtue in doctrinal work, but it is to suggest that more probing of the relationship between it and stabilization is called for, and to ask what distinguishes stability from repetition. In an appreciative survey of Vanhoozer's proposal, Anthony Thiselton commends his application of drama to the understanding of doctrine because it "allows the dynamic and tensive nature of doctrine to remain prominently in view."[63] But is doctrine as prompt actually that tensive after all? This question is heightened by what is often presented as a stable and unified cannon, the interpretation of which is determined by an equally stable "Rule of Faith." None of this is to question the normative role of the canon, but it is to ask whether the canon has to have the particular unity proposed by Vanhoozer for it to have this normative role. Take, for instance, the reference to heresy as indicating judgments that "go against the canonical grain" and that pay "scant attention" to what other players in the performance are doing. What place is then made for the judgments of fellow Christians who seek not to go *against* the "canonical grain" but to draw attention to the canonical cross grains or even the canonical knots that interrupt the normal and dominant flow of the grain?

Of course, Vanhoozer does not deny the diversity of the canon, but the theological and doctrinal significance of this diversity appears muted. Recall the comments about the canon being analogous to a "society of biblical literature." Where the diversity of the literature has most significance is in its diversity of genres. The different genres are aligned with different modes of performing the gospel's theo-drama: praising, adoring, narrating, and so on. It is true that an acknowledgment is made of Scripture's "diverse theological emphases."[64] But even a recognition of "dialogue" between the "differentiated" voices of the canon is framed by a literary construal of that diversity that, in turn, is explained as a reflection of the complexity appropriate to communicating such complex content.[65] A critical question is thus raised: Does the striking image of that diversity "wrapped around Christ" do justice to the complexity of the theological, literary, and rhetorical dynamics preserved within the canon? In an essay engaged with Vanhoozer's earlier writings, Mark Brett registers the concern that can be equally applied here. Brett suggests that Vanhoozer sits too lightly to the "conversational dynamics" evident in the canon and that he is too ready to see a unified understanding rather than engaging the "subtle detail of these 'inner-biblical conversations.'"[66] As I will highlight in the next chapter, within the canon there is disagreement, correction, dissent, innovation, agreement, and consolidation. All of this can still find its center in Christ, but in doing so it might point to a different kind of canonical unity. There is no a priori reason why a canon construed differently could not still be normative while yielding its own dynamic between stabilization and innovation in doctrine's prompting role.

Doctrine as prompt and the question of truth

If Vanhoozer's exploration of the relationship between doctrine and the Bible is in part a reaction to Lindbeck, so too is his engagement with the question of doctrine's truth. And this engagement is no less engaged with the Bible than that of doctrine's role as prompt. His overall concern is to claim a place for the cognitive dimension of truth-telling that seems to have taken a backseat in the face of the contemporary interest in performative notions of truth.

He argues that Lindbeck is right to reject a certain kind of cognitive/propositional understanding of doctrine, and he has no quibble with latter's commitment per se to performative truth. But he also contends that Lindbeck is wrong to be as ambivalent about the cognitive dimension of the church's practices as he is. For Vanhoozer, the theo-drama has a determinate content that demands something more than "modest cognitivism." His point is twofold. First, he draws attention to the now conventional claim that the contrast between literal and metaphorical language is not a contrast between the cognitive and noncognitive. With their surplus of meaning, metaphors actually stimulate—rather than deflect—cognitive activity. Along with other figures of speech metaphors are particular kinds of "cognitive instruments" that "enable *a different kind of thinking* than the historical or scientific, but a genuine thinking nonetheless."[67] Second, this "different kind of thinking" is also reflected in his use of the dramatic notion of truth that, as we saw earlier, is said to integrate the cognitive, affective, and volitional.[68] But it is also a notion of truth that is "shown, tried and proven."[69] Truth is known through being practiced. All truth claims are embedded and only known in historical circumstances. This, in fact, is the *biblical* way of truth-telling.

> The Bible itself suggests that truth is historical to the extent that it is progressively revealed over time. For example, God proves himself true because he keeps his word. Drama thus preserves the cognitive, truth-telling dimension, though its exhibit of the truth in the language of actions is richer than the merely propositional … *Drama thus*

offers an integrative perspective within which to relate propositions, experience, and narrative. Each of the above components deserves a place in an account of doctrine, but everything hinges on their proper ordering and the pattern of authority into which they fit.[70]

These comments echo those quoted earlier that pointed to the canon as a *sapiential* rather than *epistemic* criterion for the church's performance of the theo-drama. But they also make a strong claim for the biblical foundations for the historical nature of truth. Although a commonplace for contemporary discussions of truth, any acknowledgment of its historical character will always be accompanied by the specter of relativism, something to which Vanhoozer is acutely alert. His careful ordering of the triune God, the Bible, and doctrine as the source of and witnesses to truth constitutes his own attempt to resist it. In many ways, it is not a better epistemology or a better theory of truth that is his bulwark against relativism. Rather, it is this ordered "pattern of authority" that takes its coherence from the theo-drama that faith confesses. Any other discussion of the relationship between Bible, doctrine, and truth will have to be at least as careful as Vanhoozer has been in setting out this ordered pattern. But it might also have to say a little more about what it means to say that truth so construed is historical. One who does is Christine Helmer. Her work, and the notion of doctrine as catalyst, is the focus of the next section.

Doctrine as catalyst: Christine Helmer

The idea of doctrine as "catalyst" is drawn from Christine Helmer's 2014 work, *Theology and the End of Doctrine*.[71] While Helmer uses this description only in passing and doesn't highlight it at all, it crystallizes as well as any other term the status and function of doctrine that she articulates in her book. In short, she regards "the production of doctrine ... as catalyst for the living tradition of Christianity."[72] Behind this constructive proposal is a multilayered background of cultural and theological commentary that includes challenges to some of the assumptions controlling recent discussions about doctrine. While Helmer does not engage in detailed analysis of Lindbeck's *The Nature of Doctrine* itself, her own book engages the legacy it has generated.

The problem Helmer addresses is that the current state of doctrine narrows its ecclesial functions and restricts theology's public function.

The very idea of doctrine has become, she claims, "virtually a synonym for ecclesiastical authority that is inattentive to or even dismissive of human experience."[73] This is the diagnosis embodied in the book's title: dominant understandings of doctrine led to the "end" of doctrine doing the work that it should be doing. This is reinforced by the post-Enlightenment "turn to language" whereby doctrine fosters belief as "a matter of disciplined fluency"[74] in Christian discourse, with the consequence that "doctrine has moved away from reality into language."[75] On her reading, doctrine "has come to an end when by definition it cannot say anything new and when the sole measurement of doctrine's significance is its contribution as the authoritative enforcer of the church's identity."[76]

Helmer supports this reading of doctrine's current state with a detailed historical enquiry that traces the bifurcation between nature and spirit in Protestant theology. This reaches a sharp edge in the work of Emil Brunner (1889–1966) and what she regards as his serious misreading of Schleiermacher onto whom he "mapped this bifurcation,"[77] making Schleiermacher "modern theology's necessary object of attack."[78] So read, Schleiermacher is confirmed as the cause of theology's anthropological and subjectivist turn. This reading of Schleiermacher is the kind appropriated by Lindbeck, who (as we saw earlier) presented him as the primary exemplar of the experiential-expressivist type of doctrine. Helmer rejects Brunner's reading of Schleiermacher because she argues that it ignores the actual integration of the objective and subjective in Schleiermacher's work. But over and above challenging the misreading of Schleiermacher, Helmer's broader concern is to expose how the reaction to the (misread) Schleiermacher pushed doctrine toward the "end" described above. Tying doctrine to epistemology and the quest for objectivity, and combining it with a tight nexus between language and communal identity is the problem. In a pointed passage, she writes,

> The *Deus dixit* is framed as doctrine that constitutes a Christian worldview authorizing itself. All the Holy Spirit may now do is convert people to it (or not). Theology as system grounded in God's reality is replaced by Christianity as a worldview, with theology's function restricted to pointing to doctrines in their epistemic function within that worldview.[79]

The link in the above quote between theology and "God's reality" points to where Helmer locates doctrine and from where she seeks to lift it out of its epistemic narrowing. From here, she points instead to a broader understanding that the idea of a "catalyst for the living tradition of Christianity" illuminates.

Doctrine as catalyst and its possibilities

The rhetorical force of "catalyst" is very different to that of "rule" or "prompt." Where rule implies some rigidity, and prompt suggests recollection, catalyst suggests creativity and novelty. This is not to suggest that Helmer regards creativity and novelty as virtues in themselves, or that she is indifferent to continuity, which (as we will see) she certainly isn't. But it does suggest a forward-looking and productive role for doctrine; it provides critical leverage against any attempt to understand doctrine's purpose as articulating and relating "specific articulations from the past and apply[ing] them in the present."[80] For Helmer, doctrine is not to be *applied* to the present. It is to be *generated* in the present. Drawing on Schleiermacher, she presents doctrine as "discourse evoked by [Christ's] presence"; it is "grounded conceptually in the language-reality encounter between believer ... and Christ."[81] This does not mean that doctrinal formulations of the past are irrelevant or entirely without a normative role. Christology and the doctrine of the Trinity point to God's faithfulness to being and acting in the world in certain ways. In fact, this combination of present construction and existing norms is also captured to some extent in the metaphor of "catalyst." In the chemical world, a catalyst generates something new while remaining unchanged itself, thus being able to effect further novelty in subsequent reactions. The metaphor would be even stronger if we imagine the product of catalytic reactions producing agents that themselves become catalysts among other chemicals. Some of the dynamics suggested by the metaphor are contained in the following long quote:

> Doctrine is about divinity and its manifold relations to the created world. It has to do with the living reality of God. Doctrine presses towards knowledge and truth while at the same time remaining cognizant of its human origins and historical particularity. Spiritual discernment is required to see and to understand the relations that God creates and transforms in different yet often hidden ways. God cannot be domesticated by doctrine, even when doctrine insists on divine faithfulness to specific ways of relating to the world and on specific forms of divine being, as in the doctrines of the Trinity and of

Christ. Doctrine can only present its content according to the spiritual and intellectual capacities of human theologians operating under the cultural conditions of their intersubjectivities. The deepest ground of doctrine's epistemic humility is the recognition that the theologian stands before a divine reality that is capable of rejecting human efforts and of shattering human expectations with novelty.[82]

Much could be said about this rich statement. Two points will be highlighted here. The first is the way Helmer's attentiveness to the "cultural conditions" of theologians leads her specifically to address the challenges to doctrinal work posed by the realities of the non-Western churches. While calling on the Western tradition to recognize its own contingency, she warns against trading "global Christianity" off against the West. She calls instead for "mutual interaction between many predicative traditions,"[83] interaction, that is, between many doctrinal traditions each speaking about God within their respective "cultural conditions." Neither does she advocate a pluralism of doctrine without criteria. The very ground of all Christian experiences, that is, the living Christ, must also be the criteria for the justification of any particular doctrinal claim: "Theology's attunement to individual novelty is constituted by the unique Christian confession. Its fundamental capaciousness to plural predication must also be constituted on the same ground."[84] The second—and related—point is the claim that doctrine is the product of "the spiritual and intellectual capacities" of theologians. In this, she affirms the reality of the social construction of doctrine. The very term "social construction" immediately raises questions about truth and raises the fear, well cultivated in discussions of doctrine, that truth claims have no referent outside the process of their social construction. So, we turn to the issue of doctrine as catalyst and its relationship to truth.

Doctrine as catalyst and the question of truth

In turning to this topic, another specific reference to doctrine as catalyst is encountered, one that captures the replicating role of catalysts suggested above: "Doctrines are produced over time as social constructions in the terms available in any historical and cultural context and also as a catalyst to social construction."[85] Helmer makes a strong case for the sheer straightforwardness of this claim. After all, who could deny that doctrine is generated as "conversation among theologians and other Christians talking in earnest with each other about the God with whom they are in relationship"?[86] Even those resisting Helmer's openness to novelty in favor of received normative doctrines cannot deny that those received doctrines were actually the work of human agents even if sanctified by the Spirit. So why is there such nervousness about this claim? Possibilities suggested by Helmer include fears of relativism, secularism, and liberalism. Or it might also reflect a need to erase historical differences in the name of a certain understanding of apostolicity. But she argues that the key reason is to defend the view that theology is "normative all the way down."[87] For Helmer, in contrast, God in Christ—a living reality—is the norm.

What this claim means for Helmer can be presented by sketching a range of intersecting ideas. By social construction, she does not mean a process referring to or reducible to itself. She means a social construction that *is* responsible to a reality that lies *outside* that process of construction but that is also the stimulus, or catalyst, to that process: the living God. She also invests significantly in the *social* nature of this social construction. As noted above, doctrine is generated by theologians in conversation, a conversation that is multidimensional and often uneasy. This connects the social and the historical dimensions of truth. "Truth is not diminished," she writes in the passage already quoted in Chapter 1 of this book, "when it is understood as historical interpretation(s). Rather being attuned to the historical brings truth into the medium of human intersubjectivity where disagreement and explication, competing perspectives and various proposals—all are part of the process of its formulation."[88] This "process of formulation" is not, however, unstructured. When calling for the "mutual interaction" between the different doctrinal enterprises of global Christianity, she proposes a "process of mapping [doctrinal] predicates onto a conceptual grid."[89] The details of this grid are not provided, but its purpose is very clear. It is "in process"[90] as the church's collective but diverse experience of Christ's redemptive work is mapped in a way that existing concepts are confirmed, destabilized, or repositioned as new ones are added. Such mapping and categorization is an "invitation to test explanations for familiar ways of conceptualizing reality and to open up new ways to understand the categorization process."[91]

So, the concept of truth as socially constructed is not only complex, dynamic, and intersubjective but also disciplined. The intellectual, interpersonal, and spiritual rigor it involves delivers it from any cavalier charge of relativism or subjectivism. Although Helmer does not present it in just these terms, one of the points on the grid is the New Testament witness to Jesus; this does have a normative role in the formation of doctrine. It involves complex claims about the relationship between the living Christ and language. It also involves a great debt to Schleiermacher.

Doctrine as catalyst and the Bible

Helmer's contribution to the discussion of the relation between doctrine and the Bible is not focused on the status or interpretation of the Bible. The status of the Bible as Christianity's authoritative text is not defended; it is simply assumed. Its interpretation is not her concern. Her focus, borrowed from Schleiermacher, is to explore how the literature of the New Testament was produced. This is not a historical or literary exploration but a theological one. Helmer attends to the New Testament because it yields a "theological epistemology," which in turn yields doctrine. Doctrine is biblical, in part, because it shares in this epistemology. Without going into the details of her analysis of Schleiermacher, she draws on his claim (already noted in passing in Chapter 2 of this book) that the language of the New Testament was produced by the first Christian community's experience of Jesus as the Redeemer. There are links between the redemptive transformation of the first Christians and authors of the New Testament, the source of that transformation, and the literature produced. As she writes, "The cause of transformation, the person of Jesus, elicits a particular linguistic formulation that discloses the nature of the experience."[92] The experience of redemption generates titles, metaphors, and descriptions of Jesus that "in their experienced variety are knitted into the chain of concept formation by predication."[93] They become the means of identifying Jesus, and thus the "seeds of these linguistic predications are reaped as doctrine."[94]

Helmer thus claims from Schleiermacher a theological epistemology that explains the origin and the development of Christian discourse from Scripture to doctrine: "The experience of Jesus Christ is the origin of doctrine."[95] Based on this epistemology, doctrine is always related to Christ. Again drawing from Schleiermacher, Helmer argues that even though the New Testament bears witness to a relation with Christ that "transcends linguistic determination," it nevertheless cannot "be described apart from Christian discourse."[96] This is the heart of Helmer's argument for "how Scripture and doctrine have the same epistemological structure in their generation, from the earliest layers of the New Testament to contemporary global Christianity."[97] This last point about global Christianity is important because it draws attention to the orientation of this theological epistemology to the generation of diversity in relation to its Christian specificity.

On the basis of what she draws from Schleiermacher and his understanding of the production of the New Testament, Helmer proposes a very particular relationship between language and reality. But it is to be distinguished from those accounts of such a relationship (such as she sees in Lindbeck and his followers) that emphasize a fixed and stable doctrinal language being normative for Christian experience. As the terminology that follows shows, she is positing something that is neither "experiential-expressive" nor "cultural-linguistic":

> The relation between experience and language is more intimate than a standard one-directionality that expresses a prior experience or an experience that is thoroughly structured by language so as not to admit novelty. Experience, if it is interpreted at all, is "more than" its interpretation. Language is asymptotic in its attempt to capture experience.[98]

So, too, is doctrine "asymptotic." Its work is never exhausted in its role of being a "catalyst for the living tradition of Christianity."

This has been an unusual, but not an unimportant, end point for a discussion about the relationship between the Bible and doctrine. It argues for a continuity between Scripture and doctrine on the basis of the living presence of Jesus Christ, which is nevertheless normed by Scripture that provides the linguistic "seeds" for doctrine. It is not without its problems, however. The most conspicuous, one fully acknowledged by Helmer,[99] is Schleiermacher's relative disregard of the Old Testament. The "biblical" theological epistemology developed by Helmer is dependent on a particular understanding of the production of the New Testament only. Attention to the formation of the whole canon might, however, strengthen Helmer's argument with its emphasis on social construction. The particular theological reading of the New Testament's formation points to what is ostensibly a very smooth process. While the diversity of the literature is recognized, the tensions and disputes within the literature are not mentioned. This brings us to one of the questions put to Vanzhoozer in the previous section of this chapter. What role is there for the place of disagreement, correction, dissent, innovation, agreement, and consolidation that is evident in the canon? The striking thing here, with regard to Helmer, is that such a recognition would reinforce the continuity between the formation of Scripture and the formation of doctrine, the latter of which she rightly says always involves "disagreement and explication and competing perspectives." But this possibility is not explored.

Christian Doctrine

What is doctrine?

What does this engagement with this particular debate and the selected authors tell us about doctrine? It tells us that definition must include some account of doctrine's relationship to the Bible and of its truthfulness. No attempt will be made here to adjudicate between the three authors or to resolve all the issues that have been raised. Instead, some general observations about doctrine, the Bible, and truth will be drawn from the previous sections before summarizing what has been learned about doctrine.

Each of the metaphors for doctrine that have been encountered is illuminating in its own way. Certainly, "prompt" and "catalyst" crystallize what has been observed from the outset of this book: doctrine is dynamic and, at some level, open-ended. Yet both, along with "rule," point to the grounded nature of doctrine. Each of the metaphors has its own way of suggesting that doctrine is not self-generating. In fact, "prompt" and "catalyst" illuminate very well the role doctrine plays in the church navigating its way between (using Vanhoozer's terms) stabilization and innovation in its understanding and articulation of the gospel.

The issue of the Bible's authority for doctrine was not in question with any of the authors. The critical issue that emerged related to how they each construe and interpret it. Vanhoozer (with hints of similar ideas in Lindbeck) drew an analogy between the Bible and the "society of biblical literature." Helmer (echoing Schleiermacher) construed the Bible as the linguistic product of the Christian community's experience of the redemption accomplished by Christ. Each of the authors acknowledged the theological diversity of the Bible. Yet each left unaddressed the social and political realities of dissent, disagreement, and consolidation that accompany that diversity. More will be said about this in the next chapter, but there is potential here for further reflection on the continuities between the production and character of the Bible and that of doctrine, which, as Helmer put it so strongly, also involves dissent, disagreement, and consolidation.

The question of doctrine's truth is a perennial question for Christian theology. In this particular debate, the truthfulness of doctrine has been encountered under the particular pressures of the post-Enlightenment "turn to language" and the "performative" or "pragmatic" integration of truth, language, and practices. It is therefore important to note that neither Lindbeck, Vanhoozer, or Helmer were indifferent to the questions of cognition and reference which could well be sidestepped in the "turn to language." Lindbeck acknowledged this with his "modest cognitivism."

Vanhoozer addressed these issues by proposing an account of dramatic truth as integrating the "affective, volitional and cognitive." Helmer was most concerned to acknowledge the inevitable social circumstances of doctrine's production and to propose a theological epistemology that thoroughly integrated language and the experience of the living God. Yet, her use of the term "social construction" is bound to produce the anxiety that any claims so produced refer only to themselves and that they represent at least a tacit endorsement of epistemological relativism, which, in turn, implies a denial of the givenness of God's self-revelation. But Helmer's insistence on the socially produced character of doctrine is an important reminder that the fear of epistemological relativism cannot be countered by lifting doctrinal discourse above the human circumstances of its production and reception. Of course, it is possible also to speak of doctrinal work being Spirit-led and sanctified. But this must not be at the expense of acknowledging its fully human character. This involves walking the line walked by Christian theology whenever it seeks simultaneously to acknowledge the givenness of the truth that God is and the properly human actions of thinking and writing about this truth.

In a study addressing these issues with reference to postliberal theology, James K. A. Smith makes the point that because the "condition of being relative—being dependent, being contingent—is also synonymous with the conditions of creaturehood," relativism is "just a name for the human condition, the *ethos* of creaturehood."[100] For Smith, to deny contingency as a strategy for resisting relativism "would be to imagine that we can somehow transcend the conditions of creaturehood—which is usually considered diabolical, the root of all transgression."[101] Doctrine does indeed make truth claims. That is part of the answer to the question of what doctrine is. It is right for Christians to acknowledge, as Vanhoozer reminds us, that doctrine, like the canon, can be a "spiritual direction" for the performance of the gospel. It is equally important that the proper acknowledgment of doctrine's status as a human work (for it cannot be otherwise) does not diminish the church's confidence in the truth that doctrine speaks even as it tempers that confidence with humility.

Christian doctrine is a human work of witness to the gospel. It uses human language with all its possibilities and limitations to speak of a truth beyond itself. It not only guides the church by pointing back to the biblical witnesses but also opens the church to the possibility of new formulations and articulations of the gospel. Christian doctrine cannot exist without its relationship to the Bible. It not only summarizes the Bible but also interprets and illuminates the Bible as it does so. All this can be added to the ideas of doctrine as the church articulating its faith, doctrine as the focus of the exploration in the work of individual theologians as they use doctrine to construct overarching visions of the Christian faith, doctrine as made of up doctrines in their interrelationship. With all these features of doctrine identified, it is time to turn to a more integrated account of it.

CHAPTER 5
DOCTRINE AND THE CHRISTIAN SOCIAL IMAGINARY

This book began with a working definition of doctrine: *Christian doctrine is communally recognized and authoritative teaching about Christianity's beliefs and practices.* This was summarized as *communally recognized authoritative teaching*. While stating some elements of commonly held understandings of doctrine, especially doctrine's link to authority and teaching, it was noted right out at the outset that this definition raised many other questions. In the intervening chapters, some of the questions that were left begging at the outset have been asked and the definition has been expanded. It has been filled out along the following lines:

> Doctrine is the church's authoritative teaching which emerges as the church thinks, debates, discerns and prays. It can take the form of a summary of the church's faith. It can be an *ad hoc* statement or confession which clarifies or highlights some or another contentious or neglected aspect of the faith. Sometimes it is undertaken in the midst of cultural and/or ecclesiastical crises; it can also emerge in times of stability and consolidation. So produced, doctrine can provide an overall vision of the Christian faith which variously guides, attracts, inspires, challenges and comforts. But even as it offers some such vision of the whole, doctrine is nothing without particular doctrines and their interactions. Specific doctrines are often the focus of the intellectual heavy-lifting of the church's theological work. Doctrine is also the object of intellectual debate, spiritual exploration, training in discipleship, and both personal and communal formation. Doctrine is a rigorous intellectually-disciplined activity focused on the use, meaning and interpretation of concepts and texts. It is the focus of individual reflection as well as of communal decision. Doctrine is a use of language and ideas, embedded as they are in the complexities

of power and the ambiguities of life, to speak truthfully of God, the world, Christ and salvation.

This extended definition has emerged out of an engagement with actual examples of doctrine being stated, expounded, investigated, or constructed. It avoids the dangers that can attach to both overly formulaic definitions of doctrine and the definitions narrowly concerned with its cognitive nature and/or authoritative functions. It has the advantage of ensuring that the resultant understanding of doctrine is not tied to the interests of any particular confessional tradition. After all, there is always a risk that confessional divisions can be extended to the definitions of doctrine in ways that the very understanding of doctrine exacerbates the divisions. This is not a hypothetical concern. Referring to recent debates about doctrine in North America, Sameer Yadav has pointed to what he describes as "a kind of tribalism amongst theologians operating under distinct paradigms of the dogmatic task with their own literatures and conversation partners, and without much engagement with alternative paradigms."[1] He continues, "It's almost like the taxonomies and their revisions function like a noncompete clause, or an injunction to 'stay in your own lane.'"[2] That is not to say that the definition developed here could not be broader or that it could not have engaged a wider circle of examples and case studies. Nevertheless, the multifaceted character of doctrine stated above helps us to grasp that it is an activity that eludes any narrow paradigm.

Doctrine is an intellectual activity, but it is also an *activity* in a much broader sense, a sense to which the language of practice is well suited. The point is well made by James McClendon when he writes, "Just as 'medicine' denotes not merely bottles on a pharmacy shelf, but a practice, and 'law' not merely statutes, but *another* kind of practice, our practice of doctrine is far more than the individual doctrines involved. In each case the named practice is definitive for and inclusive of its ingredient doctrines, laws or medicines."[3] The point here is not the banal one that doctrine has practical implications. Nor is it simply another instance of the now commonplace insistence on the integration and mutuality of theory and practice. Indeed, the task that lies ahead in this chapter is to sketch some of the critical dimensions of the understanding of doctrine presented above. This will involve noting its various points of tension and articulating more fully and technically some of its elements and their interrelationships. To do this, I will employ the concept of the "social imaginary," specifically as defined by the Canadian philosopher Charles Taylor. It is useful because its very terms suggest a critical apparatus with which to investigate the social and imaginative elements of doctrine. Indeed, these two concepts—social and imaginary—are more fruitful for the present task than are those of "practice" and "theory." And even more fruitful for what follows is the way Taylor articulates the respective implicit and explicit elements of the social imaginary.

The social imaginary

In his *A Secular Age*, Taylor defines the "social imaginary" as the "ways people imagine their social existence, how they fit together with others, how things go between them and their fellows, the expectations which are normally met, and the deeper normative notions and images which underlie these expectations."[4] He means something "much broader and deeper than the intellectual schemes people may entertain when they think about social reality in a disengaged mode."[5] It is what is "carried in images, stories and legends"[6] and can "never be adequately expressed in the form of explicit doctrines, because of its very unlimited and indefinite nature."[7] It provides an implicit, "largely unstructured and inarticulate understanding of our whole situation."[8] In summary,

> Our social imaginary ... incorporates a sense of the normal expectations we have of each other, the kind of common understanding that enables us to carry out the collective practices that make up our social life. This incorporates some sense of how we all fit together in carrying out the common practice. This understanding is both factual and "normative"; that is, we have a sense of how things usually go, but this is interwoven with an idea of how they ought to go, of what missteps would invalidate the practice.[9]

It is an idea that helps conceptualize the mutuality between practice and understanding while being something greater than their sum: "If the understanding makes the practice possible, it is also true that it is the practice which largely carries the understanding."[10] Yet the social imaginary is not the servant of the status quo. Over time, the social imaginary can be transformed. Indeed, Taylor uses the idea to highlight the changes that led to the West becoming secular: "a set of practices in the course of their slow development and ramifications gradually changed their meaning for people, and hence helped to constitute a new social imaginary."[11] The social imaginary is a dynamic phenomenon. Nevertheless, notwithstanding the epochal changes such as those described by Taylor, the social imaginary can also extend across time, uniting members of a society from different eras. This element of the social imaginary allows the members of a given society to "imagine" their connection to those from other eras. The point is made by one of Taylor's own sources, Benedict Anderson, in his idea of nation-states as "imagined communities" where loyalty, identity, and sense of belonging transcend any given era. Such loyalty and shared identity are "*imagined* because members of even the smallest nation will never know most of their fellow-members, meet them, or even hear of them, yet in the minds of each lives the image of their communion."[12]

But another feature of the social imaginary is that it is largely *implicit*. To share a social imaginary is to share an "implicit grasp of social space."[13] Taylor contrasts this with a "theoretical description of this space, distinguishing different kinds of people, and the norms connected to them."[14] He reinforces this contrast by suggesting that the "understanding implicit in practice stands to social theory in the way my ability to get around a familiar environment stands to a (literal) map of this area. I am very well able to orient myself without ever having adopted the standpoint of overview the map offers me."[15] Yet even without the literal or explicit map, the social imaginary carries "an implicit 'map' of social space."[16] In fact, Taylor goes on to make the claim that "for most of history, and for most of social life, we function through the grasp we have on the common repertory, without benefit of theoretical overview."[17] Of course, the social imaginary is shaped by theories that are initially "held by a few people" but that, in time, "may come to infiltrate the whole society."[18] Notwithstanding Taylor's use of the categories of "theory" and "practice" in the forgoing remarks, it is the distinction between "implicit" and "explicit" that invites consideration of how such explicit phenomena as maps and the "explicit doctrines" (and even books on such things as social imaginaries) actually contribute to the implicit phenomenon of the social imaginary. After all, only a few societies would not have explicit resources such as legal codes, constitutions, and literary canons that play a role in their respective social imaginaries.

There are several ways in which these ideas can be extended to the relationship between explicit doctrine and the implicit Christian social imaginary. After all, the church is a community, the members of which have "expectations of each other," share a sense of how they "fit together in carrying out its common practices," and who together "carry images, stories and legends." Moreover, the sense of being part of the Christian community is often confirmed, reinforced, and sustained by events, experiences, and relationships that do not easily yield to clear explanation. That "literal maps" are not necessary to orient oneself to a familiar environment does not mean that such maps are not drawn or never used. Equally, the fact that explicit knowledge of doctrine may not be necessary to participate in the society of the church does not mean that doctrine is not actually playing a role, even a decisive one, in the church's social imaginary.

Using this framework, and with its various concepts and terms in mind, it is possible to address some of the critical issues associated with the understanding of doctrine developed in this book. By analogy to the idea that within the social imaginary there is a mutuality between doctrine and practice, we can explore afresh the idea of doctrine as practical wisdom. By analogy to the idea that the social imaginary and its normative function is "carried in images, stories and legends," we can explore how doctrine—being "carried" within the church's social imaginary—contributes to the church's norms, especially the Bible. By analogy to the fact that the social imaginary provides continuity across time but can also change in time, we can explore the role of doctrine in Christianity's dynamic of change and constancy.

Doctrine as practical wisdom

As already noted, the notion of doctrine as practical wisdom is now a commonplace. It is part of the wider critical response to the Enlightenment's confidence in rational, disembodied knowledge. The awareness that all knowledge is known within the confines and possibilities of embodied existence and within existing communal traditions of thought is one of the more widely held assumptions of the contemporary intellectual world. As Anthony Thiselton has pointed out, for Christian theology to place its reflection on doctrine within such assumptions "does not rest upon theological special pleading."[19] Nor is it a total surprise to Christian theologians. Two decades ago, leading practical theologian, Don Browning, commented that with the rise of practical philosophies in the twentieth century, "there is a rush among more dignified and well-established systematic and historical theologians to ask, 'After all, aren't we all practical?'"[20] The comment may well have applied to some easy targets in the world of doctrinal theology. But as observed in the examples of doctrinal theology surveyed in this book, any separation of doctrine from practice is not typical of the tradition; the historical and contemporary instances that do exist are aberrations. Ellen Charry describes such approaches to doctrine as "abnormal, shrunken, and impoverished."²¹ In her own study of some leading premodern classical theologians, Charry has documented how Christian doctrines have been taught and presented with "a moral shaping function."²² It is not that understanding and knowledge are rendered redundant. The point is that cognitive matters are not ends in themselves. Of her selected patristic theologians she writes, "Understanding God correctly was necessary in order for people to grasp their own identity as Christians and achieve true happiness in it."²³ She summarizes her interpretations of various sections of Calvin's *Institutes*, by pointing out that that for Calvin, "[k]nowing *about* God is not the point; knowing God is."²⁴ Her general point is that "[s]apience includes correct information about God but emphasizes attachment to that knowledge."²⁵

Even with these pastoral and sapiential functions of doctrine acknowledged, critical questions are raised. How, for instance, does it do this? As noted in the discussion of Lindbeck in Chapter 4, mere exposure to doctrine does not automatically produce corresponding behavior. And how does doctrine give shape not just to "knowing God," in terms of generating a strong sense of Christian identity and "true happiness," but also to the concrete forms Christian discipleship? How does it function to "lure" people through the vision it offers (to echo Sarah Coakley)? How does this formative function of doctrine actually occur? Can more be said than that it somehow diffusely "infiltrates" the church's social imaginary? Some attention needs to be given to this question if the acceptance of doctrine as practical wisdom, insightful as it is, is not to become a platitude.

One way of better understanding the relationship between doctrine and practice is to note the insight of Anthony Thiselton that doctrines are, in part, *dispositional* beliefs. Drawing on the work of philosopher H. H. Price, Thiselton notes that "[t]raditional accounts of belief ... tend to construe belief as an 'occurrence', almost a mental event."²⁶ This almost automatically separates belief (and therefore doctrines) from practice, thus isolating them from the outset and making it difficult to see how they are related. According to Thiselton, "disposition" denotes the "reservoir of knowledge, understanding, of conviction upon which the believer draws to perform appropriate belief-utterances or action."²⁷ In Price's own words, belief is a "multiform disposition, which is manifested or actualized in many different ways: not only ... in actions ... but also in emotional states such as hope and fear; in feelings of doubt, surprise and confidence ... and in inferences ... in which belief 'spreads itself' from a proposition to some of its consequences."²⁸

On this reading, if doctrine is a "belief," then it is not just a "mental event" but is already part of the processes by which human beings act. Yet, this does not answer *how* it is that doctrine and practices come to be aligned or not.

That they often are not aligned is a particular issue for Medi Ann Volpe in her *Rethinking Christian Identity: Doctrine and Discipleship*.[29] Any account of the relationship between doctrine and practice must, she writes, take note of our "failure to practice 'true discipleship'" and therefore accept "that there is more to Christian identity than the honing of our intellectual and moral skills."[30] Her work provides many insights into the "more" that is involved. Positively, and drawing heavily on Gregory of Nyssa, she argues that doctrine's chief role lies in forming the Christian imagination: it "directs desire such that it structures the imagination according to hope in God."[31] This, in turn, directs and equips the life of discipleship. "The riches of imagination," she writes, "can aid the task of discipleship, but in order to do so, the imagination itself must be trained by doctrine to nourish hope, encourage perseverance in faith, and demonstrate the love in which Christians participate as members of Christ."[32] But for doctrine to do this, it must be accompanied by ascetic practice, and, therefore, it requires "an account of the soul" both as the "seat of human capacity for the imitation of divine love" and as "that which is corrupted by sin."[33] Summarizing and endorsing Gregory's position, she sets out how doctrine and ascesis work together to turn the Christian away from sin and to live, instead, according to the truth taught in doctrine. "Right doctrine ... points the way for the soul on its journey of transformation; we ought to think of the rule function of doctrine as setting guideposts for Christian imagination. Ascetic practices provide therapy for sin, help to reorient desire toward God, and encourage growth in charity."[34] In other words, for doctrine to be properly lived requires more than resolve. It entails disciplined attention to the realities and ambiguities of human nature, and attention to the "complex of imagination, sin, desire, the vision of God and concrete practices."[35] Absent such attention, doctrine and discipleship will more easily drift apart.

Another angle on these issues is provided by Simeon Zahl in an important essay, "On the Affective Salience of Doctrines." As the title indicates, Zahl draws on concepts and insights drawn from psychology. "'Affective salience,'" he writes, "is ... where an object of our attention is understood to be 'affectively salient' to the degree that it evokes and brings to awareness particular bodily affective states."[36] Employing concrete examples from the patristic and Reformation periods[37] he demonstrates how doctrinal theologians have actually—and typically—been attentive to the connections between their doctrinal teachings and the emotional states they wish to inculcate in their readers. With particular reference to Augustine's teaching on the incarnation, but as representative of a more general trend, he notes that there is "an explicit rhetorical concern with the affective consequences of a particular doctrinal position."[38] Zahl's point is that there has been a persistent confidence that doctrine presented in certain ways can shape and even heal the emotions of Christians, and direct them to those affective states that are among the promised benefits of the Christian faith. Zahl's reading of these theologians echoes Charry's argument encountered above. His constructive suggestion is that the contemporary church enhances this established feature of doctrine by attending to psychological insights into the connection between beliefs and the emotions of those who believe them: "Attending explicitly to the affective salience of doctrines will help make contemporary theology wiser … than it has been in the past, and better able to foster creative, accurate, and affectively-compelling visions of the Christian life in the future."[39]

The preceding discussion has suggested that doctrinal theologians ought to be attentive to the processes by which doctrine does its work of shaping Christian discipleship and forming Christian communities. This is so even if the processes are not in the foreground of the church's social imaginary. Being attentive to these processes is to go beyond acknowledging that doctrine is implicit in the church's social imaginary. It is also offers the prospect of keeping doctrine and practice aligned. Further, it invites attention to the cognitive, affective, spiritual, social, and even political processes that connect thought and practice within the social imaginary.[40] As Volpe suggests, it also requires theological attention to the imagination, the soul, the reality of sin, the practices of ascesis, and the cultivation of hope.

Doctrine and the Bible

In Taylor's presentation of it, the social imaginary "carries" various "images, stories and legends" that along with its other elements form the normative role of the social imaginary. This is the case even if the image, stories, and legends are held unconsciously by most of the group that share a particular imaginary. By analogy we can think of doctrine as among the "stories and legends" forming the normative sense of the church's social imaginary. This allows us to ask about the role explicit doctrine plays in constructing such implicit and assumed norms. One obvious answer would be to suggest that

Doctrine and the Christian Social Imaginary

doctrine *is* the *norm* simpliciter.[41] Yet this immediately returns us to the question of the relationship between doctrine and the Bible. If doctrine plays a normative role, then what are *its* norms? This issue was first encountered in Chapter 1 in the discussion of confessions as *norma normata* (normed norms) and the Bible as *norma normans* (norming norm). It was also a theme running through the various theologians studied in Chapter 2, but especially Calvin, Schleiermacher, and Barth. In Chapter 4, the relation of doctrine to the Bible was a recurring issue in the responses to Lindbeck's *The Nature of Doctrine*. Obviously, much ink has been spilled in attempts to describe the relationship between doctrine and the Bible. The path followed here will be to employ a particular pair of metaphors to describe not only each of doctrine and the Bible but also their relationship.

But first, it has to be acknowledged that locating this discussion within Taylor's particular account of the social imaginary is not without possible objections. For Taylor, the social imaginary itself functions normatively for the given society. At first glance, this might suggest that the analogy will lead to the church being its own norm. Even churches that have a high view of ecclesial authority would balk at such a crudely stated position. But the analogy does not necessarily lead in that direction. Taylor's point is more subtle, as is the analogy being drawn here. For Taylor, as we have already seen, the social imaginary, including its normative role, is the product of certain "theories" and even "explicit doctrines" eventually "infiltrating the whole society." By analogy it can be suggested that within the church's social imaginary, both the Bible and doctrine "infiltrate" the church as their normative contents weave their way into the church's shared imagination through, among other things, liturgy, hymnody, polity, and pastoral care. So understood, the social imaginary is actually a very helpful analogy for thinking about how doctrine and the Bible relate to each other in carrying out their normative roles. The proposal made here is to regard doctrine as an explicit map (again employing but extending Taylor's own terms) of the church's social imaginary and the Bible as a compass.[42]

At first glance, "map" might appear to suggest something static and to be at odds with the dynamism attached to doctrine that has been highlighted throughout this book. But all maps are, in fact, contingent. Maps, even of the one location, have histories and limited currency. From time to time, the mapping of any given area needs to be modified as new territories are discovered, or as others are disrupted by geological events or erosion, or as environments are changed by human engineering. But the contingency of maps is not simply developmental; they are also frequently heavily freighted ideologically. For instance, maps of the world produced within the British Empire (and later in "Commonwealth" countries in the postcolonial era) might have more or less accurately indicated the location of national boundaries. But with their vast swathes of pink (as it usually was) denoting British rule, a particular geopolitical message was also communicated. For such reasons, maps differently configured can serve corrective functions. For instance, a recently produced map of Australia identifies the sites of the colonial massacres of indigenous Australians and thereby reconfigures many elements of Australian history and identity obscured in other maps.[43] It is clearly a map of Australia, but one highlighting a previously hidden and confronting perspective. And maps can be produced with various levels of detail depending on their intended users and uses. For all that diversity, however, maps cannot be arbitrary. They subvert their function if they are. A physical map must actually refer to the terrain. And to use the map as efficiently as possible, the user will use it in tandem with a compass. Few terrains could be navigated with a century-old map. But a century-old compass could still perform its role with a new map. By analogy, doctrine is the contingent revisable map and the Bible is the reliable and transferrable compass. Of course, the church has found that some of its doctrines do transfer across time and place, a matter that will be addressed in the next section. First, a little more needs to be said about the Bible as compass.

The idea of the Bible as compass is not unknown in Christian piety, and it is often invoked simplistically to describe the Bible as a source of personal goal setting. But that would actually be more treating the Bible as a map. The more compelling value of compass as a metaphor for the Bible lies in the fact that it points to a reality beyond itself. A compass has no value or purpose apart from its relationship to the earth's magnetic field. Similarly, the Bible's purpose is to point beyond itself to the living God. Like all metaphors, compass and map can be extended only so far, but as well as illuminating each of the Bible and doctrine, the *combination* of compass and map serves as a metaphorical description of the *relationship* between Bible and doctrine.

Being aware that the Bible as compass is ripe for simplistic appropriation, it is timely to return to another metaphor for the Bible already encountered in this book. In Chapter 4, Vanhoozer's metaphor of the Bible as a "society of biblical literature" was noted. It was used to capture the reality of the Bible's diversity. The concern I identified at the time was that it did not engage the full significance of the Bible's theological diversity. The concern extended to the treatment of the Bible in Lindbeck and Helmer. My claim was that while the theological diversity of the Bible was acknowledged, it was either too easily harmonized (Lindbeck and Vanhoozer) or noted simply as grounds for the diversity of doctrine (Helmer). I argued that what was lacking was an engagement with the *nature* of the diversity, specifically its political and social dimensions. The point can be opened up by reference to Walter Brueggemann and Rowan Williams. In his *Old Testament Theology*, Brueggemann argues that the diversity of the Old Testament reflects the ongoing history of various schools of Jewish theology, and the communities attached to them, interacting with each other though "witness, dispute and advocacy" (the terms of the book's subtitle). He is proposing an understanding of the differentiated unity of the Old Testament being the result of a process of "profound conflict and disputation through which Israel arrives at its truth-claims."[44] In other words, precisely as a body of literature, the Old Testament *preserves* tensions and conflicts in the midst of agreements. A commonly cited example of this would be the tension between those voices of the Old Testament that link blessing with obedient piety (e.g., Deuteronomy) and those that invoke lived experience to interrogate such correlations (e.g., Job and Ecclesiastes). The tensions between them cannot be resolved. Both are accepted as authoritative reference points for understanding the ways of Israel's God. In fact, it is not a benign pluralism of different views. For Brueggemann, these and other differences require the term "cross-examination" to capture their significance and function. Cross-examination, he claims, "constitutes part of the record of testimony, and it is understood in Israel as a way in which the testimony must itself be undertaken."[45] Rowan Williams's point is similar, but it is made in reference to the whole of the canon and leads to a Christological point. Echoing Brueggemann, Williams writes, "The movement of our canonical texts is frequently a quite explicit response to or rebuttal of some other position within the same canonical framework; the world it opens to us is one of uneasy relationships and discontinuities."[46] He notes the different theologies at work in the "historical" narratives of the Old Testament and within the diversity of the Gospels. This leads him to suggest that "the biblical text ... displays an inner literary history" that consists of "narrative texts reworking other narrative texts, from Chronicles and Kings to Matthew and Mark."[47] In such reworking, "the story is rewritten in the conviction that previous tellings are unbalanced or inadequate; yet the re-writing has the same risk and provisionality."[48] For Williams, the framework of this history of conflict is quite clear. Indeed, even more than having a framework, it has a *goal*.

This is his substantive Christological point. "The existence of conflict and even conscientious division," he writes, "may not be a sign of polarisation but a necessary part of that movement of the story of God's people and their language towards the one focus of Christ crucified and risen that is the movement of Scripture."[49] In many ways, Williams's image has some parallel with Vanhoozer's of the canon "wrapped around Christ," albeit with more theological diversity and dynamism incorporated into it. But his reference to "conflict and conscientious division" strikingly echo Christine Helmer's comments (already highlighted in Chapter 4) about doctrine being produced through "disagreement and explication" and in the face of "competing perspectives."

These parallels suggest a measure of continuity between the formation and nature of the canon on the one hand and the formation and nature of doctrine on the other. This does not flatten the differences in their respective authority. There is no reason why the human actions that produce Scripture need to be qualitatively different from those that produce doctrine in order for Scripture to be authoritative over doctrine. To focus on the human and social realities of the canon is not to deny that either its constitutive literature or the collection as a whole has been divinely appointed and sanctified to serve a particular authoritative role that doctrine does not have. Nor is this recognition of "conflict" and "division" within the canon to deny that Christ is the focus of the tension-filled literature. It is, however, to draw attention to certain realities of the canon that invite its readers to be as attentive as possible to the "movement of the story of God's people and their language" and to resist any temptation to short-circuit the complexities of that movement in the construction and reception of doctrine. This is not incompatible with the Bible as compass. After all, a compass needle can vibrate for a period before it finally aligns itself to the invisible force it has been constructed to detect.

Neither the Bible nor doctrine will ever be entirely implicit in the church's social imaginary. Both have accumulated high levels of visibility and presence in Christian identity and practice. Although, as noted earlier, their implicit presence in liturgy, hymnody, polity, and pastoral care also allows their normative function to be woven into and throughout the social imaginary. The preceding reflections also point to the possibility that the Bible and doctrine, precisely in their *explicit* presence, are a perennial focus of debate and discussion within the church's social imaginary and that this does not negate their normative role. It highlights that this is part of how God's truth is known, received, and articulated.

Doctrine, change, and diversity

Christianity is heavily invested in the notion of its unity. After all, generating a new community in place of previously separated communities is part of what Christianity achieved at its origin. Therefore, the theological stakes are very high in understanding the relationship between the church's unity and diversity. Much of this discussion has been honed in the church's classic language of catholicity, holiness, unity, and apostolicity. Doctrine has been a consistent element in these discussions. Often especially linked with apostolicity, it has played a role in establishing one of the threads of continuity across Christianity's ethnic, cultural, racial, and linguistic diversity. Even here, however, the reality that the church has, over time, either developed new teachings or discarded established teachings generated a rich body of discussion under the heading of "the development of doctrine."[50] More recently, the increasingly evident place of theological diversity in the canon and its reflection in the church's theological diversity has attracted significant scholarly attention, notably through the appropriation of Mikhail Bhaktin's idea of the "polyphony" of diverse voices.[51] In many ways, however, the circumstances of the contemporary world church have deflected some attention away from these discussions toward the social and political realities of the diversity of the contemporary church. Against the background of Christianity's centers of cultural, numerical, institutional, and intellectual gravity shifting from Europe to Asia and Africa, new questions are being asked about the political, ideological, and cultural dimensions of doctrinal production and reception.

For this issue, too, I suggest that the social imaginary is illuminating. The contemporary situation can be understood as the church's social imaginary being deeply reshaped by this new experience of diversity. Some of the conceptual features of Taylor's definition of the social imaginary can help describe this situation and its challenges in a helpful way. It illuminates the unity of a society across time and provides some insights for reflecting on diversity within a given time. As already highlighted several times, in Taylor's proposal, a new theory or idea "gradually infiltrates and transforms" or "penetrates and transforms" a given imaginary. By analogy, the reality of contemporary world Christianity is in the process of ideas hitherto unknown, dismissed, or ignored, and previously unasked questions, "infiltrating" and "penetrating" the whole. This may lead to doctrinal innovation that reinforces the diversity. But it also invites attention to what the "whole" is and to how it conditions the diversity. I suggest that this context invites fresh attention to the idea of Rule of Faith, the tool by which theologians and the church have summarized, to recall the remark of Kathryn Greene-McCreight quoted in Chapter 1, the "basic take" on Christianity.

But before addressing that, it is important to address some critical questions. One of the concerns, especially raised by the impact of the modern missionary movement, is that accounts of the unity of the church are too closely aligned with, and in the service of, the unity of empire. Such is the argument of contemporary Indian theologian, Y. T. Vinayaraj. "The logic of 'Oneness,'" he argues, "whether in its theological or ecclesiological [form] has always been political."[52] Vinayaraj develops a postcolonial critique of the nexus of ecclesial unity and divine oneness that lent itself to (and he argues was produced by) a collusion between church and empire. The ensuing ecclesiology traded on a political ontology of empire. The result: "When the Church becomes a sovereign power of rule and its liturgies become the celebration of the sovereign God, [the] calling of the Church is nullified and reversed. Church as a sovereign power defines its ontology unrelated to the excluded and the marginalised."[53] Behind this deficient ecclesiology, inherited from the colonizing West, is a deficient doctrine of God: "the logic of 'Oneness' has always been foundational for the Western theological tradition," subverting, he argues, the insights of Trinitarian thought.[54] He goes on to argue for an ecclesiology of marginality that is itself "a call within the call of the Church to become a 'weak church' of the Crucified God."[55] Drawing these threads together, he outlines an "ecclesiology of multitude" that "does not mean unity and diversity or commonality between units; rather it is a shared solitude—a set of relationship[s] without a single essence."[56] Notwithstanding the ironic rhetoric of "shared solitude" and the provocative refusal of a "single essence," it is important to note that Vinayaraj is not abandoning the idea of unity among Christians altogether. The solitude is, after all, "shared." What cannot be bypassed in these remarks, however, is the dissatisfaction with the discourse of "unity and diversity" and "commonality between units." Indirectly, he identifies how that discourse has been abstracted from the realities of its diversity. Vinayaraj has his own theological responses to those challenges.[57] His relevance, here, however, lies in highlighting that unity is not a benign concept. This needs to be borne in mind when considering the role of doctrine in the unity of the church.

John Flett articulates overlapping concerns in his *Apostolicity: The Ecumenical Question in World Christian Perspective*. Flett challenges received definitions of apostolicity, especially as employed in the modern missionary and the contemporary ecumenical movements. Apostolicity came to be linked to the continuity of particular cultural and ecclesiastical forms detached from the work of the Spirit and removed from any Christological norm. Accordingly, cross-cultural missionary transmission becomes a form of colonization "with all that this entails for uneven power relationships, paternalism, building relationships of dependence and, finally, maintaining a state of Christian infancy."[58] He argues for an alternative understanding of apostolicity by separating it from "a lineal cultural expression of the gospel."[59] This allows for the recognition of "the pluriformity of the church through its temporal course."[60] Drawing on the discipline of "world Christianity,"[61] he contends that this notion of apostolicity refuses the "controlling assumptions of Protestant/Catholic schism and its cartography of the ecclesial landscape."[62] Resisting this cartography allows the church to be seen in its "pluriform" and "polycentric" nature. These are not denials of apostolicity but rather manifestations of it. In a comment that echoes Vinayaraj, he writes, "To take unity seriously is to take Christian pluralism seriously."[63] These reflections lead to an extended definition of apostolicity:

> It is not the continuity of a cultural body in a lineal historical course ... Apostolicity, the historical continuity of the church, rests in the event of cross-cultural encounter and the processes of conversion through the local appropriation of the gospel. This history is not the settled and measured development of a cultural entity but is marked by multiple instances of cross-cultural encounter and sometimes radical shifts in thinking.[64]

On the basis of extensive exegetical engagement with the biblical witness to apostolicity, Flett also points to the New Testament's "complex picture of the apostle"[65] and also to its consistent emphasis on apostolicity's "christological ground" on which basis the apostle points "beyond the self and to Christ."[66] Apostolicity "means that the church does not possess its own identity. The church finds this identity in the history of Jesus Christ."[67] And because the church lives from and in the history of Jesus Christ, "it takes the form of participation in his being sent to and for the world and thus the integration of multiple histories into his and only so by the testimony of the Spirit."[68] Flett's contribution to the present discussion is to highlight that there can be no account of the church's unity that does not fully engage its de facto diversity. With Vinayaraj, he points, with exegetical, historical, and doctrinal backing, to the fact that unity and diversity are mutually defining.

By engaging both Vinayaraj and Flett, albeit briefly, the need to frame the discussion of change and diversity in ways that acknowledge the social realities of the church has been highlighted. I've suggested that the new realities of the world church are fostering inevitable and long-term changes in the church's social imaginary. To that general concern with change, both of our writers also help us to see that even ideas of unity and diversity are themselves in ferment and that the associated changes in the church's social imaginary involves interactions between multiple histories, complex power relations, and diverse intellectual conversation partners.

These realities shape the context in which doctrine, as defined at the outset of this chapter, does its work. Doctrinal theologians will not be able to ignore them. It will shape their ongoing work of using doctrine to generate visions of Christianity; it will influence their work of exploring, teaching, and developing particular doctrines (which, as we observed in Chapters 2 and 3, they are doing). There is no reason in this context not to continue to engage the church's great creeds. This prompts us to return to the issues raised earlier concerning the status of "doctrinal maps" that are transferrable across time and place. How do we assess the resilience of those "maps" that have proved transferrable and resilient? It is entirely legitimate to answer that with claims about the "leading of the Spirit." Yet, such claims should not automatically justify an unqualified normative role for such maps. Recall the comments of John Behr, quoted in Chapter 1, about the emergence of the most transferrable of all Christian "doctrinal maps," the Nicene-Constantinopolitan Creed. Behr argues that this Creed "became detached from its original context as a rule of faith in a particular context," and then only after its expansion at Constantinople it became a "standard and universal point of reference, fixed even in its very wording." This is a helpful reminder that that which *became* universal did not begin as such. Its resilience is to be honored but always in the context of the particular issues it was originally addressing. Awareness of the particularity of its origin does not disqualify its use and even its authority, but it does help determine the scope of its authority and use. Behr's observation that the Creed began as a "Rule of Faith" in a particular context is an invitation to reflect on what such contemporary rules might be and how they might function. A principal reason for this is that rules of faith *tend* not to be encumbered with the conceptual density and innovation that is seen in, for instance, the Nicene Creed and the Chalcedonian definition. They can assist in getting beneath the "fixedness of the wording" of established Creed and open up the underlying claims. They also tend to be free (albeit not entirely) of the polemics characteristic of the Reformation Confessions. Such features have been present in the Rules of faith noted in passing in this book: those of Irenaeus in Chapter 1 and Lindbeck and Vanhoozer in Chapter 4. Even if they do employ context-specific concepts, and even if they are not free of polemics, the idea of a Rule of Faith that seeks to summarize a broad sense of what Christianity is, and that stays close to biblical idiom in doing so, is, I suggest, valuable in this present context of the complicated and freighted diversity that characterizes contemporary Christianity and its social imaginary.

While not using the language of Rule of Faith, and not specifically addressing the question of doctrine, the following comments from Nigerian theologian Teresa Okure point to the significance of biblical idiom and framework for addressing the issue of the "global Jesus." In an essay addressing that very topic, she identifies what it is about Jesus that makes him "known, loved and followed by peoples of all nations, languages, cultures in all ages in their diverse expressions."[69] But all efforts "to understand and appreciate the global nature of Jesus are to be located within biblical history. More specifically, Jesus is to be located in the biblical accounts of creation and fall (protology) as well as salvation and redemption (soteriology), seen comprehensively as God's work of love and mercy for humanity."[70] She continues,

> Taken out of this biblical context of protology and soteriology, the discussion of Jesus in his global significance for humanity and his consequent reception by every age, loses much of its meaning and causes irresolvable problems, for then the question becomes a square peg in a round whole. The biblical history of creation and salvation provides the only authentic (in the etymological sense of "that which is proper to itself") context for asking and answering the question of the global Jesus. If one situates the question in the context of other creation stories, soteriologies and ideologies, one cannot expect to obtain adequate answers to the question.[71]

The summary she offers here is itself contestable, but it is a powerful challenge to any doctrinal innovation to be measured by its commitment to the breadth of the story that the biblical accounts of Jesus, even in their diversity, assume about his status and significance. Indeed, this allows me to return to the observations I made in Chapter 1 about the messianic interpretation of Jesus, providing the conceptual framework for the theological coherence of the claims made about him by those who first proclaimed him. When this framework is lost, as elements of the church's history demonstrates, Jesus as the focus of the messianic hope, is obscured. This is not at all to deny the legitimacy of conceptual innovation in doctrinal description of Jesus, or of creation or salvation. As we were reminded by Rowan Williams in Chapter 1, such innovation is actually necessary to sustain the enduring claims of the founding story. But particular conceptual innovations can never be the ultimate norm of doctrinal work. Ultimately, that is the role of the foundational story as presented in the biblical witness.

Concerns similar to those of Okure have been articulated by American theologian, Sameer Yadav, who was quoted earlier in this chapter. He too proposes something like a Rule of Faith (again, my term, not his). In his case, it is developed as a way of breaking through the tendency of theologians to address doctrine within their own confessional traditions. His summary focuses on creation, sin, the calling of Israel, the coming of Christ as Israel's Messiah, his reconciling life, death, resurrection and ascension, and the ongoing work of the Spirit in church.[72] For Yadav, the task of doctrinal work "is the task of determining the meaning, reference, or significance of some such story."[73] He recognizes that "there is no one commonly accepted way that Christians have told the Christian story about God's creating and saving work,"[74] but he claims that doctrinal proposals that lack reflection on some such account of "God's creation and redemption through Christ" appear "vaguely incoherent and self-contradictory."[75] Yadav also suggests that doctrine concerns itself with the truth of this narrative, which is not *just* a narrative. Doctrinal work investigates for Christians "what it is to which their story ontologically commits them."[76] This entails attention to the narrative's "truthmarkers."[77] While Yadav's major concern is to introduce some criteria for disputes about definitions of doctrine, I suggest that his concerns are also relevant to the engagement with diversity of doctrine's content. His and Okure's summaries, or other similar contemporary or ancient rules of faith, can serve a role that is normative but mediating in this time when the church's social imaginary is being transformed by new ideas, questions, and proposals. Such summaries can be means of conversation between competing, alternative, or even complementary doctrinal proposals.

*****

This chapter began with an expanded definition of doctrine. It was informed by the engagement with doctrine and doctrines conducted in the previous four chapters. In this chapter, Charles Taylor's version of the "social imaginary" has been used to frame a number of the critical issues associated with the proposed definition. This framing has been conceptually illuminating, but it has also served as a reminder of the ecclesial location of doctrine. There is an outstanding matter related to the definition of doctrine, and for it we must leave behind the social imaginary. It is the question of the doctrine's truthfulness. A reflection on this topic will be the focus of the brief concluding chapter.

CHAPTER 6
CONCLUSION

The last sentence of the definition of doctrine proposed at the beginning of the previous chapter addressed the question of doctrine's truthfulness: *Doctrine is a use of language and ideas, embedded as they are in the complexities of power and the ambiguities of life, to speak truthfully of God, the world, Christ and salvation.* How to speak of the truthfulness of doctrine is an issue that has arisen at various times in the course of this book. It did so with particular acuteness in Chapter 4 in the study of Lindbeck, Vanhoozer, and Helmer. There the issue was framed by the "turn to language" and the investment each of them made in "performative" or "pragmatic" notions of truth. We encountered debates about doctrinal truth being "intrasystematic" or whether it shared in some "ontological correspondence" to the realities it confessed. The sharpest edge of the discussion was Helmer's use of the term "social construction" to describe the nature of doctrinal production. It states the obvious fact that all doctrine is produced through, to recall her words, "conversation among theologians and other Christians talking in earnest with each other about the God with whom they are in relationship." On the other hand, the term "social construction" raises a concern not only that doctrine is the product of those social relationships and interactions but also that it only ever refers back to them rather than to any external referent. Another concern is the fear of relativism: if doctrine is only ever the product of the social context in which it is produced, there is no independent vantage point from which to determine the truth of the doctrinal claim. The brief engagement with the response to these concerns by James Smith highlighted that the fear of relativism should not be used to deny the creaturely nature of doctrinal claims. Doctrine cannot transcend the conditions of creaturehood. Certainly, it is possible for the church to receive some doctrines as "Spirit-led" and ascribe them a certain authority on that basis. But that claim can only be made within the constraints of creaturehood, sanctified creaturehood to be sure. But it still depends on human discernment of, and consensus about, the Spirit's work. That in no way denies the integrity of, or disallows, such a claim about the Spirit to be made. It is simply to note its limits.

On the other hand, to note its limits is not to endorse skepticism. When discussing the plurality of the Reformed Confessions in Chapter 1, some comments of John Webster were quoted, which, in summary, stated that to acknowledge the penultimate nature of doctrinal claims is "worlds apart" from the idea that doctrine is "merely one not very good attempt at pining down a God we cannot really know." Similar issues were raised, albeit in significantly different terms, by Sarah Coakley. Her own insistence that her apophatic commitment to the ongoing "destabilizing" of human knowledge of God was not to be confused with "mere verbal play" or "deferral of meaning." In the same chapter, we also noted Karl Rahner's comments about the "adequacy" of Christian truth claims notwithstanding their "limits." Christian faith confesses that God is known, albeit within the limits of human finitude. As I observed toward the end of Chapter 4, being aware of the promise and the limits of human talk about God involves walking the line walked by Christian theology whenever it seeks simultaneously to acknowledge the givenness of the truth that God is, and the properly human actions of thinking and writing about this truth. The work of Christian doctrine walks this line; doctrine shares in the promise and limits of all Christian talk of God.

This last observation also means that there can be no discussion of the truthfulness of Christian doctrine that separates doctrine from the Bible and its witness to the gospel. At the end of my exposition of Kevin Vanhoozer in Chapter 4, I referred to the order he outlined in his discussion of the historical character of truth: first there was the theo-drama to which the Bible refers, to which, in turn, doctrine refers. There can be no definitive account of doctrine's truthfulness that abstracts it from this matrix or this order. Doctrine does not stand alone, nor can accounts of its truthfulness. Certainly, theologians can develop ad hoc epistemological and metaphysical arguments to explain and defend the truthfulness of doctrine. Doctrinal theologians in particular will contribute to such arguments with attention to, for instance, revelation, pneumatology, and anthropology. These and other doctrines shape the Christian understanding of how Christians speak about God. None of these arguments, however, can ever *secure* the truthfulness of doctrine. When discussing the truthfulness of doctrinal claims, the doctrinal theologian has a particular responsibility to attend to the possibilities and limits of the language and concepts that doctrine employs. In the end, doctrinal work proceeds with the confidence that in the gospel there are realities that can be articulated and communicated.

Conclusion

There is, of course, a term with a long Christian pedigree that illuminates the finitude and limits of human writing and speech about God in their relationship to God. The term is witness. It is a notion that points to the responsiveness of human speech about God. Its metaphorical possibilities lie in the fact that, by definition, it is intentionally not self-referential; it assumes a prior reality to which it is a response. The category of witness is often used to establish the relative status of doctrine and Scripture vis-à-vis each other and Jesus Christ. But here the idea of witness is being invoked in order to draw attention to the *character* it gives to the acts of human writing and speech about God. Of course, so understood, witness properly invites epistemological reflection and ideological alertness. While not ignoring those issues, the positive roles of witness are gathered together in these remarks from Craig Hovey's *Bearing True Witness*:

> In contrast to the kinds of discourses prized by the dispassionate modern mind, witness devotes itself to a wholly different kind of rigor and undertakes a divergent association with what is real. It does not give general accounts of axiomatic truths since such truths (if they indeed are truths) require only reason and no testimony. Attentive to particulars, witness will not police its speech when it cannot make sense of what it sees using reason alone. Nor does it smooth over the rough road of the unforeseen and unpredictable, because these are precisely the things the make it necessary to have witnesses in the first place. Witness reaches for whatever it can in the effort to be true to things that may be either clear or opaque, but especially the latter, things that in their tangled relationships with immense variety in life and the world do not yield easily to explanation.[1]

Doctrine is not a means for any Christian, any theologian, or any church institution to escape those "tangled relationships." Proper recognition of them is a necessary step in allowing doctrine to fulfill its particular vocation in the church's work of bearing witness to the living God.

NOTES

Chapter 1

1. This slogan is associated with the twentieth-century ecumenical movement. On the background to its use and its significance, see Geoffrey Wainwright, "Does Doctrine Still Divide?" *Ecclesiology* 2 (2005): 11–34.
2. Alister E. McGrath, *The Genesis of Doctrine: A Study in the Foundation of Doctrinal Criticism* (Grand Rapids, MI: Eerdmans, 1997), 1.
3. Karl Barth, *CD* I/2, 768–9.
4. See Second Vatican Council, "Dogmatic Constitution on Divine Revelation, *Dei Verbum* 18 November, 1965," sec. 2.10 in *Vatican Council II: The Basic Sixteen Documents: Constitutions, Decrees, Declarations. A Completely Revised Translation in Inclusive Language*, ed. Austin Flannery, O. P. (Northport, NY: Costello, 1996).
5. Christine Helmer, *Theology and the End of Doctrine* (Louisville, KY: WJKP, 2014), 167–8.
6. Ibid., 168.
7. The term "majority world" refers to what is also sometimes spoken of as "the global south." In the context of contemporary Christian theological writing, the relevant term here might also be "world Christianities." I use "majority world" because it captures the fact that the non-Western forms of Christianity being referred to here are located in regions of the world holding the majority of the world's population and that non-Western Christians now outnumber the Christians of Europe, North America, and Australasia.
8. It cannot be pointed out often enough that "Christ" is not a surname. As the English translation of the Greek *christos*, itself a translation of the Hebrew *mashiach*, it is a title given to Jesus of Nazareth.
9. Even if a mission to the Gentiles is a de facto reality by the time the Gospels emerge, those same Gospels bear witness to the ambiguity of Jesus' own engagement with Gentiles (e.g., Mt. 10:5-6; cf. 8:10-12 and 15:21).
10. For an overview of the issues, see Daniel J. Harrington SJ, *The Church According to the New Testament: What the Wisdom and Witness of Early Christianity Teach Us Today* (Chicago, IL: Sheed and Ward, 2001), 159–71.
11. See, e.g., David G. Horrell, "Leadership Patterns and the Development of Ideology in Early Christianity," in *Social-Scientific Approaches to New Testament Interpretation*, ed. David G. Horrell (Edinburgh: T&T Clark, 1999), 309–37.

Notes

12. On the nature of messianism, see Joseph A. Fitzmyer, *The One Who Is to Come* (Grand Rapids, MI: Eerdmans, 2007), especially 82–133. For an overview, see Paul Spilsbury, "Messiah," in *Jesus the Complete Guide*, ed. Leslie Houlden (London: Continuum, 2005), 598–602.
13. See *Didache: The Teaching of the Twelve Apostles* in *The Apostolic Fathers*, vol. 1, trans. Barth D. Ehrman, Loeb Classical Library (Cambridge, MA: Harvard University Press, 2003), 417–43. For the historical and theological background, see Johnathan A. Draper, "The Apostolic Fathers: *The Didache*," *Expository Times* 117 (2006): 177–81.
14. For details of these and other references see Johnathan A. Draper, "The Didache," in *The Writings of the Apostolic Fathers*, ed. Paul Foster (London: T&T Clark, 2007), 13–20 (13).
15. This "Two Ways" tradition is also present in the *Community Rule* of the Essenes. Beyond the *Didache*, its presence in early Christian literature is found in Jesus' teaching on the wide and narrow gates in Mt. 7:13-14 and in the final sections of *The Epistle of Barnabus*. See Draper, "The Didache."
16. *Didache*, 1.
17. See Draper, "The Didache," 17.
18. As Draper notes, the kind of Jewish-Christian communities suggested by the concerns of the *Didache* were "marginalised and even demonized as heretics." See Draper, "The Didache," 20.
19. On this public and "reasonable" aspect of such rules, see Eric Osborn, "Reason and the Rule of Faith in the Second Century AD," in *The Making of Orthodoxy: Essays in Honour of Henry Chadwick*, ed. Rowan Williams (Cambridge: Cambridge University Press, 1989), 41–61.
20. Kathryn Greene-McCreight, "Rule of Faith," in *Dictionary for Theological Interpretation of the Bible*, ed. Kevin J. Vanhoozer (London: SPCK, 2005), 703–4 (703).
21. This translation is by Alister E. McGrath in *The Christian Theology Reader*, 5th ed. (Chichester: Wiley-Blackwell, 2017), 157. A less colloquial translation of this text, set within the full text of the English translation of *The Demonstration*, can be found in Iain M. MacKenzie, *Irenaeus's Demonstration of the Apostolic Preaching: A Theological Commentary and Translation* (Aldershot: Ashgate, 2002), 1–28 (3).
22. See, e.g., St. Irenaeus of Lyon, *Against the Heresies*, 1.1.8 and 2.25.2, Ancient Christian Writers, Nos. 55 (New York: Paulist Press, 1992) and 65 (New York: Newman Press, 2012).
23. Eric Osborn, *Irenaeus of Lyons* (Cambridge: Cambridge University Press, 2001), 160.
24. See Tertullian, *Against Praxeas II*, in *The Ante-Nicence Fathers: Translations of the Fathers down to A.D. 325*, vol 3, American edition (Edinburgh: T&T Clark, 1993).

Notes

25. See ibid., VIII.
26. Stephen R. Holmes, *The Quest for the Trinity: The Doctrine of God in Scripture, History and Modernity* (Downers Grove, IL: IVP Academic, 2012), 81.
27. Access to Arius's own arguments is another dimension of the complexity of this issue. Only a small selection of his writings have survived, and until recently the "Arian" position was assumed to be what his critics, especially Athanasius, claimed it to be. On these matters, and both the ancient and contemporary debates about Arianism, see David Rankin, "Arianism," in *The Early Christian World*, ed. Philip F. Esler (Abingdon: Routledge, 2017), 905–20.
28. "Arius's Letter to Eusebius of Nicomedia," in *The Trinitarian Controversy*, Sources of Early Christian Thought, ed. and trans. William G. Rusch (Philadelphia, PA: Fortress Press, 1980), 30.
29. Frances M. Young, *From Nicea to Chalcedon: A Guide to the Literature and Its Background*, 2nd ed. (London: SCM, 2010), 47.
30. For a discussion of the specifics of Arius's theology and his underlying biblical exegesis, see Rowan Williams, *Arius: Heresy and Tradition*, rev. ed. (Grand Rapids, MI: Eerdmans, 2001), 107–16.
31. On the immediate theological and historical backgrounds to the Council, discussions about the number and identity of the bishops present, and the events which unfolded at their meeting, see Williams, *Arius*, 48–71.
32. Wolfram Kinzig, *Faith in Formulae: A Collection of Early Christian Creeds and Creed-related Texts*, vol. 1, Oxford Early Christian Texts (Oxford: Oxford University Press, 2017), 290–1.
33. See Lewis Ayres, *Nicea and Its Legacy* (Oxford: Oxford University Press, 2004), 93.
34. Holmes, *The Quest for the Trinity*, 88.
35. John Behr, *The Nicene Faith Part 1*, Formation of Christian Theology, vol. 2, (Crestwood, NY: St. Vladimir's Seminary Press, 2002), 27.
36. The *homoians* were so called because of their preference for speaking of the Son being "like," *homoios*, the Father rather than the "same," *homo*.
37. "Athanasius's Orations against the Arians, Book 1," in *The Trinitarian Controversy*, ed. Rusch, 80.
38. Ibid., 116–17. On this, see Frances Young, "The 'Mind' of Scripture: Theological Readings of the Bible in the Fathers," *International Journal of Systematic Theology* 7 (2005): 126–41.
39. Behr, *The Nicene Faith*, 151.
40. Williams, *Arius*, 235.
41. Robert Louis Wilken, *The Spirit of Early Christian Thought: Seeking the Face of God* (New Haven, CT: Yale University Press, 2003), xvi–xvii.
42. See Arthur C. Cochrane, ed., *Reformed Confessions of the Sixteenth Century* (Louisville, KY: WJKP, 2003).

Notes

43. *The Geneva Confession of 1536*, in Cochrane, *Reformed Confessions*, 120.
44. *The Geneva Confession of 1536*, Article 1, in Cochrane, *Reformed Confessions*, 120.
45. *The First Helvetic Confession of* 1536, Article 2, in Cochrane, *Reformed Confessions*, 100.
46. *A Simple Confession and Exposition of the Orthodox Faith: The Second Helvetic Confession of 1566*, chapter 2, in Cochrane, *Reformed Confessions*, 226.
47. Council of Trent, Session 4, "Second Decree: Acceptance of the Latin Vulgate Edition of the Bible; Rule on the Manner of Interpreting Sacred Scripture etc.," in *Decrees of the Ecumenical Councils, vol. 2, Trent to Vatican II*, ed. and trans. Norman P. Tanner SJ (London: Sheed and Ward, 1990), 664.
48. James T. Dennison Jr., "The Westminster Confession of Faith (1646)," in *Reformed Confessions of the 16th and 17th Centuries in English Translation: Vol 4, 1600–1693*, ed. James T. Dennison Jr. (Grand Rapids, MI: Reformation Heritage Books, 2014), 231.
49. "The Westminster Confession of Faith," I.i in Dennison, *Reformed Confessions*, 231–3 (233).
50. Ibid., I.i, 234.
51. Ibid., I.ii, 234.
52. Ibid., I.ii, 235.
53. Ibid.
54. Ibid., I.v, 235.
55. Ibid., I.x, 236.
56. E.g., *The First Helvetic Confession* (1536), *The Lausanne Articles* (1536), *The Geneva Confession* (1536), and *The Second Helvetic Confession* (1566).
57. John Webster, *Word and Church: Essays in Christian Dogmatics* (Edinburgh: T&T Clark, 2001), 9.
58. Shawn Bawulski and Stephen R. Holmes, *Christian Theology: The Classics* (London: Routledge, 2014), 123.
59. On this issue, and for a discussion of what should and should not be included in any such collection (such as his own), see Cochrane's introduction ("Concerning Collections of Reformed Confessions") in his *Reformed Confessions,* 12–31.
60. Dirkie Smit, "Trends and Directions in Reformed Theology," *The Expository Times* 122 (2011): 313–26 (318).
61. Webster, *Confessing God*, 80–1.
62. Ibid., 81.
63. For much of what follows, in addition to the specific references cited, I am significantly indebted to my colleague, Rev. Ockert Meyer, for his unpublished paper presented at a conference in Sydney in 2014, "Basis of Union and the Importance of Creeds."

64. All references to the text of Belhar are to the English translation of the Afrikaans text included in Presbyterian Church (USA), *The Book of Confessions* (Louisville, KY: Office the General Assembly, 2016), 299–306.
65. Belhar, 2
66. Belhar, 3.
67. Belhar, 4.
68. Belhar also drew on earlier and similarly influential confession, namely the 1934 Barmen Declaration of Germany's Confessing Church. See D. J. Smit, "Barmen and Belhar in conversation—a South African perspective," *Nederduitse Gereformeerde Teologiese Tydskrif* 47 (2006), accessed September 11, 2018, http://ojs.reformedjournals.co.za/index.php/ngtt/article/view/1197/1666.
69. The most recent example is that of the Presbyterian Church (USA), which added it to its *The Book of Confessions* in 2016. This follows its adoption by other Reformed churches in North America and the even earlier adoption by churches in Namibia and Belgium.

Chapter 2

1. For a brief summary of Origen's impact, see Joseph W. Trigg, *Origen* (London: Routledge, 1998), 62–6.
2. Ronald E. Heine, *Origen: Scholarship in the Service of the Church* (Oxford: Oxford University Press, 2010), 131.
3. John Behr, "Introduction," in *Princ.*, xvi–lxxxviii (xxix).
4. *Princ.* Pr.1.
5. *Princ.* Pr.2.
6. Ibid.
7. *Princ.* Pr.3.
8. Ibid.
9. Ibid.
10. Ibid.
11. *Princ.* Pr.4.
12. *Princ.* Pr.10. The "precept" quoted here is Hos. 10:12.
13. *Princ.* Pr.4.
14. *Princ.* Pr.10.
15. *Princ.* Pr.8.
16. *Princ.* Pr.9.

Notes

17. For a detailed discussion of these controversies, see Henri Crouzel, *Origen*, trans. A. S. Worrall (Edinburgh: T&T Clark, 1989), 181–204.
18. David Ivan Rankin, *From Clement to Origen: The Social and Historical Context of the Church Fathers* (Aldershot: Ashgate, 2006), 138.
19. Rowan Williams, "Origen," in *The First Christian Theologians: An Introduction to Theology in the Early Church*, ed. G. R. Evans (Malden, MA: Blackwell, 2004), 132–42 (139).
20. Ibid., 139.
21. On this, see the influential modern biography by Peter Brown, *Augustine of Hippo: A Biography*, rev. ed. (Berkeley: University of California Press, 2000).
22. Henry Chadwick notes the following, in relation to the *Confessions*: "Augustine understood his own story as a microcosm of the entire story of the creation, the fall into the abyss of chaos and formlessness, the 'conversion' of the creaturely order to the love of God as it experiences griping pains of homesickness." Henry Chadwick, *Augustine* (Oxford: Oxford University Press, 1986), 86.
23. *Conf.* V.xiv/25.
24. Ibid., XI.xxii/28.
25. For further discussion of these and other issues, see Rowan Williams, *On Augustine* (London: Bloomsbury, 2016).
26. The writing of this text was broken off in 397 and only resumed in 426.
27. *Doctr. Chr.* Preface 1.
28. Ibid., Preface 9.
29. Ibid., Preface 11.
30. Ibid., 1.86
31. Ibid.
32. See ibid., 1.16–23.
33. See ibid., 1.26–29.
34. Ibid., 1.30.
35. The Latin "enchridion" means a short handbook or book of instructions.
36. *Ench.*1,4.
37. Ibid.
38. *Ench.* 31.118.
39. *Faith and the Creed 1*, trans. Michael G. Campbell, OSA, in *The Works of Saint Augustine: A Translation of the 21st Century*, vol. 1/8, ed. Boniface Ramsey (Hyde Park: New City Press, 2005), 155–74 (155).
40. Philipp W. Rosemann, *Peter Lombard* (Oxford: Oxford University Press, 2004), 17.
41. Ibid.
42. Ibid., 18.

Notes

43. According to Rosemann, the technical reading of structured text books replaced the "contemplative and ruminative" styles of reading characteristic of the earlier medieval era. See Philipp W. Rosemann, *The Story of a Great Medieval Book: Peter Lombard's Sentences* (Peterborough, Ontario: Broadview, 2007), 25.
44. Marcia L. Colish, "Peter Lombard," in *The Medieval Theologians: An Introduction to Theology in the Medieval Period*, ed. G. R. Evans (Oxford: Blackwell, 2001), 168–83 (169).
45. *Sentences*, Prologue 2.
46. *Sentences*, Prologue 4.
47. Ibid.
48. *Sentences*, Prologue 5.
49. *Sentences*, Prologue 4.
50. For a helpful summary of the Lombard's own theological emphases, see Colish, "Peter Lombard."
51. *Sentences*, 4, dist. ix, chap. 2.
52. See Rosemann, *The Story of a Great Medieval Book*, 27–52.
53. Ibid., 60-70.
54. See, e.g., this comment by Thomas O'Meara:

    > Too often, Aquinas has been presented in a digest of texts, in boring summaries, or in authoritarian lists of conclusions—and often they offered a static Aristotelianism rather than a vital Christianity … But his theology illustrates the Gospel of Christ, precisely because the gospel is the truth about a real realm, the kingdom of God, a supernatural order to which life points and which revelation expresses.

    Thomas F. O'Meara, OP, *Thomas Aquinas: Theologian* (Notre Dame: University of Notre Dame Press, 1997), 45.
55. *ST* Foreword.
56. *ST* 1a, q1.
57. See *ST* 2a2ae, q1, a8.
58. *ST* 1a, q1, a8.
59. ST 1a, q1, a7.
60. *ST* 1a, q1, a1.
61. *ST* 1a, q1, a8.
62. *ST* 1a, q1, a10.
63. *ST* 1a, q1, a4.
64. Nicholas M. Healy, "Aquinas, Thomas," in *The Cambridge Dictionary of Christian Theology*, ed. Ian McFarland, David A. S. Fergusson, Karen Kilby, and Iain R. Torrance (Cambridge: Cambridge University Press, 2011), 30–1 (31).

Notes

65. Timothy Radcliffe, "Dominican Spirituality," in *The Cambridge Companion to The Summa Theologiae*, ed. Philip McCosker and Denys Turner (Cambridge: Cambridge University Press, 2016), 23–33 (27).
66. Ibid., 26.
67. The others being Hildegard of Bingen (1098–1179), Terese of Avila (1500–1569), and Thérèse of Lisieux (1873–1897).
68. In particular, see Tina Beattie, *Theology after Postmodernity: Divining the Void—A Lacanian Reading of Thomas Aquinas* (Oxford: Oxford University Press, 2013), 365–87.
69. For summary accounts of her life and wide-ranging influence, see Carolyn Muessig, "Introduction," in *A Companion to Catherine of Siena*, ed. Carolyn Muessig, George Ferozogo, and Beverly Mayne Kienzle (Leiden: Brill, 2012), 1–21; Guiliana Cavallini, OP, *Catherine of Siena* (London: Geoffrey Chapman, 1998); and Suzanne Noffke, OP, "Introduction," in *Catherine of Sienna: The Dialogue*, trans. Suzanne Noffke, OP (London: SPCK, 1980), 1–11. For recent overviews of her theology and its reception, see the various essays in Muessig et al., *A Companion*.
70. *Dialogue* 1.
71. Cited from Caffarini's *Processus* in Susan Noffke, OP, "Introduction," in *Dialogue*, 1–22 (13–14).
72. *Dialogue* 25.
73. *Dialogue* 26.
74. Ibid.
75. Ibid.
76. *Dialogue* 27.
77. *Dialogue* 29.
78. Ibid.
79. Ibid.
80. Karen Scott, "Mystical Death, Bodily Death: Catherine of Sienna and Raymond of Capua on the Mystic's Encounter with God," in *Gendered Voices: Medieval Saints and Their Interpreters*, ed. Catherine M. Mooney (Philadelphia: University of Pennsylvania Press, 1999), 135–67 (143), cited in Beattie, *Theology after Postmodernity*, 369.
81. Beattie, *Theology after Postmodernity*, 370.
82. See, e.g., Randall Zachman, *John Calvin as Teacher, Pastor and Theologian: The Shape of His Writing and Thought* (Grand Rapids, MI: Baker, 2006).
83. John Calvin, "John Calvin to the Reader," in *Inst.*, 3–5 (3).
84. Cited in John T. McNeill, "Introduction," in *Inst.*, xxix–lxxi (xxxiii). Italics in original.
85. John Calvin, "Prefatory Address to King Francis I of France," in *Inst.*, 9–31 (9–10).

86. Calvin, "John Calvin to the Reader," 4.
87. Zachman, *John Calvin*, 101.
88. Ibid., 100.
89. *Inst.* I.vii.4.
90. *Inst.* I.vv.4.
91. *Inst.* IV.viii.9.
92. *Inst.* IV.viii.10.
93. *Inst.* IV.viii.9.
94. *Inst.* I.ix.1.
95. *Inst.* I.ix.2.
96. Murray Rae, "Calvin on the Authority of Scripture," in *Calvin: The Man and the Legacy*, ed. Murray Rae, Peter Matheson, and Brett Knowles (Adelaide: ATF Theology, 2014), 79–96 (84).
97. *Inst.* I.i.1.
98. *Inst.* I.xviii.4.
99. As noted in Chapter 1. See John Webster, *Holy Scripture: A Dogmatic Sketch*, Current Issues in Theology (Cambridge: Cambridge University Press, 2003).
100. The Enlightenment critique of Christianity will be discussed in more detail in the following chapter.
101. See Immanuel Kant, *Critique of Pure Reason*, ed. and trans. Paul Guyer and Allen W. Wood, The Cambridge Edition of the Works of Immanuel Kant (Cambridge: Cambridge University Press, 1998), 354–65.
102. Friedrich Schleiermacher, *On Religion: Speeches to Its Cultured Despisers* (Cambridge: Cambridge University Press, 1988), 102.
103. Ibid.
104. Ibid., 136.
105. Ibid.
106. For a survey of the history of the text's reception, see Richard Crouter, *Friedrich Schleiermacher: Between Enlightenment and Romanticism* (Cambridge: Cambridge University Press, 2005), 248–70.
107. For consistency with my use of the 2015 English translation by Terrence Tice et al., I follow the translators' omission of the definite article in the title of the recent English translation of *Der christliche Glaube*. For the reasons for this omission, see Terrence Tice et al., "Concerning This Translation," *CF*, vol. 1, xix–xxv (xxii).
108. *CF* §11. For a discussion of how redemption shapes the whole structure of *Christian Faith* and the understanding of doctrine presented in it, see Dietrich Korsch, "Dogmatics of Redemption: The Nature and Status of Christian Doctrine within the *Glaubenslehre*," in *Schleiermacher, the Study of Religion,*

and the Future of Theology: A Transatlantic Dialogue, ed. Brent W. Sockness and Wilhelm Gräb (Berlin: Walter de Gruyter, 2010), 179–88.

109. *CF* §15. Note that *Gemützustände* is related to the *Gefühl* of *The Speeches* and likewise points to the comprehensiveness of the human encounter with God, although here it is more directly related to the Christian experience of redemption.

110. *CF* §16.

111. *CF* §11.2.

112. Walter E. Wyman Jr., "The Cognitive Status of the Religious Consciousness," in *Schleiermacher, the Study of Religion, and the Future of Theology: A Transatlantic Dialogue*, ed. Brent W. Sockness and Wilhelm Gräb (Berlin: Walter de Gruyter, 2010), 189–202 (195).

113. *CF* §15.2.

114. Helmer, *Theology and the End of Doctrine*, 134.

115. *CF* §16.3.

116. *CF* §16.Postscript.

117. Ibid.

118. See *CF* §17.2.

119. *CF* §17.2.

120. *CF* §18.1.

121. Ibid.

122. *CF* §19.

123. *CF* §19.3.

124. *CF* §17.1.

125. *CF* §129.

126. *CF* §129.2.

127. See, e.g., Paul T. Nimmo, "Schleiermacher on Scripture and the Work of Jesus Christ," *International Journal of Systematic Theology* 31 (2015): 61–90. Drawing particular attention to the late appearance of Scripture in *CF*, Nimmo worries that the preceding doctrines have emerged from the religious self-consciousness abstracted from Scripture (see 73). He also draws attention to Schleiermacher's disregard of the Old Testament, by any measure a major problem (Nimmo describes it as "aporetic" (75)) for any doctrine of Scripture.

128. *CF* §170.1.

129. He sees a need for further consideration of the issues at stake in the classical disputes between the Sabellian and Athanasian positions. See *CF* §172.3.

130. *CF* §170.1.

131. See Francis Schüssler Fiorenza, "Schleiermacher's understanding of God as triune," in *The Cambridge Companion to Friedrich Schleiermacher*, ed. Jacqueline Marina (Cambridge: Cambridge University Press, 2005), 151–70.

132. Karl Barth, *The Epistle to the Romans*, 6th ed. (London: Oxford University Press, 1968), 318.
133. For the English translation of The Theological Declaration of Barmen (1934), see Cochrane, *Reformed Confessions*, 332–6.
134. See Christiane Tietz, "Karl Barth and Charlotte von Kirschbaum," *Theology Today* 74.2 (2017): 86–111.
135. In particular see Bruce L. McCormack, *Karl Barth's Critically Realistic Dialectical Theology: Its Genesis and Development* (Oxford: Clarendon, 1995); and John Webster, *Barth's Earlier Theology: Four Studies* (London: T&T Clark, 2005).
136. Barth's comments on Schleiermacher are extensive but are most accessible in his *The Theology of Schleiermacher: Lecturers at Göttingen, Winter Semester 1923/24* (Grand Rapids, MI: Eerdmans, 1982).
137. Karl Barth, *The Word of God and the Word of Man*, trans. Douglas Horton (New York: Harper & Row), 196.
138. On this reading of Barth, see Bruce. L. McCormack, *Orthodox and Modern: Studies in the Theology of Karl Barth* (Grand Rapids, MI: Baker, 2008), 21–39.
139. *CD* I/1, 88–124.
140. See *Inst.* III.xxi. According to Calvin, God's will for human is twofold: some humans are eternally predestined to salvation and some to damnation. In Barth's hands, God's single will to save all reflects God's unified being, which is love.
141. *CD* II/1, 11.
142. *CD* III/2, x.
143. For helpful diagrammatic presentations of this structure and commentary upon it, see Eberhard Jüngel, *Karl Barth: A Theological Legacy* (Philadelphia, PA: Westminster, 1986), 47–8; and Paul T. Nimmo, *Barth: A Guide for the Perplexed* (London: Bloomsbury T&T Clark, 2017), 111.
144. *CD* IV/3, 136.
145. *CD* II/1, 861–9.
146. *CD* I/2, 862.
147. *CD* I/2, 867.
148. *CD* I/2, 869.
149. William Stacy Johnson, *The Mystery of God: Karl Barth and the Postmodern Foundations of Theology* (Louisville, KY: WJKP, 1997), 33. Stacey's discussion of this metaphor helpfully locates it in the context of a different but similar metaphor used by Barth in his earlier works.
150. *CD* I/2, 768–9.
151. *CD* I/2, 868.

Notes

152. Karl Barth, *Evangelical Theology: An Introduction* (Grand Rapids, MI: Eerdmans, 1963), 166.
153. *CD* I/1, xv.
154. *CD* I/1, 277.
155. *CD* I/1, 280.
156. *CD* I/1, 281.
157. *CD* I/2, 860.
158. *CD* 1/2, 870.
159. *CD* I/1, 16.
160. On Barth's *use* of the Bible, see David F. Ford, *God and Barth's Story: Biblical Narrative and the Theological Method of Karl Barth in the Church Dogmatics* (Frankfurt: Peter Lang, 1985).
161. Joseph L. Mangina, *Karl Barth: Theologian of Christian Witness* (Louisville, KY: WJKP, 2004), 48.
162. Karl Rahner, *Foundations of Christian Faith: An Introduction to the Idea of Christianity* (New York: Crossroad, 1978).
163. Karl Raher and Adolf Darlap, eds., *Sacramentum Mundi: An Encyclopaedia of Theology*, 6 vols. (London: Burns and Oates, 1968–70); and Karl Rahner and Herbert Vorgrimler, *Theological Dictionary* (New York: Herder and Herder, 1965).
164. The German title is *Schriften zur Theologie*, which ostensibly is less exploratory than *Investigations*, but the latter is consistent with the overall nature of the contents.
165. "Nature and Grace," *TI* IV, 165–88 (177).
166. Ibid.
167. "Observations on the Problem of the 'Anonymous Christian'," *TI* XIV, 280–94 (288).
168. Ibid.
169. "The Concept of Mystery in Catholic Theology," *TI* IV, 54–5.
170. For overviews of these matters, see Karen Kilby, *Karl Rahner: A Brief Introduction* (New York: Herder and Herder, 1997); and Thomas F. O'Meara, OP, *God in the World: A Guide to Rahner's Theology* (Collegeville, PA: Liturgical, 2007).
171. On this, see Karen Kilby, *Karl Rahner: Theology and Philosophy* (London: Routledge, 2004), especially 70–144, and also some brief remarks in Mark F. Fischer, *The Foundations of Karl Rahner: A Paraphrase of the Foundation of Christian Faith with Introduction and Indices* (New York: Herder and Herder, 2004), vii–xxvii.
172. See especially "Anonymous Christians," *TI* IV, 390–8, and "Atheism and Implicit Christianity," *TI* IV, 145–64.

173. "The Prospects for Dogmatic Theology," *TI* I, 1–19.
174. Ibid., 4.
175. Ibid., 6.
176. Ibid., 9.
177. Ibid., 12.
178. Ibid., 15.
179. "The Development of Dogma," *TI* I, 39–77.
180. Ibid., 39.
181. Ibid., 42.
182. Ibid., 42.
183. Ibid., 45.
184. Ibid.
185. Ibid., 43–4.
186. Ibid., 42.
187. Ibid.
188. Ibid., 75.
189. Ibid., 76.
190. Ibid., 77.
191. Part of these controversies is the role of the papacy in the magisterium. Rahner's thoughts on this relationship can be traced in his *Foundations*, 378–87.
192. A much more detailed example of how Rahner systematically orders doctrinal topics is his essay, "A Scheme for a Treatise of Dogmatic Theology," *TI* I, 19–39.
193. Rahner, *Foundations*, 448.
194. Ibid., 449.
195. Ibid.
196. Ibid., 450.
197. Ibid., 451.
198. Ibid., 453.
199. See ibid., 454–9, for the creeds and his comments upon them.
200. Ibid., 454.
201. For some of the discussion, see Janice McRandal, "Sarah Coakley and the Future of Systematic Theology," *Pacifica* 24.3 (2011): 300–14; Lin Marie Tonstad, *God and Difference: The Trinity, Sexuality, and the Transformation of Finitude* (New York: Routledge, 2016), 98–132.

Notes

202. Sarah Coakley, *God, Sexuality and the Self: An Essay "On the Trinity"* (Cambridge: Cambridge University Press, 2013), xv.
203. Ibid.
204. Ibid., 89.
205. Ibid., 90.
206. Ibid.
207. Ibid., 41.
208. Ibid., 90.
209. Ibid., 41.
210. Ibid.
211. Ibid.
212. Ibid., 42.
213. See ibid., 43.
214. Ibid., 51.
215. Ibid., 48.
216. For some lines of criticism, see Michael Allen, "Dogmatics as Aesthetics," in *The Task of Dogmatics: Explorations in Theological Method*, ed. Oliver D. Crisp and Fred Sanders (Grand Rapids, MI: Zondervan, 2017), 194–5.
217. Coakley, *God, Sexuality and the Self*, 45–6.
218. Ibid.
219. Ibid.
220. Sarah Coakley in an interview with Rupert Shortt in his *God's Advocates: Christian Thinkers in Conversation* (London: DLT, 2005), 71.
221. Allen, "Dogmatics as Aesthetics," 193.
222. Tonstad, *God and Difference*, 108.
223. See Anthony C. Thiselton, *The Hermeneutics of Doctrine* (Grand Rapids, MI: Eerdmans, 2007), 137–41, and more generally the whole of chapter 7 (119–43), which is developed under the theme of "coherence and polyphony."
224. Ibid., 139.
225. Ibid., 141.
226. Gale Heide, *Timeless Truths in the Hands of History: A Short History of System in Theology* (Eugene, OR: Pickwick, 2012).
227. The center of the story Heide tells is the place given to rationality in Kant and Hegel (ibid., 147–85) and the way the work of these two figures influenced modern theology. While acknowledging the rejection of such understandings of rationality in Kierkegaard and Barth, Heide is not so sanguine about the turn to existentialism and narrative associated with them. Heide believes that both sit too lightly to the proper place of system in Christian theology.

Notes

Chapter 3

1. Dorinda Outram, *The Enlightenment: New Approaches to European History*, 3rd ed. (Cambridge: Cambridge University Press, 2013), 42.
2. Gertrude Himmelfarb, *The Roads to Modernity: The British, French and American Enlightenments* (New York: Vintage, 2008), 20. In a summary of their respective distinctive features she writes, "The British Enlightenment represents the 'sociology of virtue', the French the 'ideology of reason', the American 'the politics of liberty'" (19).
3. Immanuel Kant, "What Is Enlightenment," in *The Enlightenment: A Sourcebook and Reader*, ed. Paul Hyland, Olga Gomez, and Francesca Greensides (London: Routledge, 2003), 54–8 (54).
4. Ibid., 58.
5. Ibid.
6. For much of the following, see Alister E. McGrath, *The Genesis of Doctrine: A Study in the Foundation of Doctrinal Criticism* (Grand Rapids, MI: Eerdmans, 1990), 145–51.
7. G. E. Lessing, "On the Proof of the Power of the Spirit," in *Lessing's Theological Writings*, ed. H. Chadwick (Stanford, CA: Stanford University Press, 1956), 51–6 (53).
8. Adolf von Harnack, *Outlines of the History of Dogma*, trans. Edwin Knox Mitchell (London: Hodder and Stoughton, 1893), 5.
9. Ibid.
10. Ibid., 7.
11. Ibid., 8.
12. For further on these matters, see Alister E. McGrath, *The Making of Modern German Christology 1750–1990*, 2nd ed. (Apollos: Leicester, 1994), 89–98.
13. As used here, "the study of Jesus" is shorthand for the attention given to Jesus in such disciplines as New Testament Studies, Historical Jesus Studies, and the study of Christian Origins.
14. Jürgen Moltmann, *The Theology of Hope: On the Ground and Implications of a Christian Eschatology*, trans. James Leitch (London: SCM, 1967).
15. Jürgen Moltmann, *The Crucified God: The Cross of Christ as the Foundation and Criticism of Christian Theology*, trans. R. A Wilson and John Bowden (London: SCM, 1974).
16. Jürgen Moltmann, *The Way of Jesus Christ: Christology in Messianic Dimensions*, trans. Margaret Kohl (London: SCM, 1990).
17. Ibid., 137.
18. Ibid., 136.
19. Ibid.

Notes

20. Ibid.
21. Ibid., 138.
22. Ibid., 150.
23. Ibid.
24. For discussions of these and other matters, see Richard Bauckham (ed.), *God Will Be All in All: The Eschatology of Jürgen Moltmann* (Minneapolis, MN: Fortress, 2001); and Richard Bauckham, *The Theology of Jürgen Moltmann* (Edinburgh: T&T Clark, 1994), especially 199–212.
25. For a brief overview of the deeply problematic treatment of gender in Enlightenment thought but also the appropriation of Enlightenment rhetoric by early advocates of women's rights, see Outram, *The Enlightenment*, 84–98.
26. For a helpful summary of these issues, see Janice McRandal, *Christian Doctrine and the Grammar of Difference: A Contribution to Feminist Systematic Theology* (Minneapolis, MN: Fortress, 2015), 1–18.
27. See *CD* I/1, 209–304.
28. See Karl Rahner, *The Trinity*, trans. Joseph Donceel (New York: Crossroad, 1997), 10–15.
29. Elizabeth A. Johnson, *She Who Is: The Mystery of God in Feminist Theological Discourse* (New York: Crossroad, 1996).
30. Ibid., 17.
31. Ibid., 10.
32. Ibid., 105.
33. Ibid., 200.
34. Ibid., 193.
35. Ibid., 21.
36. Ibid., 199.
37. See ibid., 194–7.
38. Ibid., 213–14.
39. Ibid., 218.
40. Ibid., 223.
41. Ibid., 219.
42. Ibid., 215.
43. For a discussion of such concerns, precisely in relation to Johnson's work, see Veli-Matti Kärkkäinen, *The Trinity: Global Perspectives* (Louisville, KY: WJKP, 2007), 208–10.
44. Johnson, *She Who Is*, 211.
45. See Cherith Fee Nordling, *Knowing God by Name: A Conversation between Elizabeth A. Johnson and Karl Barth* (New York: Peter Lang, 2010), especially 250–61. Nordling's critique is very detailed and raises important questions

about the revisionist nature of Johnson's work and many of her underlying assumptions.

46. For a summary, see Moltmann, *The Way of Jesus Christ*, 274–80.

47. Although drawing directly on the English writings and translations of these two theologians, I am also indebted for what follows to the following literature: Edmond Tang, "The Cosmic Christ—the Search for a Chinese Theology," *Studies in World Christianity* 1 (1995): 131–42; Miika Ruokanen, "K.H. Ting's Contribution to the Contextualization of Christianity in China," *Modern Theology* 25 (2009): 107–22; Alexander Chow, "Wang Weifan's Cosmic Christ," *Modern Theology* 32 (2016): 384–96; Wen Ge, "The Cosmic Christ and China: An Exploration of Bishop K.H. Ting's Legacy of Contextual China," *Ny Mission* 25 (2013): 72–89; and Yongtau Chen, *The Chinese Christology of T.C. Chao* (Leiden: Brill, 2017), 293–309.

48. Reported in Tang, "The Cosmic Christ," 136.

49. K. H. Ting, *Love Never Ends: Papers by K. H. Ting*, ed. Janice Wickeri (Nanjing: Yilin, 2000), 408.

50. E.g., Col. 1:15-20; Eph. 1:20-23; Jn 1:1-14; and Heb. 1:1-4.

51. Ting, *Love Never Ends*, 144.

52. Ibid., 145.

53. Ibid., 144.

54. Ibid., 413.

55. Ibid., 145.

56. Ibid., 415.

57. See ibid., 409. Ting's willingness to critique Christologies produced by the Enlightenment is overlooked in Simon Chan's inclusion of Ting among several Asian theologians who, he says, engaged in "uncritical assimilation of Enlightenment epistemology and the resultant lack of theological discernment." Simon Chan, *Grassroots Asian Theology: Thinking the Faith from the Ground Up* (Downers Grove, IL: IVP Academic, 2014), 24.

58. Ting, *Love Never Ends*, 418.

59. Wang Weifan, "Chinese Theology and Its Cultural Sources," *Chinese Theological Review* 11 (1995): 44–8 (45).

60. For a brief discussion of this reference, see Chow, "Wang Weifan's Cosmic Christ," 386.

61. See Archie Lee, "Contextual Theology in East Asia," in *The Modern Theologians: An Introduction to Christian Theology since 1918*, ed. David F. Ford and Rachel Muers, 3rd ed. (Oxford: Blackwell, 2005), 518–34 (526–8).

62. See his summary in Wang Weifan, "Chinese Traditional Culture and Its Influence on Chinese Theological Reflection," *Chinese Theological Review* 13 (1999): 1–11 (1–4).

Notes

63. Wang Weifan, "The Word Was Here Made Flesh," *Chinese Theological Review* 8 (1993): 92–9 (94).
64. Wang, "Chinese Traditional Culture," 7.
65. Wang, "Chinese Theology and Its Cultural Sources," 45.
66. Ibid.
67. Ibid., 48.
68. Wang, "The Word Was Here Made Flesh," 95.
69. Certainly there are other Chinese theologians who do make foundationalist appeals to traditional Chinese religions and traditions. For an overview of other Chinese developments of Cosmic Christology, see Tang, "The Cosmic Christ." Wang is more subtle. As Alexander Chow notes, Wang's appeal to *shengshen* is "not so much formulated as a mystery of Christ behind other religions as it is about how other religious and philosophical traditions can guide the articulation of Christian faith and theology" (Chow, "Wang Wiefan's Cosmic Christ," 394).
70. Joachim Gentz, *Understanding Chinese Religions* (Edinburgh: Dunedin, 2013), 45.
71. See Robert Eric Frykenberg, *Christianity in India: From Beginnings to the Present*, Oxford History of the Christian Church (Oxford: Oxford University Press, 2008), 92–115.
72. Hielke T. Wolters, "M. M. Thomas and the Pilgrimage of Justice and Peace," in *The Life, Legacy and Theology of M. M. Thomas: "Only Participants Earn the Right to be Prophets,"* ed. Jesudas Atyhyal, George Zachariah, and Monica Melancthon (London: Routledge, 2016), 61–81 (77).
73. In the preface to his *The Acknowledged Christ of the Indian Renaissance* (London: SCM, 1969), M. M. Thomas declares both his innocence "of any ambition to be a systematic theologian" and that his reflections on the "truth of Jesus Christ … in concrete situations of history" are "fragmentary and unsystematic, but they constitute living theology" (ix).
74. M. M. Thomas, *Salvation and Humanization: Some Crucial Issues of the Theology of Mission in Contemporary India* (Bangalore: CLS, 1971), 1–19.
75. Jesudas M. Athyal, "M. M. Thomas's Theology of Society: An Overview," in *Life, Legacy and Theology of M. M. Thomas*, ed. Athyal, Zachariah, and Melancthon, 9–29 (10).
76. Thomas, *Salvation and Humanization*, 2.
77. Ibid., 8.
78. Ibid.
79. Ibid., 8–9.
80. Ibid., 10.
81. Ibid.

Notes

82. Ibid., 18.
83. Ibid.
84. Ibid. 14.
85. E.g., Santano K. Patro, "Locating 'Humanisation of M. M. Thomas in Feminist Hermeneutics," in *Reclaiming Manyness: Re-Reading M.M. Thomas in the Light of Indian Christian Theologies*, ed. P. G George and Y. T. Vinayaraj (Serampore: Department of Research, South Asian Theological Research Institute, 2015), 48–66.
86. On these issues, see Peter Harrison, *The Territories of Science and Religion* (Chicago, IL: University of Chicago Press, 2014).
87. See Adrian Thatcher, *Redeeming Gender* (Oxford: Oxford University Press, 2016), 11–112.
88. Megan K. DeFranza, *Sex Difference in Christian Theology: Male, Female and Intersex in the Image of God* (Grand Rapids, MI: Eerdmans, 2015).
89. Ibid., 24.
90. See ibid., 23–67, for her discussion of scientific data and the response by intersex people.
91. Ibid., 9.
92. Ibid.
93. Ibid., 83.
94. Ibid., 104.
95. Ibid., 105.
96. Ibid., 161.
97. Ibid., 238.
98. Ibid., 177.
99. Ibid.
100. Ibid.
101. Ibid., 169.
102. Ibid., 238.
103. Ibid., 286.
104. Two alternatives are common. One is to use scientific data in order to accept gender diversity as a theologically neutral natural variable and therefore subordinated to more theologically defined notions of relationality. The other is to insist on the male–female gender binary and to deem any nonbinary sex or gender, regardless of its scientific explanation, as a pathology consequent upon the fall.
105. Kathryn Tanner, *Theories of Culture: A New Agenda for Theology* (Minneapolis, MN: Fortress, 1997), 117.

Notes

106. Nicolas Lash, *Believing Three Ways in One God: A Reading of the Apostles' Creed* (London: SCM, 1992), 33.

Chapter 4

1. Ronald T. Michener, *Postliberal Theology: A Guide for the Perplexed* (London: Bloomsbury, 2013), 3.
2. Many of these issues are discussed and analyzed in Paul J. DeHart, *The Trial of the Witnesses: The Rise and Decline of Postliberal Theology* (Oxford: Blackwell, 2006), especially 32–41; and John Allan Knight, *Liberalism Versus Postliberalism: The Great Divide in Twentieth-Century Theology* (Oxford: Oxford University Press, 2013), especially 155–224. For a quite specific critique of Lindbeck's particular dependence on nontheological resources, see Mike Higton, "Frei's Christology and Lindbeck's Cultural-Linguistic Theory," *Scottish Journal of Theology* 50 (1997): 83–95. Nevertheless, see Higton's more recent defense of the *theological* character of Lindbeck's project, "George Lindbeck and the Christological Nature of Doctrine," *Criswell Theological Review* 13.1 (2015): 47–61.
3. For a critical study of the priority of the ecumenical context of *The Nature of Doctrine*, see Mike Higton, "Reconstructing the Nature of Doctrine," *Modern Theology* 30 (2014): 1–31.
4. George A. Lindbeck, *Religion and Theology in a Postliberal Age* (Philadelphia: Westminster, 1984), 16, 21.
5. Ibid., 18.
6. Ibid., 39.
7. Ibid., 22.
8. Ibid., 33.
9. Simeon Zahl, "On the Affective Salience of Doctrines," *Modern Theology* 31 (2015): 428–44 (429).
10. E.g., Zahl, "On the Affective Salience," and Medi Ann Volpe, *Rethinking Christian Identity: Doctrine and Discipleship* (Chichester: Wiley-Blackwell, 2013), both of whom critique but seek to build on Lindbeck. A more extensive account of the practice- and emotion-forming role of doctrine, although not developed in dialogue with Lindbeck, is Ellen T. Charry, *By the Renewing of Your Minds: The Pastoral Function of Christian Doctrine* (Oxford: Oxford University Press, 1997). The contributions of Zahl, Volpe, and Charry will be taken up later in this book.
11. Lindbeck, *The Nature of Doctrine*, 51.
12. See ibid., 64.
13. Ibid.
14. Ibid., 65.

15. Ibid.
16. Ibid., 66.
17. Ibid., 68.
18. Ibid., 94.
19. Ibid., 114–15.
20. Ibid., 116.
21. Ibid., 117.
22. Ibid., 118.
23. Ibid., 33.
24. For the idea of realistic narratives, Lindbeck draws on Hans Frei, *The Eclipse of Biblical Narrative: A Study in Eighteenth and Nineteenth Century Hermeneutics* (New Haven, CT: Yale University Press, 1974).
25. Lindbeck, *The Nature of Doctrine*, 120.
26. Ibid., 120.
27. See especially the discussion in ibid., 121–3.
28. Ibid., 121.
29. Ibid.
30. For a more extensive, and slightly more sympathetic, account of Lindbeck's engagement with the Bible, see Higton, "George Lindbeck and the Christological Nature of Doctrine," 50–1.
31. McGrath, *Genesis of Doctrine*, 28.
32. Kevin J. Vanhoozer, *The Drama of Doctrine: A Canonical-Linguistic Approach to Christian Theology* (Louisville, KY: WJKP, 2005).
33. Ibid., 17.
34. Ibid., 39.
35. Ibid., 65. Employing categories developed by the Swiss Catholic theologian Hans Urs von Balthasar (1905–1988) and before him German philosopher G. W. F. Hegel (1770–1831), Vanhoozer develops the dramatic theme through its distinction from "epic" and "lyric" (83–102).
36. The theological legitimacy of the appeal to speech act theory is encapsulated in this claim: "God's communicative acts include both deed-words like the cross and speech-acts like the canon" (66). For a further account on the theoretical background to speech act theory, see J. L. Austin, *How to Do Things with Words*, 2nd ed., ed. J. O. Urmson and Marina Sbsià (Cambridge, MA: Harvard University Press, 1975).
37. Anthony C. Thiselton, *The Hermeneutics of Doctrine* (Grand Rapids, MI: Eerdmans, 2007), 77–8.
38. Vanhoozer, *The Drama of Doctrine*, 102.

Notes

39. Ibid., 107. Italics in original. Vanhoozer makes extensive use of italics. All italics in the quotations that follow are in the original.
40. Ibid., 106.
41. Ibid., 67.
42. Ibid., 226.
43. Ibid.
44. Ibid., 227–8.
45. Ibid., 228.
46. Ibid.
47. Ibid., 229.
48. Ibid.
49. Ibid., 237.
50. Ibid., 453.
51. Ibid.
52. Ibid.
53. Ibid.
54. Ibid., 452.
55. Ibid., 216.
56. Ibid., 237.
57. See ibid., 168.
58. Ibid., 424.
59. Ibid.
60. Ibid.
61. Ibid., 205.
62. Ibid., 204.
63. Thiselton, *The Hermeneutics of Doctrine*, 77.
64. Vanhoozer, *The Drama of Doctrine*, 227. See also his specific engagement with the issue of diverse New Testament theologies in his "Is the Theology of the New Testament One or Many? Between (the Rock) of Systematic Theology and (the Hard Place of) Historical Occasionalism," in *Reconsidering the Relationship between Biblical and Systematic Theology in the New Testament*, ed. Benjamin E. Reynolds, Brian Lugioyo, and Kevin J. Vanhoozer (Tübingen: Mohr Siebeck, 2014), 16–37. Even in this essay, while the diversity of theologies is fully acknowledged, the impulse, I believe, is to affirm a unity that underplays the significance and character of the diversity.
65. E.g., in a discussion about the kind of realism suggested by the canon: "Some forms are more adequate for communicating or rendering a certain content than others." Vanhoozer, *Drama of Doctrine*, 290.

66. Mark G. Brett, *Political Trauma and Healing: Biblical Ethics for a Postcolonial World* (Grand Rapids, MI: Eerdmans, 2016), 71–2.
67. Vanhoozer, *The Drama of Doctrine*, 89.
68. Ibid., 100.
69. Ibid., 101.
70. Ibid.
71. Christine Helmer, *Theology and the End of Doctrine* (Louisville, KY: WJKP, 2014).
72. Ibid., 131–2.
73. See ibid., 1.
74. Ibid., 15.
75. Ibid., 19. This is a slightly problematic formulation since it implies that language is distinct from reality, which is exactly the opposite of Helmer's constructive position (as will be seen). Her legitimate concern in this particular remark might be better stated as a concern that doctrinal language has been presented as the sole and truncated point of access to God's reality.
76. Ibid., 7.
77. Ibid., 55.
78. Ibid.
79. Ibid., 105. The specific proposal that draws this particular charge, and that is presented as emblematic of the entire problem, is that of Lindbeck's erstwhile student, Bruce Marshall, in his book *Trinity and Truth* (Cambridge: Cambridge University Press, 2000).
80. Ibid., 105.
81. See ibid., 134.
82. See ibid., 165.
83. See ibid., 137.
84. See ibid., 137–8.
85. Ibid., 164.
86. Ibid., 152.
87. Ibid., 151.
88. Ibid., 167.
89. Ibid., 139.
90. Ibid., 140.
91. Ibid., 141.
92. Ibid., 126.
93. Ibid., 128.
94. Ibid.
95. Ibid., 131.

Notes

96. Ibid., 122.
97. Ibid., 146.
98. Ibid., 135.
99. See ibid., 117.
100. James K. A. Smith, *Who's Afraid of Relativism? Community, Contingency and Creaturehood* (Grand Rapids, MI: Baker, 2014), 180.
101. Ibid.

Chapter 5

1. Sameer Yadav, "Christian Doctrine as Ontological Commitment to a Narrative," in *The Task of Dogmatics: Explorations in Theological Method*, ed. Oliver D. Crisp and Fred Sanders (Grand Rapids, MI: Zondervan, 2017), 70–86 (85–6).
2. Ibid., 86.
3. James W. McClendon, *Doctrine: Systematic Theology*, vol. 2 (Waco, TX: Baylor University Press, 2012), 29. Alasdair McIntyre's influential definition of practice also lies in the background here. See Alasdair McIntyre, *After Virtue*, 3rd ed. (London: Duckworth, 2007), 187.
4. Charles Taylor, *A Secular Age* (Cambridge, MA: Belknap, 2007), 171.
5. Ibid.
6. Ibid., 172.
7. Ibid., 173.
8. Ibid., 172.
9. Ibid.
10. Ibid., 173.
11. Ibid., 176. The change he describes is that from a social imaginary in which "it was virtually impossible not to believe in God" to one where "many of us find this not only easy but inescapable" (25). It was a shift from an "enchanted world" to an "immanent frame" (see 539–43).
12. Benedict Anderson, *Imagined Communities: Reflections on the Origin and Spread of Nationalism* (London: Verso, 1983), 15, cited in Douglas Hedley, *Living Forms of the Imagination* (London: T&T Clark, 2008), 246, in Hedley's own discussion of Taylor. For Taylor's own engagement with Anderson, see *A Secular Age*, 208–9, 713.
13. Taylor, *A Secular Age*, 173.
14. Ibid.
15. Ibid.
16. Ibid.

17. Ibid.
18. Ibid., 172.
19. Thiselton, *The Hermeneutics of Doctrine*, 97. This claim comes at the end of a chapter (81–97) where Thiselton surveys the various thinkers and intellectual movements that lie behind this current intellectual climate. He draws especially on the work Ludwig Wittgenstein (1889–1951), Hans Georg Gadamer (1900–2002), and Paul Ricoeur (1913–2005). He also engages extensively with Wittgenstein in an earlier chapter (19–26).
20. Don S. Browning, *A Fundamental Practical Theology: Descriptive and Strategic Proposals* (Minneapolis, MN: Fortress, 1996), 3.
21. Ellen T. Charry, *By the Renewing of Your Minds: The Pastoral Function of Christian Doctrine* (New York: Oxford University Press, 1997), 237.
22. Ibid., 19.
23. Ibid., 229.
24. Ibid., 211.
25. Ibid., 4.
26. Thiselton, *The Hermeneutics of Doctrine*, 19.
27. Ibid., 31.
28. H. H. Price, *Belief* (London: Allen & Unwin, 1969), 293, quoted in Thiselton, *The Hermeneutics of Doctrine*, 31.
29. Medi Ann Volpe, *Rethinking Christian Identity: Doctrine and Discipleship* (Chichester: Wiley-Blackwell, 2013).
30. Ibid., 13.
31. Ibid., 234.
32. Ibid., 236.
33. Ibid., 10.
34. Ibid., 224.
35. Ibid., 217.
36. Zahl, "Affective Salience," 431.
37. Specifically Augustine, Gregory of Nyssa, Calvin, the Council of Trent, and (at greatest length) Philip Melancthon.
38. Zahl, "Affective Salience," 433.
39. Ibid., 444.
40. On the political processes that both generate and are served by doctrine, see Hugh Nicholson, "The Political Nature of Doctrine: A Critique of Lindbeck in the Light of Recent Scholarship," *Heythrop Journal* 48 (2007): 858–77. Responding to Lindbeck, Nicholson proposes that doctrines are formed in response to social opposition and that they are more like "the mobilizing slogans of political discourse" (868) than rules. Nicholson's argument is illuminating,

but much of its force rests on a narrowing of doctrine to its social-demarcating and authoritative roles.

41. E.g., Kevin Vanhoozer who, in an admittedly passing "nod to Charles Taylor," describes the Christian social imaginary as "the biblically normed imaginary of the church, the society of Jesus Christ." See Kevin Vanhoozer, "Analytics, Poetics, and the Mission of Dogmatic Discourse," in *The Task of Dogmatics: Explorations in Theological Method*, ed. Oliver D. Crisp and Fred Sanders (Grand Rapids, MI: Zondervan, 2017), 23–48 (43).

42. There are overlaps between what follows here and the proposal to consider doctrine as maps in Serene Jones and Paul Lakeland (eds.), *Constructive Theology: A Contemporary Approach to Contemporary Themes* (Minneapolis, MN: Fortress, 2005), 9–18; and Serene Jones, *Feminist Theory and Christian Theology: Cartographies of Grace*, Guides to Theological Inquiry (Minneapolis, MN: Fortress, 2000), 19–21. What it developed in the present proposal is the relationship between doctrine as map and the Bible as compass. In this respect, it differs also from Kevin Vanhoozer's proposal to consider the Bible as both map and compass (*The Drama of Doctrine*, 294–6).

43. The map was produced by The Centre for 21st Century Humanities at the University of Newcastle and is available via this webpage, which includes an introduction: https://c21ch.newcastle.edu.au/colonialmassacres/.

44. Walter Brueggemann, *Old Testament Theology: Testimony, Dispute and Advocacy* (Minneapolis, MN: Fortress, 1997), xvi.

45. Ibid., 317.

46. Rowan Williams, *On Christian Theology* (Oxford: Blackwell, 2000), 53.

47. Rowan Williams, "Historical Criticism and Sacred Text," in *Reading Texts, Seeking Wisdom: Scripture and Theology*, ed. David F. Ford and Graham Stanton (London: SCM, 2003), 217–18 (221).

48. Williams, *On Christian Theology*, 55.

49. Ibid., 57.

50. Much of the discussion around the development of doctrine was generated by Cardinal John Henry Newman's 1845 work on this topic. Essentially, Newman held that the proliferation of doctrinal teachings beyond the apostolic age could be explained as the expansion and growing comprehension of what was contained in the original apostolic teaching. Newman developed certain criteria by which to determine the faithfulness of subsequent doctrines and to identify corrupt doctrines. See John Henry Newman, *An Essay on the Development of Christian Doctrine* (London: Longmans, Green, 1903). For overviews of Newman's position and various alternatives, see Peter Toon, *The Development of Doctrine in the Church* (Grand Rapids, MI: Eerdmans, 1979).

51. See, e.g., Thiselton, *The Hermeneutics of Doctrine*, 134–44, and Kevin J. Vanhoozer, *Remythologizing Theology: Divine Action, Passion and Authorship*, Cambridge Studies in Christian Doctrine (Cambridge: Cambridge University Press, 2010), 305–29. The text on which these authors draw is

Mikhail Bhaktin, *Problems with Dostoevsky's Poetics*, trans. Carol Emmerson (Minneapolis: University of Minnesota Press, 1984).

52. Y. T. Vinayaraj, "Ecclesiology with(out) Margins: Defining Church in the Context of Empire," in *Rekindling the Divine Gifts: Meaning, Mediation and Methods: Theological Education and Formation of Clergy*, ed. M. C. Thomas and Shiby Varghese (Kottayam: Marthoma Theological Seminary, 2016), 81–93 (87).
53. Ibid.
54. Ibid., 88. Such criticism is, of course, present within the Western tradition itself. See Jürgen Moltmann, *The Trinity and the Kingdom of God*, trans. Margaret Kohl (London: SCM, 1981), 191–201.
55. Ibid., 96.
56. Ibid., 95.
57. See Y. T. Vinayaraj, *Intercessions: Theology, Liturgy, and Politics* (Delhi: ISPCK, 2015), especially "Ecumenism and Marginality" (83–96), where the issues discussed above are brought into conversation with the nature of the modern ecumenical movement.
58. John G. Flett, *Apostolicity: The Ecumenical Question in World Christian Perspective* (Downers Grove, IL: IVP Academic, 2016), 181.
59. Ibid., 284.
60. Ibid.
61. See Dale T. Irvin, "What Is World Christianity?" in *World Christianity: Perspectives and Insights*, ed. Jonathan Y. Tan, and Anh Q. Tran (Maryknoll, NY: Orbis Books, 2016), 3–27.
62. Flett, *Apostolicity*, 284.
63. Ibid., 288.
64. Ibid.
65. Ibid., 325.
66. Ibid., 327.
67. Ibid., 328.
68. Ibid.
69. Teresa Okure, SHCJ, "The Global Jesus," in *The Cambridge Companion to Jesus*, ed. Marcus Bockmuehl (Cambridge: Cambridge University Press, 2001), 237–49 (249).
70. Ibid., 237.
71. Ibid., 237–8.
72. See Yadav, "Christian Doctrine as Ontological Commitment," 76.
73. Ibid., 77.
74. Ibid.

Notes

75. Ibid.
76. Ibid., 79.
77. See ibid., 79–84.

Chapter 6

1. Craig Hovey, *Bearing True Witness: Truthfulness in Christian Practice* (Grand Rapids, MI: Eerdmans, 2011), 58.

RECOMMENDED READING

Sources of further reading about the details of the various topics included in this book can be found in the notes throughout. The following list provides significant texts for further study of the key themes addressed in this book.

Histories of Doctrine and Theology

Gonzalez, Justo L. *A History of Christian Thought*, 3 vols. 2nd ed. Nashville, TN: Abingdon, 1987.
Miles, Margaret. *The Word Made Flesh: A History of Christian Thought*. Malden, MA: Blackwell, 2005.
Oden, Thomas C., ed. *Ancient Christian Doctrine*. 5 vols. Downers Grove, IL: IVP Academic, 2009–10.
Pelikan, Jaroslav. *The Christian Tradition: A History of the Development of Doctrine*, 5 vols. Chicago, IL: University of Chicago Press, 1971–89.

Creeds and Confessions of Faith

Allen, Michael. "Confessions." In *The Cambridge Companion to Reformed Theology*, edited by Paul T. Nimmo and David A. S. Fergusson, 28–43. Cambridge: Cambridge University Press, 2016.
Pelikan, Jaroslav. *Credo: Historical and Theological Guide to Creeds and Confessions of Faith in the Christian Tradition*. New Haven, CT: Yale University Press, 2003.
Pelikan, Jaroslav, and Valerie R. Hotchkiss, eds. *Creeds and Confessions of Faith in the Christian Tradition*, 4 vols. New Haven, CT: Yale University Press, 2003.
Rohls, Jan. *Reformed Confessions: From Zurich to Barmen*, translated by John F. Hoffmeyer. Columbia Series in Reformed Theology. Louisville, KY: WJKP, 1998.

The Nature and Functions of Doctrine

Crisp, Oliver D., and Fred Sanders, eds. *The Task of Dogmatics: Explorations in Theological Method*. Grand Rapids, MI: Zondervan, 2017.

Recommended Reading

Gunton, Colin. "A Rose by Any Other Name? From 'Christian Doctrine' to 'Systematic Theology.'" *International Journal of Systematic Theology* 1.1 (1998): 4–22.

Heyduck, Richard. *The Recovery of Doctrine in the Contemporary Church: An Essay in Philosophical Theology*. Waco, TX: Baylor University Press, 2002.

Hütter, Reinhard. *Suffering Divine Things: Theology as Church Practice*. Grand Rapids, MI: Eerdmans, 2000.

Loughlin, Gerard. "The Basis and Authority of Doctrine." In *The Cambridge Companion to Christian Doctrine*, edited by Colin E. Gunton, 41–64. Cambridge: Cambridge University Press, 1997.

Vanhoozer, Kevin. *Faith Speaking Understanding: Performing the Drama of Doctrine*. Louisville, KY: WJKP, 2014.

Doctrine and Scripture

Bockmuehl, Markus, and Alan J. Torrance, eds. *Scripture's Doctrine and Theology's Bible: How the New Testament Shapes Christian Dogmatics*. Grand Rapids, MI: Baker, 2008.

Crisp, Oliver, and Fred Sanders, eds. *The Voice of God in the Text of Scripture*. Grand Rapids, MI: Zondervan, 2016.

Holcomb, Justin S., ed. *Christian Theologies of Scripture: A Comparative Introduction*. New York: New York University Press, 2006.

Martin, Dale. *Biblical Truths: The Meaning of Scripture in the Twenty-First Century*. New Haven, CT: Yale University Press, 2017.

Sonderegger, Katherine. "Holy Scripture as Sacred Ground." In *The Task of Dogmatics: Explorations in Theological Method*, edited by Oliver D. Crisp and Fred Sanders, 131–43. Grand Rapids, MI: Zondervan, 2017.

Work, Telford. *Living and Active: Scripture in the Economy of Salvation*. Grand Rapids, MI: Eerdmans, 2002.

Young, Frances. *Biblical Exegesis and the Formation of Christian Culture*. Cambridge: Cambridge University Press, 2007.

Doctrine and Feminism

Johnson, Elisabeth, ed. *The Strength of Her Witness: Jesus Christ in the Global Voices of Women*. Maryknoll, NY: Orbis Books, 2018.

Kim, Grace Ji-Sun, and Jenny Daggers, eds. *Reimagining with Christian Doctrines: Responding to Global Gender Injustices*. New York: Palgrave Macmillan, 2014.

LaCugna, Catherine Mowry, ed. *Freeing Theology: The Essentials of Theology in Feminist Perspective*. San Francisco, CA: HarperSanFrancisco, 1993.

Parsons, Susan Frank, ed. *The Cambridge Companion to Feminist Theology.* Cambridge: Cambridge University Press, 2006.
Pau, Amy Plantinga, and Serene Jones, eds. *Feminist and Womanist Essays in Reformed Dogmatics.* Columbia Series in Reformed Theology. Louisville, KY: WJKP, 2006.

Doctrine and the Majority World

Bediako, Kwame. *Theology and Identity: The Impact of Culture upon Christian Thought in the Second Century and in Modern Africa.* Eugene, OR: Wipf & Stock, 2011.
Carroll, Seforosa. "Weaving New Spaces: Christological Perspectives from Oceania (Pacifica) and the Oceanic Diaspora." *Studies in World Christianity* 10.1 (2004): 72–92.
Chan, Simon. *Pentecostal Theology: An Essay on the Development of Doctrine.* Journal of Pentecostal Supplement Series 38. Blandford Forum, UK: Deo, 2011.
Chow, Alexander. *Theosis, Sino-Christian Theology and the Second Chinese Enlightenment: Heaven and Humanity in Unity.* London: Palgrave, 2013.
Phan, Peter C. *Being Religious Interreligiously: Asian Perspectives on Interfaith Dialogue.* Maryknoll, NY: Orbis Books, 2004.
Tan, Jonathan Y., and Anh Q. Tran, SJ, eds. *World Christianity: Perspectives and Insights: Essays in Honour of Peter C. Phan.* Maryknoll, NY: Orbis Books, 2016.

Doctrine and Truth

Long, D. Stephen. *Speaking of God: Theology, Language and Truth.* Grand Rapids, MI: Eerdmans, 2009.
Moore, Andrew. *Realism and Christian Faith: God, Grammar and Meaning.* Cambridge: Cambridge University Press, 2003.
Murphy, Francesca Aran. *God Is Not a Story: Realism Revisited.* Oxford: Oxford University Press, 2007.
Murphy, Nancy. *Beyond Liberalism and Fundamentalism: How Modern and Postmodern Philosophy Set the Theological Agenda.* Harrisburg, PA: TPI, 1996.

INDEX

Affective Salience of Doctrine 135
Allen, Michael 76, 166 n.216
Anderson, Benedict 132, 176 n.12
anthropology 61, 64, 82, 98, 99–103
Apostles' Creed 35–6, 71–2
apostolic authority 6–7
Apostolicity (Flett) 142
apostolicity, notion of 142–3
Aquinas, Thomas 37, 40–5, 67, 76, 77, 93, 159 n.54
Arius 13–14
Arian theology 13–17 155 n.27
Athanasius 15, 16
Augustine of Hippo 31–6
Austin, J. L. 173 n.36

Barmen Declaration 62, 157 n.68
Barth, Karl 3, 61–7, 76–8, 88, 163 n.136, 164 n.160
Basil of Caesarea 15
Bauckham, Richard 168 n.24
Beattie, Tina 48
Behr, John 14, 15, 28, 144
Belgic Confession 25
Belhar Confession 24–6
Bhaktin, Mikhail 141, 178 n.51
Bible. *See also* doctrine
  as compass 137–40
  and doctrine as catalyst 124–5
  and doctrine as prompt 114–18
  and doctrine as rules 111–12
Book of Changes (Zhou Dynasty) 95, 96
Brett, Mark 117
Brown, Peter 158 n.21
Browning, Don 133
Brueggemann, Walter 139
Brunner, Emil 120

Caffarini, Tommaso 46
Calvin, John 18, 49–55, 76, 77, 134, 163 n.138
Canons of Dort 25

Catherine of Siena 45–9
Cavallini, Guiliana 160 n.69
Chadwick, Henry 158 n.22
Charry, Ellen 134, 172 n.10
Chinese Christians and cosmic Christology 92–6
Chow, Alexander 170 n.69
Christendom 62, 91, 92, 97
Christian Faith (Schleiermacher) 57–60
Christology 64, 73, 121, 140
  cosmic 91–7
  Hellenization critique of 85
Church Dogmatics (Barth) 62–7, 78
Coakley, Sarah 72–6, 77, 78
coherence of doctrines 11, 15, 23
  system as 79
Colish, Marcia L. 159 n.50
confessions of faith 12, 16, 18–24
  Augsburg 18
  Belgic 25
  Belhar 24–6
  First Helvetic 19
  Geneva 19
  multiplicity of 23, 115
  Protestant theology and 22
  Reformation 17–23, 26, 105, 145, 150
  Second Helvetic 19
  Westminster 20–3
Confessions (Augustine of Hippo) 32–4
Constantine, Emperor 14
contemplation, practice of 75–6
Copernican Revolution 55
Council of Constantinople 15
Council of Trent 19–20
Crouter, Richard 161 n.106
Crouzel, Henri 158 n.17

DeFranza, Megan 100–2, 171 n.88
DeHart, Paul J. 172 n.2
Dei verbum 68
development of doctrine, notion of 59
Dialogue, The (Catherine of Siena) 46–8

Index

Didache, The 8–10
dispossession of theological knowledge 75
doctrine
   and anthropology 99–103
   and Bible 136–40
   as catalyst 119–21
      and Bible 124–5
      and possibilities 121–2
      and question of truth 122–4
   change and diversity and 141–7
   and cosmic Christology 91–7
   as dispositional beliefs 134
   Enlightenment and 82–5
   experiential-expressivist type, 108
   in majority world 91–8
   New Testament origins of 5–8
   as practical wisdom 133–6
   as prompt 112–13
      and Bible 114–18
      and question of truth 118–19
   as rules 106–7
      and question of truth 109–11
      and Bible 111–12
   and study of Jesus 85–8
   and women 88–91
   working definition of 1, 26, 79–80, 126–8, 129
dogmatic propositions 58
dogmatics 64–5
Dogmengeschichte (history of dogma) 84–5, 86
Drama of Doctrine, The (Vanhoozer) 112–19
Draper, Johnathan A. 154 nn.13–14, 18

ecclesial authority 120
   rejection of 53
Enchiridion on Faith, Hope and Love, The (Augustine of Hippo) 32, 34–5, 78
Enlightenment 79, 81–2
   and doctrine 82–5
   emancipatory forces of 88
   knowledge and 99–100
Eucharist 39
Eunomius 15
eunuchs, biblical witness to 101
Eusebius of Caesarea 28

"Faith and Creed" (Augustine of Hippo) 35–6
Farel, Guillame 50
feminist theology 72–6, 88–91, 104

Fitzmyer, Joseph A. 154 n.12
Flett, John 142, 143, 144
Ford, David F. 164 n.160
Foundations of Christian Faith (Rahner) 68, 71
Frei, Hans 173 n.24
friendship, metaphor of 90

gender 45, 48–9, 72, 74, 77, 82, 89, 100–3
Greek philosophy, doctrinal tradition's relationship with 4–5, 82–5
Greene-McCreight, Kathryn 10, 142
Gregory of Nazianzus 15
Gregory of Nyssa 15, 135

Hales, Alexander 40
Harnack, Adolf von 84–6
Harrington, Daniel J. SJ 153 n.10
Healy, Nicholas 44
Heide, Gale 79, 166 n.227
Heidegger, Martin 67
Heidelberg Catechism 25
Heine, Ronald 28
Hellenization thesis 17, 83–5
Helmer, Christine 4, 59, 105, 119–25, 127, 175 n.75
Hermeneutics of Doctrine (Thiselton) 79
Higton, Mike 172 nn.2–3, 173 n.30
Himmelfarb, Gertrude 82–3, 167 n.2
Holmes, Stephen 14, 26
Holy Spirit 10–11, 22, 120
   inward testimony of 53
   as prompt 114–15
   witness of 48
homoians 15, 155 n.36
homoousios 14, 15, 16, 17, 26
Hovey, Craig 151
humanization and salvation 98–9

imago Dei 91, 100, 101, 102
Indian theology 97–9
Institutes of the Christian Religion (Calvin) 49–55, 78, 134
intersex, theological implications of 100–4
intrasystematic truth 109–10
intratextual theology 111
Irenaeus 10, 11, 22

Jesus
   and doctrine (*see* doctrine)
   human nature of 85–8

Index

proclamation as Messiah 5–8
Johnson, Elizabeth A. 89–91
Johnson, William Stacy 65, 163 n.149
Jones, Serene 178 n.42
Jüngel, Eberhard 163 n.143

Kant, Immanuel 55–6, 83
Kärkkäinen, Veli-Matti 168 n.43
Kilby, Karen 164 n.170
Kinzig, Wolfram 14
Kirschbaum, Charlotte von 62
Knight, John Allan 172 n.2
Korsch, Dietrich 161 n.108

Lakeland, Paul 178 n.42
Lao Tze 94
Lash, Nicholas 104
Lessing, G. E. 84
Lindbeck, George 105, 106–12, 114, 118, 126, 137, 172 nn.2, 10, 173 n.24
literal sense, of Scripture 43
logos 93
Lombard, Peter 36–40, 77
Lord's Prayer 35
Loyola, Ignatius 68
Lumen gentium 68
Luther, Martin 50

McClendon, James 130
McCormack, Bruce. L. 163 n.138
McGrath, Alister E. 2, 167 nn.6, 12
McIntyre, Alasdair 176 n.3
McRandal, Janice 168 n.26
majority world 91–9, 153 n.7
Mangina, Joseph 67
Marshall, Bruce 175 n.79
Martyr, Justin 93
Meyer, Ockert 156 n.63
modest cognitivism 110
Moltmann, Jürgen 85, 179 n.54
  on personhood of Jesus 86–8
Muessig, Carolyn 160 n.69

Nature of Doctrine, The (Lindbeck) 105–12 119, 137
Newman, John Henry 178 n.50
Nicene-Constantinopolitan Creed, 144
  regulative principles of 110
  Trinity and 12–17
Nicholson, Hugh 177 n.40

Nimmo, Paul T. 162 n.127
Noffke, Suzanne 160 n.69
Nordling, Cherith Fee 168–9 n.45
nouvelle théologie 68

Okure, Teresa 145
O'Meara, Thomas F. 159 n.54, 164 n.170
On Christian Teaching (Augustine of Hippo) 32, 33–4
On Faith and the Creed (Augustine of Hippo) 32
On Religion: Speeches to its Cultured Despisers (Schleiermacher) 55, 56, 57
ontological truth 110
Origen of Alexandria 28–31, 76
Osborn, Eric 11, 154 n.19
Outram, Dorinda 81, 168 n.25

performative/pragmatic notion, of truth 109
Pope Paul III 19
postliberal theology 106, 127
Price, H. H. 134
propositionalist type, of doctrine 107

Radcliffe, Timothy 45
Rahner, Karl 63, 67–72, 76, 77, 88, 165 nn.191–2
  on creeds 71–2
  on magisterium 70–1
Rankin, David 31, 155 n.27
reason and revelation, relationship between 43
redemption 11, 12, 93, 161 n.108
  Christ as source of life in creation and 95
  Christian 58
  creation in covenantal relationship with 64
  drama of 113
  experience of 124
  God, creation and 44
religion
  as gigantic proposition 109
  modern understandings of 108
Rethinking Christian Identity (Volpe) 135
revelation, doctrine of 21
revised Scriptural principle 114
Rosemann, Philipp 37, 40, 159 n.43
"Rule of Faith" 10–12, 22, 112, 142, 144, 145
  doctrine as prompt and 116, 117
Ruokanen, Miika 169 n.47

187

Index

sacramental signs, notion of 39–40
"Salvation and Humanization" (Thomas) 98
Schleiermacher, Friedrich 55, 56–61, 76, 77, 88, 107, 124–5, 163 n.136
  Barth on 62–3
  misreading of 120
  views of 56–7
Scott, Karen 48
Secular Age, A (Taylor) 131
Sentences (Lombard) 36–40, 78
Sex Difference in Christian Theology (DeFranza) 100
shengsheng shen (ever generating God) 94–6
She Who Is (Johnson) 89
Smit, Dirkie 23
Smith, James K. A. 127
social construction, of truth 122, 123, 127
social imaginary 129–33. See also doctrine
Spilsbury, Paul 154 n.12
Summa contra Gentiles (Aquinas) 41
Summa Theologiae (Aquinas) 37, 41–5 76, 78
system in theology 78–9

Tang, Edmond 169 n.47, 170 n.69
Tanner, Kathryn 104
Taylor, Charles 130, 131, 132, 137, 176 nn.11–12
Tertullian 10, 12
Theological Investigations (Rahner) 68
théologie totale 74, 78
Theology and the End of Doctrine (Helmer) 119
Theology of Hope, The (Moltmann) 86
Thiselton, Anthony 79, 117, 133, 134, 177 n.19
Thomas, Madathilparampil Mammen 97–9, 103, 170 n.73
Tice, Terrence 161 n.107
Ting, K. H. 92, 93–4, 96, 104, 169 n.57

Toon, Peter 178 n.50
Trigg, Joseph W. 157 n.1
Trinity 12, 121
  and analogy to Word of God 63
  contemplation and 75
  as copestone 61
  doctrine and women and 88–91
  and Nicene-Constantinopolitan Creed 12–17
  sexual desire and 73

Vanhoozer, Kevin 105, 112–19, 125, 126, 127, 138, 173 nn.35, 39, 174 nn.64–5, 178 n.41
Vinayaraj, Y. T. 142, 143, 144, 179 n.57
Volpe, Medi Ann 135, 136, 172 n.10

Wainwright, Geoffrey 153 n.1
Wang Weifan 92, 94–6, 104, 169 n.62
Way of Jesus Christ, The (Moltmann) 86
Webster, John 23
Wen Ge 169 n.47
Westminster Confession of Faith 20–3
"What is Enlightenment?" (Kant) 83
Wilken, Robert Louis 17
Williams, Rowan 16, 31, 91, 139, 146, 155 nn.30–1, 158 n.25
witness, notion of 151
World Alliance of Reformed Churches 25
world Christianity 91–9, 141, 143, 153 n.7

Yadav, Sameer 130, 146
Yelikewen 95
Yongtao Chen 169 n.47

Zachman, Randall 52, 53
Zahl, Simeon 109, 135, 136, 172 n.10
Zwingli, Huldrych 18